VIRGINIA COLONIAL ABSTRACTS

Vol. VIII
Essex County - Wills and Deeds
1711 - 1714

*This book is a consolidation of
two volumes into one
with two separate indexes*

Compiled By:
Beverley Fleet

Southern Historical Press, Inc.
Greenville, South Carolina

This volume was reproduced from
1940 editions located in the
Publisher's private library

All rights reserved. No part of this publication may be reproduced,
stored in a retrieval system, transmitted in any form, posted
on to the web in any form or by any means without
the prior written permission of the publisher.

Please direct all correspondence and orders to:

www.southernhistoricalpress.com
or
**SOUTHERN HISTORICAL PRESS, Inc.
PO BOX 1267
Greenville, SC   29601
southernhistoricalpress@gmail.com**

Originally published: Richmond, VA.   1940
ISBN #0-89308-790-4
All rights Reserved.
Printed in the United States of America

PREFACE

The records of Essex County are remarkably complete. That is for war ridden Virginia. The originals are in Tappahannock.

Record Book No. 14, Wills and Deeds, 1711 - 1718, not indexed, came to be in such bad condition it had to be withdrawn from use. These abstracts were the last notes taken. As I turned the pages, gingorly, parts would fall into hundreds of fragments in my lap. These I gathered up and placed in envelopes to be used in the future restoration of this immense old book. The Archives Division of the Virginia State Library had a photostat copy made, thanks to the interest of Mrs. Martha Woodroof Hiden. This may be consulted by anyone who has the car fare or legs long enough to walk to Richmond.

July 10th 1940.   Beverley Fleet.

8-E

Essex County, Virginia.
Deeds and Wills
No. 14.

page 1. Lease and Release. 10 and 11 October 1711. ffrancis Gouldman and Martha Gouldman of the parish of St. Ann, Essex Co., Gent etc., Executors of the last will and testament of Edward Gouldman late of sd parish, sell Samuel Thacker that plantation whereon William Williams lately dwelt, 150 acres, adj. land of Wm. Howlett and of Matrum Wright, part of a tract formerly called Buttons Range, granted to Thomas Button deceased by patent dated 19th July 1666 and by his will bequeathed to his brother Robert Button, this said will dated 1 March 1669; and by said Robert Button conveyed to Folin Baker, and confirmed to him by order of the General Court at James Citty dated 27 October 1688, and conveyed by Baker to William Williams by deed dated in the year 1694, and conveyed by Williams to Edward Gouldman dec'd. by deed dated 8 February 1705, and by his will dated 3 Nov. 1709 directed to be sold.

Witnesses   signed   ffrancis Gouldman (seal)
Wm. Thompson
Aug't Smith   The marke of
Salvator Muscoe   Martha   M   Gouldman (seal)

Recorded   8 9ber 1711 (8th Nov. 1711)
Richard Buckner   Cl Cur.

page 3. Lease and Release. 7 and 8 November 1711. William Scott of St. Ann's Par., Essex Co., planter, sells Gawin Corbin of Christ Church Par. Middlesex Co., 156 acres known as the Indian Town Island and Mad'm Surkings Field and Ball Eagle Neck in St. Ann's Par., Essex Co., adj. Portobacco bay, granted to said Scott 25th April 1704.

Witnesses   signed   William Scott (seal)
Paul Micou
Jno Lomax
Richard Buckner

Recorded   8 Nov. 1711
Richard Buckner   Cl Cur.

page 5. Lease and Release. 7 and 8 November 1711. Robert Parker, planter of St. Ann's Par. Essex Co., sells to Peter Godfrey of So. Farnham Par., chirurgeon, 55 acres on So. side of Rappahannock River on the Maine Creek side commonly called Occupa'con Creek, being part of a dividend bequeathed Ludowick and John Rowzee by their father Edward Rowzee in his will. About 30 square feet reserved being "the burying place lying betwixt the present dwelling house and the Creek now known by sundry graves".

Wit:
ffrancis Gouldman
Aug't Smith
Leo Tarent

signed Robert Parker (seal)

Power of Atty. Elinor and Margaret Parker to Mr Leonard Tarent to ack. dower rights to Mr. Peter Godfrey of plantation "lately purchased of Robert Parker Son of the said Elinor and husband of me the said Margarett".

Wit:
Tho Williamsons mark
Ja Alderson

signed Elinor Parker
Margarett Parker
(both signatures by mark)

Recorded 8 November 1711

page 7.   Part of the Estate of Rich'd Ripley Dec'd

To one hand mill	2.	0.	0
To one caske	0	3.	6
To 2 hogs	0	15.	0
To 1 pair of wool cards	0	1.	0
To 1 stear	2	5.	0

signed James x Landrum
William x Golding

Presented by Eliz'a Ripley Exx of Richard Ripley Dec'd to Essex County Court the 8th day of November 1711 and is Recorded.

page 7. Deed of Gift. John Barker, planter, of St. Ann's parish gives "my two kinsmen John Diskin and Dan'l Diskin" both of St. Ann's Par., each a 3 yr. old heifer. Dated 11 Oct. 1711.

Wit:
Joshua Righcraft
Tho Newman

signed John Barker
Penelophe Barker

Recorded 9th day of 9ber 1711
(9th Nov. 1711)

page 8. "To the Worshipful her Maj'ts Justices
George Loyd Humbly showeth
That the marke of his Stock is a Crop on the right Ear and a Crop and Slitt on the left Ear which he humbly prays may be Recorded and Shall pray it
Truly Recorded
Test
Richard Buckner   Cl Cur.

page 8. An inventory of the Estate of Roger Prosser, Deceased. Listed and amounting to L 13. 02. 8
signed   Larkin Chew
Thomas x Hillard
Jno Long

Presented by Katherine Prosser, admx of Roger Prosser.

Rec. 9 Nov. 1711

page 8. Petition of William Thompson "humbly showeth that your pet'rs ffather Wm Thompson Clerk Dec'east having a quarter in this county" never recorded his mark for cattle. That mark be recorded. No date shown.

page 8. Jno. Copeland complains that Henry Rose owes him 800 lb. tobo. "and has illegally absented himself out of this county". Requests attachment agt. Rose's estate. Dated 27 7ber (Sept) 1711.
signed Francis Meriwether
"By virtue of the within attachm't I have atteacht Eight hundred and fifty pounds of Sweet Sented tobo and caske of the Estate of Henry Rose in the hands of Henry Woodnot
William Covington
Sub Sher: E C ".

8-E   4

page 8. Bond. 100 pounds Sterl. Henry Long as Admr. of Est. of Simon Boulin, Dec'd. Dated 10 day of 9'ber 1711 (10 Nov. 1711)

Wit: signed   Henry Long
Ja Alderson   Richard Long
Robt Parker   Henry Brice

          Rec. 10 Nov. 1711.

page 9. Bond. Five thousand pounds Sterl. Elizabeth Loyde, Admr. Stephen Loyde, dec'd. Dated 13 December 1711.

Wit: signed   Eliza Loyde
Ja Alderson   Jno Lomax
Robert Jones   Paul Micou
                                       Rich'd Buckner

          Rec. 13 Dec. 1711.

page 9. Will of David Jameson. Dated 2 Dec. 1711. Prob. 13 Dec. 1711. To wife Mary Jameson 250 acres 'where I now live'. All personal property. She sole exor.

Wit: signed   David x Jameson
Samll Stallord
David Willson
Robert Retterford his mark

Bond. L 200. Mary Jameson, Admr. Dated 13 December 1711.
Wit: signed   Mary Jameson
Ja Alderson   Jno Lomax
Robt Parker   Wm Woodford

         Rec. 13 Dec. 1711.

page 9. Bond. L 100. Richard Wilton Admr. Est. of Richard Wilton, Deceased. Dated 13th day of X'ber 1711. (13th Dec. 1711)
Wit: signed   Richd Willton
Ja Alderson   Tho Merit
Robt Parker   Jno Strang

         Rec. 13 Dec. 1711.

page 10. Lease and Release. 20 and 21 Nov. 1711. Samuel Prosser, planter, of St. Mary's Par. in Essex Co., sells Joseph Trawhere, 'Taler', of same par. and Co., 57 acres, adj. land of Robert Kay, the line crossing Prossers Creek and to land of said Trawhere purchased of Roger Prosser. The name also appears in the two Indentures as 'Throhere' and as 'Trowher'.

Wit: signed   Saml Prosser
John Catlett
Robert Kay junr
John Morgan   Rec. 13 Dec. 1711.

page 12. Lease and Release. 12 and 13 Dec. 1711. John Mills the younger, planter, of South Farnham Par. Essex Co., sells to Henry Byrom, 'Gunn Smith', of same Par. and Co., 40 acres, bordering on the mouth of a Gut issueing out of Gilson's Creek a little below an Island in the Marsh by the mouth of a Great Swamp called the old plantation swamp, to Evans point, it being a point of land formerly sold by John Mills, grandfather to the sd John Mills, to John Evans deceased, from thence on the land which Peter Byrom and the afsd Henry Byrom now liveth on.

Wit: signed   John Mills Junr
Ro Brooke Junr
Wm Covington Junr
Salvator Muscoe   Rec. 13 Dec. 1711.

page 14. Lease and Release. 11 and 12 Dec. 1711. Elias Blackburn, planter, of St. Ann's Par. sells to Martin Kemp,'Black Smith',of Sittenburn Par., Richmond Co., 50 acres in St. A. Par., bounded by land of Charles Brown and the Beever Dams of the head of Blackburn Creek.
                                  signed   Elias Blackburn
Wit:
James Boughan Jr
Wm Covington Jr
Rich'd Kemp

Martha Blackburn wife of sd Elias Blackburn relinq. Right of Dower.
                     Rec. 13 Dec. 1711.

8-E

page 15. Indenture. 8 Dec. 1711. John Spires of St. Ann's Par., sells to Jeremiah Bessill of afsd Par., 80 acres, part of land where Spires now lives, on E. side of Occupa'con Run and land of Capt Edward Rowzee.

         signed John Spires

Wit:
Robert Jones
William Jones his mark
Richard Gouggee (sic) Rec. 13 Dec. 1711.

page 16. Bond. L 100. John Mills Junr as guardian of Anthony North an orphan. Dated 14 ffeby 1711.

Wit: signed John Mills (seal)
Ja Alderson   Thomas Munday "
              Rich'd Long "

page 16. Appraisal of Estate of David Jemison, dec'd according to Court order dated 13 Dec. 1711. Totals L 113. 18. 11
Includes:
"To one Cattaile bed furniture and bedstead 02. 10. 00
 To one hatt and his Wearing cloathes at   05. 00. 00
 To one knife and fork Razor and hone   00. 05. 06

          signed Samuel Stallord
              Bucken Browne
              John Andrews

     Recorded 14 Feb. 1711/12

page 17. Will of Elizabeth Reeves of Essex Co. Dated 4 May 1709. Probated 14 Feb. 1711/12.
"I give unto my six children Elizabeth, Henry, Rebeckah, Joseph, Martha and Mary Ten Shillings Sterling money in some convenient time after my decease".
"I give unto my Grandson Edward Moseley a young bay horse"

The Will of Elizabeth Reeves (continued)

"I give unto my Grandson Thomas Munday one young black horse to him and his heirs for Ever"

"I give and bequeath all the Remaining part of my Estate not yet bequeathed unto my Daughter Ann Reeves and her heirs lawfully begotten of her body for ever"

Daughter Ann Reeves to be "my whole and sole executor"

"It is my desire that my Exor Give unto my Servant Boy Samuel Henley at the time of his freedom one good suit of cloathes and one Two year old heiffer".

Wit: signed   Elizabeth x Reeves
Thomas Munday
John Ja -
Timmotha Dayle

"Know all men by these presents that we Edw'd Coleman and Ann his wife, Robert Coleman and Thomas Munday are holden and firmly bound unto Saml Thacker of the County of Essex gent x x in behalf of the Court of the afor'sd County of Essex in the x x sum of Two hundred pounds Sterling x x x this 14th day of ffebry 1711

x x x the above bound Edw'd Coleman and Ann his wife late Ann Reeves who at a Court held for Essex County the day and year above sd had a Certificate Granted for obtaining a probat of the last will and Testament of Elizabeth Reeves deceased x x "

Wit: signed   Edwd Coleman
Ja Alderson   Ann Coleman
Robt Parker   Robt Coleman
                                                           Thomas Munday

Recorded   14 February 1711/12

page 18. "An acco't or an Inventory of the Estate of Mr John ffoster Dec'ed Brought before us the Subscribers, and in an obedience to an ord'r of Essex Court Dated the 11th day of October 1711 Do appraise the same as follows (Viz)"

The inventory includes:
"Craft

1	Great New Sloop	55.	00.	00
1	old Do Sloope and Rigging	35.	00.	00
1	large new flatt	10.	00.	00
2	old large flatts	12.	00.	00
1	small boat	2.	10.	00 "

(continued)

Inventory of the Estate of Mr John ffoster (continued)

Negroes

Dick a Ship Carpenter	50.	00.	00
Tom a Sawer	35.	00.	00
Roger another Sawer	35.	00.	00
Peter a Ladd	30.	00.	00
Betty a woman	27.	10.	00
ffrank a Gerl	18.	00.	00

Household Goods

Include:

2	Double pistolls	3.	10.	00
1	Old Silver quart Tankard and 3 buckles	5.	00.	00
12	old knives and forks	0.	02.	00
1	spy glass	0.	01.	00

This long inventory totals L 458. 17. 0 1/2

"Inventoried and appraised this 2d day of November 1711"

                       signed   John Dangerfeild
                                    Fran: Moore
                                    Leo: Tarent

"At a Court held for Essex County the 14th Day of ffebry 1711
   This Inventory and appraisal was presented on oath by Paul Micou Ex'r of John ffoster Deceased and is Recorded.
                          Test
                               Richard Buckner Cl Cur "

page 20. An Inventory of the Estate of Richard Wilton, deceased, taken by Court Order dated 13 Dec. 1711. The inventory is signed by:

                                    John Graves
                                    Thomas Munday
                                    John Merritt

Richard Wilton, Admr. of Richard Wilton, dec'd., presented this inventory 14 February 1711/12.

page 21.   "Essex County December the 8th 1711
In the Name of God Amen.

Then William Bonnitt late of this County lying sick and at the point of Death, but in his perfect sense and memory uttered his last will and bequests of all his worldly Goods and Chattels. These following words he said calling us the subscribers to Justifie and to witness that if he Dyed that he did give all that he had to Robert Bell Except his Bed and he did Give his bed to Robert Bells boy, one of the Subscribers asked him which boy he answered Robert and Departed within two or three hours after these words, which the Subscribers are ready to Depose x x x as witness our hands.

At a Court held for Essex   Thomas Brooke
County the 14th day of   Richard Brooke
ffebry 1711   Dennis Dougherte
                                 his mark   "

Bond. L 100 Sterl. Robert Bell as Admr. Est. of Wm. Bonnit. Dated 14 Feb. 1711/12.
Wit: signed   sign
Ja Alderson   Robert Bell
Rich'd Wilton   sign
                                   Henry Woodnot
                                   sign
                                   Owen Owens

                    Recorded   14 February 1711/12

page 21. Lease and Release. 26 and 27 January 1711/12. William Underwood, Gent'l., of Sittinburn Par., Richmond Co., sells John Combes and Richard Tutt, planters of the same county, 400 acres in St Maries Par., Essex Co., Bounded: Beginning at a Beach on SW side of punius Inn run, the land of John Meadows and Henry Peters, this land sold by Warwick Cammock to Amory Butler 30 April 1679.

Wit: signed   Wm Underwood
Tim Atkinson
Jno Skey
Alex Somervile

Power of Atty. Wm Underwood to "my Trusty and welbeloved friend Timothy Atkinson of St Anns Parish and county of Essex" to ack. lease and release. Dated 26 Janry 1711/12.

Wit: signed   Wm Underwood
Allex Somerville
Jno Skey
                    Recorded   14 Feb. 1711/12

page 23. Deed. William Combes of St Maries Par. Richmond Co., sells to Richard Tutt of Sittenbourne Par. same Co., 200 acres, being part of 600 acres in St Maries Par. Essex Co. (part of foregoing) "and further I Mary wife of the said Wm Combs x x confirm x unto x Richard Tutt x x all my x x rights x ". Dated 3o Jany. 1711/12.

Wit: signed   Wm Combes
Joseph Dinker   Mary Combes
John x Combes
Tim Atkinson

Power of Atty. "William Combes and Mary my Wife of St Maries parish in the County of Richmond Planters" to Timothy Atkinson to ack. deed. Dated 30 Jan. 1711/12

Wit: signed   Wm Combes
John x Combes   Mary Combes
Thomas x Harvey
Jno Skey

                    Recorded 14 February 1711/12

page 23. Power of Atty. John Whiteside of the "Kingdome of Great Britain" to "my Trusty and welbeloved friend Wm Daingerfield of the Colony of Virg'a Gent" to collect debts, especially from Mr. David Berrick in Richmond County. Dated 17 July 1711.

Wit:
Henry x Wood   signed   Jno Whiteside
ffrancis Paget

                    Proved by oath of ffrancis Paget
                    Recorded 14 February 1711/12

page 23. Deed. 9 Jan. 1711/12. Wm Willis of Westmorland Co., planter, and Mary his wife "Daughter heir apparent of Thomas Kirk Dec'd", sells Charles Brown of Essex Co., land, acreage not shown, in Essex Co., it being granted unto James Coghill 24 March 1664, and by Coghill assigned to afsd Kirk.

Wit: signed   William x Willis
Arthur Bowers   Mary x Willis
Richard Goode
                    Rec. 14 Feb. 1711/12

Note: St. Mary's Parish was in Essex County and also in Richmond County. B.F.

page 24. Lease and Release. 15 Feb. 1711/12. William Stoaks of St. Anns Par., planter, sells Nathaniel ffogg of the same Par., "Endholder"('Inholder' is inhabitant, obsolete), 100 acres in St. A's Par., adj. land of Thomas Davis, land of James Hollaway and that of George Loyd.

Wit: signed
Robert Jones   the marke of
Jno Gibson   William Stoakes

Rec. 14 Feb. 1711/12

page 26. Lease and Release. 12 and 13 March 1711/12. Richd. Long of St. Marys Par., Essex Co., planter, sells John Rackloy of So. Farn. Par., Essex Co., planter, 200 acres in St Mary's Par. Essex Co., adj. land of Samuel Ellit.

Wit: signed the marke of
John Hill   Richard Long
William x Grinnall
Salvator Muscoo   Rec. 13 March 1711/12

page 28. Lease. 9 August 1711. Timothy Hay of Essex Co., planter sells Robert Beverley of the County of King and Queen, Gent., two tracts of land in Essex Co., one containing 210 acres bounded according to deed made by Nicholas ffranklin to George Loyd dated 30 May 1705, the other containing 118 1/2 acres in two parcels bounded according to a deed made by William Cole to the sd George Loyd dated 9 Dec. 1705, along with 2 negroes named Harry and Sarah commonly worked on the 118 acres.

Witnesses as below.   signed   Timothy x Hay
see Release.
                       Recorded 13 March 1711/12

page 28. Release. 10 August 1711. "Whereas the said Timothy is indebted to Mr John Cleveland Mercht in Liverpool in Great Britain Thirty six pounds one shilling Sterl which came into the said Roberts hands to receive, and whereas the said Timothy for payment thereof hath drawn bills of Exchange payable to the said John on Mr John Wright Mercht in London bearing date the day before the date of these presents, x x the said Timothy Hay for and in consideration of the sd debt and the better Assureing the paymt of the said Bills of Exchange x x x hath sold x x x unto the said

(continued)

Release Timothy Hay. 1711 (continued)

Robert Beverley x x x Two severall Tracts or seats of Land x x"

Wit:
Ja Alderson
Richard Buckner
Reu'b Welch
Thomas Harwar
Isaac Webb

signed Timothy Hay
　　　　　his mark

Recorded 13 March 1711/12

page 29. Deed. 13 March 1711/12. ffrancis Awbrey of Copel Par., Westmorland Co., sells ffrancis Gouldman of St. Anns Par., Essex Co., 200 acres in So. Farn. Par. in Essex Co., sd land purchased by Mr Henry Awbrey of Edward Hill Esq., by Deed dated 29 April 1692 (it being 400 acres) and by the said Henry Awbrey in his will given the said ffrancis Awbrey. The sd land lying at the lower end of a Patent of 1200 acres formerly granted to Mr. Thomas Gouldman and next adjoining to the land of Patrick Camell.

Wit:
John X Doughty
ffrancis X Cofflin
Edward Waller

signed ffrancis Awbrey

page 30. Power of Atty. ffrances Awbrey wife of ffrancis Awbrey to "my good friend James Alderson" to ack. right of dower in foregoing. Dated 11 March 1711/12.

Wit:
Tho Baker
Thomas Peach
William Martin his marke
Jno Awbrey

signed
　　her
ffrancis Awbrey
　　mark

Recorded 13 March 1711/12.

page 30. Inventory of Est. of Will Bonnitt, Deceased. Ordered by Court 14 Feb. 1711/12. Totals L 12. 14. 00

signed William Broocke
　　　　Richard Broocke
　　　　Nicho's Smith Jun'r

Sworn before Francis Meriwether.
"Presented on oath by Robert Bell Exor of the Nuncupative Will of Will Bonnitt dec'd to Essex County Court the 13th day of March VII and is Recorded"

page 30. Inventory of the Est. of Mrs. Elizabeth Reeves, Dec'd., ordered by Court 14 Feby. 1711/12. Totals L. 73. 20. 10

                          signed Will Daingerfield
                                     John Mills
                                     Will Greenell his mark

"Appraisers Sworn by me
                Joseph Smith"

                Recorded   13 March 1711/12

page 32. Will of John Waters of South Farnham Parish. Dated 18th Jany. 1709/10. Probated 13 March 1711/12.
"to my beloved Wife Catherine her utmost due according to Law and equity"
"Item my Will and further pleasure is that the remainder of my estate be equally divided between my five Daughters and paid them as Soone as they attain the age of Eighteen years or day of marriage"
"Item I will and bequeath unto my Daughter Catherine all the land x x lying x x in New Kent County x x", she failing in heirs to the next daughter by seniority.
All land in Essex Co. to daughter Winifred.
To John Hines "all my Carpenters tooles"
To "my Godson Henry Young my Gunne and one redd pyed heiffer the said Gunne being now at my brother in Laws Jno Morriss"
To Godson Jno. Sarle "my Gunne now present at my brother Youngs"
Exors: wife Catherine and Mr. William Young.

Wit: signed   John Waters
Catherine x Young
John x Hines
Peter Godfrey

"At a Court held for Essex County the 13th day of March 1711 Edward Price and Katherine his wife Executrix and William Young Ex'or in this will named Presented the said Will in Court and made oath thereto, and being proved by the oath of Peter Godfrey one of the witnesses hereto is Recorded
                                Test   Richard Buckner   Cl Cur"

page 33. Bond. L 500 Sterling. Dated 13 March 1711/12.
                            signed
Wit: Edw'd Price
Ja Alderson   Kath x Price
Wm Covington junr   Will Young
                                  Isaac Webb
                                  Wm Covington

page 33. Lease and Release. 9 and 10 April 1712. William Berry and Margarett his wife of Richmond Co., planter, sells Samuel Short of Essex Co., planter, 310 acres in Essex, being part of a patent granted to Enoch Doughty for 4763 acres, and bounded by land of Joseph Callay and that of ffrancis Browning, the line running to an oak and a pine standing nigh the head of a branch of Matapony.

Wit:
Edward Coleman
Ephriam Paget
John Boughan

signed William Berry
Margret Berry

Recorded 10 April 1712.

page 35. Lease and Release. 8 and 9 April 1712. Richard Edwards of St. Ann's Par., planter and Mary his wife sell to John Andrews of the same Par., planter, 250 acres, the plantation where they now live, bounded by a line shown on patent formerly granted to Thos. Page deceased, whereof sd land is a part, to a great branch of Popeman which divided the land of James Boulware from this land, being also a part of the aforementioned patent, which land was by David Jameson late of Essex Co., deceased in his will dated 2nd December 1711 bequeathed to his wife Mary, now Mary Edwards wife of Richard Edwards.

Wit:
Ja Alderson
Tho Newman
Thomas Ayres his mark.

signed Richard x Edwards
Mary x Edwards

Recorded 10 April 1712.

page 37. Deed. 12 March 1711/12. Daniel Tucker of St. Ann's Par., sells Cornelius Sale of the same Par., for 2200 lb. tobo., 100 acres in St. A. Par., on SW bank of Occupation Creek, adj. land of Robert Gaines, the land of Thomas Parker, the land of Robert Moss and the land of Will: Bates. This land formerly conveyed by Deed of Gift from Robert Moss and Rebeccah Moss, dated 2 September 1679 to Laomedon Tucker (sic, this name appears under various spellings) and from him devised to Daniel Tucker.

Wit:
Daniel Hayes
Robert Mayfield
Jonathan Clark

signed Daniel Tucker

(continued)

Deed. Tucker to Sale (continued)

"At a Court held for Essex County the 10th day of Aprill 1712
Daniel Tucker acknowledged this his Deed to Cornelius Sale and Eliz'a Tucker wife to the said Daniel and Casandra Goulding Relinquished their right of Dower of and to the Land by this Deed Conveyed which on mo'con is Recorded
        Test
          Richard Buckner C Cur "

page 38. Lease and Release. 13 and 14 March 1711/12. Jno. Rackley of So. Farnham Par., planter, sells Richard Long of St. Mary's Par., Essex Co., 400 acres in St. Mary's Par., about 12 miles above Nanzemond Town on S. side of Rappa. River, behind the land of John Gillett.
Wit: signed John x Rackley
Saml Prosser
Jonathan Tapley
Salvator Muscoe
      Recorded 10 April 1712.

page 39. "This Indenture made at Glasgow the twenty first day of November one Thousand seven hundred and Eleven years between John McCai Son of William McCai Cordener in Glasgow dec'd of the one party and David Leitch Merchant of the other party Witnesseth that the said John McCai doth hereby Covenant promise and grant to and with the said David Leitch his heirs Exor's Adm'rs and Assignes from the day of the date hereof untill the first and next arrivall at Virginia and after for and during the space of six years to serve in such Service and imployment in Virginia as the sd David Leitch and his assigns shall there imploy him according to the Custom of the Country and in like kind and consideration whereof the said David Leitch is to pay for passage to find and allow him meat drink apparell and Lodging dureing the said terme or time and at the End of the same to pay unto him the usual allowance according to the Custome of the Country and in like kind. In witness whereof the said parties above mentioned to the Indenture have interchangeably Set their hands and Seals the day and year first above written
Signed sealed and   signed   his
Delivered in presence of   John x McCai
Jo McGilchriss   mark
Jo Mcmerkins

These do Certifie that the above John McCaj appeared before me

The Indenture of Charles McCai (in error John McCai) continued.

Peter Murdock one of the baillies of the burgh of Glasgow and declared he had willingly of his own Consent Sign'd Seal'd and Deliver'd the above Indenture and was no ways forced thereunto In Testimony whereof I have Sub'd these presents at Glasgow the Twenty first day of December 1711 years
                                          Peter Murdock "

"Att a Court held for Essex County the 10th Day of April 1712.   David Leitch appeared and showed that the Servant boy ment and intended to be bound by these Indentures and by him sold to John Waggoner is named Charles McCai and that his being writ John McCai in this Indenture was by mistake of the person drawing the same, and moved that this Indenture be Recorded with this Endorsement to show the mistake aforesd, to which the said Waggoner appearing Consented, wherefore this Indenture is Recorded
                              Test
                              Richard Buckner   Cl Cur   "

page 40. Deed. 10 April 1712. William Harding of So. Farnham Par., Essex Co., sells land to Owen Owens and Mary his wife of same Par., "Whereas Peter Harrood late of the said County was in his lifetime seized of a plantation x x and by his last will x x Devised the same to the said Mary then his wife for and during her natural life, the reversion of which said Land is Vested in the said William Harding and his heirs". Harding disposes of his interest to the Owens for 1/2 of the land.

Wit: signed   William x Harding
Timothy Driscoll
Samll Coates
Fran: Moore   Recorded 10 April 1712.

page 40. Deed. 10 April 1712. Owen Owens and Mary his wife, of South Farnham Parish, sell to William Harding of the same parish, the other half of the land (above) left by Peter Harrood.

Witnesses   signed Owen x Owens
as above.   Mary X Owens

page 41. "Know all men by these presents that we Nath'll ffogg Ephriam Paget Richard Buckner and Augt Smith are held and firmly bound unto our Sovereign Lady Ann by the Grace of God of Great Britain ffrance and Ireland Queen Defender of the ffaith in the Sum of Ten Thousand pounds of Tobacco convenient in the County of Essex To which payment well and truly to be made to our said Sovereign Lady the Queen her heirs and successors we bind our Selves and every of us our and every of our heirs Exor's and Adm't'rs Jointly and Severally firmly by these presents In witness whereof we have hereunto sett our hands and seals the 11th day of Aprill 1712.

    The Condi'oon of this obligation is such that whereas the above bound Nat'l fogg and Ephriam Paget have obtained a Lycence to keep an ordinary at the house where they now dwell in this County of Essex If therefore they the said Nath'l and Ephriam do constantly find and provide in their said ordinary good wholesome and cleanly Lodgings and Dyett for travellers and stableage and fodder and provender or pasturage and provender as the season shall require for their horses for and during the terme of one year from the 11th day of March 1711 and shall not suffer or per- mitt any unlawfull gaming in their house nor on the Sabbath day suffer any to tiple or drink more than is necessary Then this obligation to be nul void and of none effect, otherwise to be and remain in full force power and virtue

Wit:	signed	Nath ffogg	(seal)
Ja Alderson		Ephriam Paget	"
Geo Loyd		Richd Buckner	"
		Augt Smith	"

Acknowledged in Essex County Court the 11th day of Aprill 1712 and is Recorded

                        Test
                            Richard Buckner   Cl our   "

page 41. Bond of George Loyd to keep an ordinary. 10000 lb. tobo. Dated 11 April 1712.

Wit:	signed	Geo Loyde
Nath fogg		Henry Boughan
Robert Jones		his mark
		John Boughan

                Recorded 11 April 1712.

page 42.

"Virginia   Alexander Spotswood her Maj'ts Lieu't Governor and
 (seale)   Comander in Chief of the Colony and Dominion of Virg'a
             To ffrancis Meriwether Saml Thacker Jno Lomax Joseph
Smith Henry Robinson William Woodford Paul Micou William Daingerfield Leonard Tarent and William Young Gentlemen all of the County of Essex, Greeting Whereas by an Act of the Gen'll Assembly begun at her Maj'tie Anns Royall Capitol the Twenty third day of October in the fourth year of the Reign of our Sovereign Lady Anne of England and Anno Dm'ous one Thousand seven hundred and five Entitled an Act for the Speedy and Easy prosecution of slaves committing Capital Crimes It is Enacted that every Slave Committing such offense as by the Law ought to be satisfied by the death of the offender or loss of member shall be forthwith Comitted to the Com'on Goal of the County within wch such offense shall be com'itted there to be safely kept and that the Sheriff of such County upon such Comitment shall forthwith Certifie such Comitment with the cause thereof to the Governor or Commander in Chief of this her Majesties Colony and Dominion for the time being who is thereupon desired and Impowered to Issue out a Comission of Oyer and Terminer directed to such persons of the County as he shall think fit which persons forthwith after the Receipt of such Comission are Impowered and required to Cause the offender to be Publickly Indicted and arrainged at the Court house of the said County and to take for evidence the Confession of the party or the Oath of Two Credible witnesses or of one with pregnant Circumstances without the Soleminty of a Jury and the offender being by them found Guilty to pass such Judgment upon such offender as the Law provides in the like crimes and on Such Judgment to award Execution

And whereas It hath been Represented to me by Richard Covington Gent'lman Sheriff of the said County of Essex

That four negro Slaves (to wit) Jam'ey a negro man slave and nanney a negro woman slave belonging to Colo John Catlett of the said County of Essex and George a negro man Slave and Bridget a negro woman slave belonging to Mrs Anne Hay of the County of Middlesex are Com'itted to and remaine in the Com'on Goal of the said County of Essex on Suspicion of their being guilty of breaking open the house of one Hugh Jones in the said County of Essex and a Lockt Chest in the said house and stealing sundry Goods and apparell of Considerable value belonging to the said Jones and his wife and hath prayed that a Com'ission may Issue for the tryal of the said slaves x x x x "

page 43. Lease and Release. 8 and 11 April 1712. Thos Pettit of St. Stephens Par. King & Queen Co., sells Robt. Coleman of So. Farn. Par., Essex Co., 486 acres in Essex Co., bounded by land of Robt. and John Pleas and that of Capt. Richard Wyatt. This land being part of a patent granted Mr Geo. Morris and John Long 29th Sept. 1667. It is also bordering the land of Katherine Long, now wife of Capt. Richd. Wyatt, and was by deed of gift, made by Geo. Morris, transferred to Thomas Pettit and Katherine Long the now wife of Capt. Richd. Wyatt.

Wit:
Richard Buckner
Will Young.

signed Tho Pettit

Recorded 8 May 1712.

page 45. Lease and Release. 7 and 8 May 1712. Richard Long of St Marys Par. Essex Co., sells Thomas and John Powell of same Par. and Co., 316 acres, Long's part of 1149 acres in Essex Co., granted to said Long, Andrew Harrison Sen'r and Samuel Elliot.

Wit:
Geo Loyde
A Somervell
Salvator Muscoe

signed Richard Long
       his mark

Recorded 8 May 1712

page 48. Bond. L 500 Sterl. 8 May 1712. John Seager Admr. Est. of Winefred Webb, dec'd.

Wit:
Robert Jones
Zach Lewis

signed John Seager
       Will Young
       Benj ffisher

Recorded 8 May 1712.

page 48. Lease and Release. 6 and 7 May 1712. John Andrews, planter, of St. Ann's Par., Essex Co., sells Richard Edwards, planter, of same Par. and Co., 250 acres "which the said John Andrews purchased of the aforesaid Richard Edwards and Mary his wife late Mary Jameson x x the eighth and ninth days of Aprill in this present year 1712". This land part of a patent granted to Thomas Page deceased.

Wit:
Wm Covington Jun'r
P'r Godfrey
Ja Alderson

signed   John Andrews

Recorded 8 May 1712

page 50. Bond. L 500 Sterl. Jaell Williams as Admr of Est. of James Harrison dec'd. Dated 8 May 1712.

Wit:
Aug't Smith
Ja Alderson

signed   Jaell x Williams
Samuell Short
Richd Long

Recorded 8 May 1712

page 50. Bond. L 500 Sterl. Jaell Williams as Admr of Est of William Williams dec'd. Dated 8 May 1712.

Wit:
Aug't Smith
Ja Alderson

signed   Jaell x Williams
Samuel Short
Tho's Griffin

Recorded 8 May 1712.

page 51. Bond. L 100 Sterl. Tho Harwar as Admr. of Est of Thomas Lough dec'd. Dated 8 May 1712.

Wit:
Ja Alderson
Robt Parker

signed   Tho Harwar
Richard Covington
Leo Tarent

Recorded 8 May 1712

page 51. Bond. L 100. Robert (or Roben - plainly Robert in signature and in following entry) Thomas junr as Admr. of Est. of John Thomas Dec'd. Dated 8 May 1712.

Wit:
Robt. Jones
Ja Alderson

signed Robert Thomas Junr
Tho's Griffin
Richard x Long

Recorded 8 May 1712

page 52. Bond. L 100. Robert Thomas junr as Admr of Est of Catherine Thomas dec'd. Dated 8 May 1712.

Wit:
Ja Alderson
Robert Jones

signed Robert Thomas Junr
Thomas Griffin
Rich'd Long

Recorded 8 May 1712

page 52. Lease and Release. 6 and 7 May 1712. Timothy Hay of St. Anns Par. Essex Co., planter, sells John Hart, planter, of same Par. and Co., for 5900 lb. tobo., 118 acres in Essex Co., bounded by Portobacco path, Wyatt's, etc.

Wit:
Daniel Hays
A Somervell
William Hart

signed Timothy Hay

Recorded 8 May 1712.

page 54. Bond. "Richard Covington has obtained a Comission for the office of Sheriff of Essex County during her Maj'ts pleasure". L 1000 Sterl. Dated 9th May 1712.

Wit:
Ja Alderson
Wm Covington Junr

signed Rich'd Covington
Wm Covington
Will Young

Recorded 9th May 1712
Test
Richard Buckner Cl Cur.

page 55. Deed. Robert Richardson of So. Farnham Par. sells Henry Shackelford of sd Par. and Co., 110 acres in same Par., adj. land of John Gills (or Hills or Cills), the land of Henry Boughan and Crompills Quarter branch. Dated 19 Dec. 1711.

Wit: signed Robard Richason
John Haile   his mark
Jno Pickett
      Rec. 12 June 1712.

page 56. Deed. Robert Richardson of So. Farn. Par. sells Henry Shackelford of same Par., for 3300 lb. tobo., 100 acres known by the name of Cadds neck (Codd's neck ?), on S. side of a main Powsan that runneth into Piscataway Creek, bounded by Midle branch, Dividing branch, Crampills Quarter, all lying between land of Thomas Evitts and land of Robt Richardson.

Wit: signed Rob Richonson
Wm Allen   his mark
John Haile
      Rec. 13 Sept 1711.

page 57. Assignment of title of above by Henry Shackelford to Robert Richason. Dated 11 June 1712.

Wit: signed Henry Shackelford
Tho Brown His mark
John Stiles His mark

(Note. The above entries are not clear to me. B.F.)

page 57. Deed of Gift. William Hudson and Rebeckah his wife give for "naturall affection that we do bear towards our son Edward Hudson", 116 acres belonging to a patent of John Long dated 1667 lying on S. side of Rappahannock River, adj land of Wm Hudson, land of Henry Woodnott and that of James Allieson. If said Edward Hudson dies without heirs the land to return to his younger bros., Isaac Hudson and John Hudson. Dated 16 May 1712.

Wit: signed William Hudson
Jno Vass   his mark
John Parker   Rebeckkah Hudson
             her mark

      Rec. 12 June 1712

page 58. Lease and Release. 11 and 12 June 1712. Robert Kay of Essex Co., sells William Stanard of Middlesex Co., 130 acres in freshes of Rappa., over against Nanzimon Town, along land formerly John Paynes and by him sold to John Haslewood, along Prossers line to lower end of poquoson a little above Thomas Dickasons Landing, according to a papent granted Robert Kay dated 6th June 1699.

Wit: signed   Robert Kay
Robert Coleman
John Hawkins
Richard Kemp
Robert Parker   Rec. 12 June 1712

page 60. Inventory of Est. of William Williams according to order of Court 9th June 1712.
Includes:

1 serv't woman two years 1/2 to (serve) called Marg'ry Thomas	05. 60. 00
To a parcel of books	00. 10. 06
To one Cane and Sword	00. 02. 06
To i pale 2 piggins & a noggen	00. 04. 00

Valuation of inventory totals L 143. 01. 2

                         signed   Charles Taliaferro
                                   ffran Thornton
                                   Robert Slaughter
                                       his mark

Note: A piggin was a small wooden vessel with erect handle used as a dipper. A noggen was a small mug or wooden cup measure equaling one gill. Note the relative valuation of the 'i pale' etc. and the cane and sword.   B. F.

page 61. The Inventory of Mr James Harrisons Estate appraised according to Order of Court by us the Subscribers this 9th June 1712. Produced by Jaell Williams Admx.
Includes:

To Money due in England	64. 09. 00
To one sundial	00. 02. 00
To one parcell of books	03. 00. 00

Total valuation L 94. 00. 00

                         signed   Charles Taliaferro
                                   ffran Thornton
                                   Robert x Slaughter

page 61. Inventory of Estate of John and Katherine Thomas, dec'd., taken by order of Court 8 May 1712 and sworn before Mr. John Lomax. Includes:

ffive old turned Virg'a chairs without bottoms at	00. 01. 08
one indifferent good fether bed and bedstead and cord at	04. 06. 00
Two old vessels of brass one of them full of holes att	00. 00. 06
One pestle made of an old gun barrell att	00. 01. 00
one Silver Thimble and one Silver shirt buckle and two brass shirt buttons att	00. 02. 00
one pair of old bodies and one apron i yard of Linen att	00. 04. 09
five old Ragged caps and one old Ragged petticoat and wastcoat att	00. 01. 09

Inventory presented 12 June 1712 by Robert Thomas, Admr.

                        signed   Tho x Hilliard
                                Robert Kay
                                Jno Ellit (or Ellils)

page 63. "A Commission of Oyer and Terminer for the Tryal of Jack and Cockey negroes in Essex County", dated Williamsburg 27th May 1712, from Alexander Spotswood, to try two negroes belonging to M'ris Anne Hay of Middlesex Co., for suspicion of breaking open the house of Hugh Jones of Essex Co.

page 64. "A Commission of the Peace for Essex County". Instructions to ffrancis Meriwether, Richard Covington, Samuel Thacker, John Lomax, Joseph Smith, Henry Robinson, William Woodford Paul Micou, Wm Daingerfield, William Young and Leonard Tarent, Gent'l "justices to keep our peace in the County of Essex." Dated 16th June 1712.

                        signed   A Spotswood

page 65. Instructions regarding administering oaths &c to the Justices of Essex County.

page 65. Deed of Trust. 10 July 1712. "James Alderson of St Anns Parish in the County of Essex and Ann his wife of the one part and John Hunter of the Parish and County aforesaid of the other part   Whereas she the said Anne is seized in ffee of the Plantation and Land which the said James and Anne now live upon formerly the Land and plantation of Capt Thomas Gregson (late husband of the said Anne) which said land was by him purchased of William Harper and James Boughan Dec'ed, and some other Land formerly taken up by the said Gregson, and by him Given and Devised to the said Anne by his last will x x". James and Ann Alderson deed to John Hunter their home property so that if he outlives his wife he may have use of the plantation during lifetime. She to dispose of it by will as she sees fit, possession to be given at his death.

Wit:
Geo Loyde
Thomas Streshly Junr
Robt Brooking

signed Ja Alderson
Ann Alderson

Rec. 10 July 1712.

page 66. Deed of Trust as above. Same dates, signatures and witnesses. Three negroes. "And whereas by the Law of the Land negroes are Declared to be real Estate and to disend as Land and Estates of Inheritance".

page 67. Lease and Release. 7 and 8 July 1712. Wm Stokes, planter, of St. Anns Par., Essex Co., sells Arthur Mackdonel, planter, of the same Par. and Co., for 500 lb. tobo., 50 acres, part of a greater tract in St. Anns Par., adj. Foggs land.

Wit:
Daniel Hayes
Thomas Sorsbe
Robt Moss

signed William Stokes

Rec. 10 July 1712.

page 70. Deed. 10 July 1712. Thomas Short, planter, of St. Anns Par., Essex Co., sells William Ayrnold "of the parish of - in the county of King William planter", for L 20 Sterl., 197 acres, being part of a patent of 393 acres granted to Nathaniel Bentley 24th Sept. 1658 and conveyed to the said Thomas Short by Thomas Bartlett and Patience his wife, daughter and heir of said Nathaniel Bentley by Deed dated 10th July 1712, lying in St. Ann's Parish, bounded

8-E

Deed. Short to Ayrnold (continued)

by John Martins cleared Ground, etc.

Wit: signed   Thomas Short
John Boughan
John Martin
James Boughan   Rec. 10 July 1712.

page 71. June 7th 1712. Inventory of the Est. of Thomas Lough, dec'd., by order of Court 8th May 1712.

"Vizt   To an old horse   01. 00. 00
To a chest an old Trunk 4 small books and
    Lyninge   01. 00. 00
To a Coat Jackett and breeches 1 pr old
    stockings 1 pr drawers   01. 00. 00
To a Small pockett book   00. 00. 06
                                                         ----
                                                         03. 00. 06

To his share of Tobacco of the crop   852
To a hhd of Tobacco at Mr Webbs   1052

                                      1904 @ 5 per cent
                                                         04. 15. 02

To 8 barrels of Indian corne at 5/ per barrel   02. 00. 00
To Cash   15. 17. 06
To more cash due   35. 00. 00
                                                         ----
                                                         60. 13. 02

This being the Estate of Thomas Lough that was presen't to us and acc't Given by Mr Thomas Harwar

Something omitted   1 small looking glass
                    1 small Tinn pott
                    Some good for nothing Tob
                       at my Quarter

                          signed   Isaac Webb
                                   Joshua Booton
                                   Edw Adcocke

Presented by Thomas Harwar Admr of Thomas Lough Decd on oath to Essex County Court the 10th day of July 1712, and is Recorded
                           Test
                               Richard Buckner   Cl Cur   "

page 71. Deed. 10 July 1712. ffrancis Pearce, planter, of South Farnham Par., Essex Co., sells Benjamin Fisher, planter, of same Par. and Co., for L 30., 70 acres, part of a patent of 440 acres granted John Pigg dated 22 Dec. 1682, in So. F. Par., bounded by Jonathan Fisher's line, Piscataway Creek, line running to mouth of William Covington's Mill Creek, etc.

Wit:
David Willson
William x Price
John Boughan

signed Francis Pearse
his mark

Elizabeth Pearce, wife to Francis, appeared and relinquished dower rights.

Recorded 10 July 1712.

page 73. The Will of John Jinkinson.
Dated 4th of 7'ber 1710 (4th Sept. 1710). Prob. 11 July 1712. Gives wife, Elizabeth Jinkinson, dwelling plantation and all personal property during life. To his daughter Jane at wife's death. Wife to be Exor.

"Item my will and desire is that my said Daughter do dwell on my plantation with her mother in Law Dureing her good behavior and that Doctor Henry Rose be Guardian over my said Daughter to Curb her as may appear necessary during her minority and at the decease of her said Mother to see she be no ways wrong'd of what may then be her due In witness whereof I have hereto sett my seale this 4th of 7'ber 1710"

Wit:
Vincent Vash (mark)
Ann Vash (mark)
Henry Rose

signed John Jinkinson

(Note: The above name shown 'Vash' in the record is Vass. B.F.)

page 73. Bond. L 200. William Davis as Guardian for Mary Vergitt. Dated 10 July 1712.

signed Wm Davis
Thomas Bartlett
Thomas Peatross

Recorded 10 July 1712.

page 74. Mortgage. Augustine Smith, Gent., of Essex County, deeds to Robert Beverley of King and Queen Co., Gent., 10 slaves to guar. pmt of L 137. 10. 00 and 1963 lb. tobo.

Wit: signed Augustine Smith
Chr Beverley
Isaac Walters
Arthur Hughes   Rec. 14 Aug. 1712.

page 75. Deed. 4th July 1712. Thomas Bartlett and Patience his wife, of St. Anns Par. Essex Co., she the daughter of Nathaniel Bentlet dec'd, sell Thomas Short of same Par., for L 20., 395 acres formerly granted Nath'l Bentley by patent dated 29 Sept. 1698, in St. A. Par.

Wit: signed Thomas x Bartlett
A Somervell   Patience x Bartlett
John x Bondall
                  Rec. 14 Aug. 1712.

page 76. The Will of Major James Boughan.

"Robert Coleman of the Parish of So Farnham in the County of Essex Gent aged about fifty six years Doposeth and saith that on the fourteenth day of January in the year of our Lord x x 1711 x x this Deponent was sent for by Major James Boughan late Dec'd in his life time to come to him the said Boughan x x the said Boughan did then desire this Deponent to make his x x will x x x First I give and bequeath unto my loving daughter Frances Stark the wife of John Stark x x Land x in King William County containing about two hundred acres Purchased by me of Henry Kirby x x x and my bay mare

    x x I give unto my Grandson Thomas Stark the colt that now belongs to my bay mare

    x x I give unto my loving daughter Elizabeth ffisher one gold ring of Twenty shillings

    I give unto Susanna Jones one Cow and calf and one gold ring of Twenty shillings

    I give and bequeath unto my loving son John Boughan one gold ring of Twenty shillings price

    I lend unto my Brother Henry Boughan one Third part of my water mill dureing his natural life x x and I give my Brother Henry all my wearing cloaths

    I give and bequeath unto my beloved Grandson James Boughan the son of my son James Boughan all my land and plantation whereon I now live together with my water mill and all that tract of

8-E

The Will of Major James Boughan (continued)

Land I bought of the Holts together with my old Plantation and Land and a Small Island of Land and Marsh lying before my doore", he failing in heirs then to "Grandson John Boughan son of my son James Boughan", and he failing in heirs to brother Henry Boughan and he failing to heir next of blood.

Balance of Estate to son James Boughan, he to be sole Exor. Dated 14th January 1711. "And this Deponent further saith that after he made the will x x the said Major James Boughan did sign and seal publish and declare the said will so made by this Deponent to be his last will and Testament in the presence of this Deponent one John Chamberlain Anne Atkins and the aforesaid Susanna Jones and that the said Major James Boughan then did bid the said Chamberlain Atkins and this Deponent to take notice that he the said Major James Boughan was not mad nor drunk but was in his right Senses x x".

                                 signed   Robert Coleman

page 77. "At a Court held for Essex County the 11th day of July 1712 Robert Coleman made oath to this his Deposition which by the order of August Court 1712 is Recorded as the will of James Boughan Decd"

                                 Test
                                      Richard Buckner   Cl Cur

page 77. "John Chamberlain of the Parish of South Farnham in the county of Essex planter aged about one and twenty years Deposeth and saith", relative to Major James Boughan's signature to his will.
Sworn to 11 July 1712.   signed   John Chamberlain

page 77. "Anne Atkins a servant woman that did belong to Major James Boughan late dec'd in his lifetime" swears as to the signature to his will. Dated 15 Aug. 1712

                                 signed   Anne Atkins
                                         her mark

page 77. Bond. L 500 Sterl. 15 Aug. 1712. James Boughan, John Boughan and Benj ffisher as Admrs. of the Est. of James Boughan deceased
Wit: signed   James Boughan
Ja Alderson   John Boughan
Robert Jones   Benj'a ffisher
                                                   Aug't Smith
                                                   Wm Thompson
                                                   John Pickett

                               Rec. 15 Aug. 1712

page 78. Lease and Release. 26 and 27 Sept. 1712. Mathew Collins, planter, and Mary his wife of Essex Co., sell Paul Micou of the same Co., 'Sirgurgeon', 250 acres formerly belonging to Henry Peter in St Anns Par., upon Rappahannock River "just over against the Land of Silvester Thacker", bounded on the W. side by land the sd. Mathew Collins and Mary his wife sold to William Scott.
Wit:
William Scott   signed   Matthew x Collins
Thomas Peatross   Mary x Collins
Robert Cooke
         Rec. 9 Oct. 1712.

page 80. Lease and Release. 26 and 27 Sept. 1712. Paul Micou, chirurgeon, of Essex Co., sells Mathew Collins, planter, of the same Co., 406 acres, "it being part of a Divident of four thousand two hundred acres of land formerly granted to John Meders and Henry Peter by patent dated 17th of Aprill 1667 it being the same seat or Tract of land formerly sold by the said Mathew Collins to the said Paul Micou as appears by a Deed of Sale bearing date March the tenth one Thousand Seven hundred and seven", in St. Mary's Parish.
Wit: signed   Paul Micou
William Scott
Thomas Peatross

page 81. Power of Atty. Margarett Micou to John Lomax, Gentleman, to ack sale by "my husband Paul Micou" to Collins.

Wit: Signed   Margaret Micou
Thomas Peatross
Thomas Meades

         Recorded 9 October 1712.

page 81. Lease and Release. 11 and 12 August 1712. John Willard, planter, of St. Anns Par., Essex Co., and Sarah his wife sell to John Retterford (Rutherford ?) planter, of same Par. and Co., 40 acres, formerly bought by James Coghill Dec'd of Vallentine Allen Dec'd, by deed dated 2 March 1664, and sold by Coghill to William Brown late dec'd, by deed dated 1 August 1682. Land in St. Ann's Par., bounded by Cockell Shell Creek and the land of John Lampart dec'd.

     Also 100 acres formerly bought by the said William Browne of George Lampart dec'd out of said Lamparts tract which land was by said William Brown late of the County of Essex, deceased, in his last will dated 11 Nov. 1705, bequeathed to his daughter Sarah, now Sarah Willard, the burying place excepted being about 15 ft. square.

Wit: signed John x Williad
Samll Stallord   Sarah x Willard
John Wriding
William Hakes
       Rec. 9 Oct. 1712.

page 83. Bond. L 500 Sterl. 9 Oct. 1712. Martha Parker Admr. Est. John Parker deceased.

Wit: signed Martha Parker
Ja Alderson   Jno Pickett
Robt Jones   Arth: x Bowers
              Charles Gresham

       Rec. 9 Oct. 1712.

page 84. Will of Richard Hutchens.
Dated 1 Jan. 1710/11. Probated 9 Oct. 1712.
To daughter Catherine a feather bed, etc. Balance of Est. to wife Jane, she Exor with Robert Parsons.

Wit: signed Richard x Hutchens
John Williams Junr
John x Twisdell

Bond. L 500 Sterl. Jane Hutchens and Robert Parsons, Exrs of Richard Hutchens, deceased. Dated 9 Oct. 1712.

Wit: signed Jane x Hutchens
Ja Alderson   Robert x Parsons
Robert Parker   John x Gatewood
              John Cheyney

      Rec. 9th Oct. 1712.

page 85. Lease and Release. 10 and 11 December 1712. Jonathan ffisher and Benjamin ffisher, planters, both of So. Farnham Par.

Essex Co., sell Joseph Smith, merchant, of same Par. and Co., 268 acres, a part thereof being a part of a patent formerly granted to Samuel Perry and the other part being part of a patent formerly granted Robert Young, in So. Farn. Par., on S. side of Piscataway Creek. Bounds: "Beginning at the mouth of a small creek called Covingtons mill creek runing up the several Courses of Piscataway Main Creek to the mouth of a small Creek called Perry litle Creek where now the said ffishers mill stands and runing thence up the Several Courses of the said litle Creek x x"

Wit: signed Jonathan ffisher
John Boughan   Benja ffisher
Salvator Muscoe
Jos Baker

                Recorded 11 December 1712.

page 87. Deed of Partition. 1 Dec. 1712. "E'manuel Jones of the parish of Petsworth in the County of Gloucester in the Colony of Virginia Clerk" and Joshua Boughton, planter, of So. Farnham Par., Essex Co. Whereas the said Emanuel and Joshua jointly purchased to them x x of one Henry Woodnot and Elizabeth his wife, 620 acres in So. Farn. Par., by Ind. dated 5 Dec. 1705, surveyed by Harry Beverley on 25 Aug. 1705. Joshua Boughton's part surveyed by Thomas Cooke 3 Sept. 1712. The boundry touching Croswells Corner and being near Hudson's plantation.

Wit: signed E'manuel Jones
Henry Robinson
Reub'n Welch

                Recorded 11 Dec. 1712.

page 88. Deed as foregoing. Signed Joshua Boughton his mark.

                Recorded 11 Dec. 1712.

page 88. November 11 1712. An Inventory and appraisment of the Estate of Richard Hutchings Dec'd of this County. List includes usual cattle, hogs, etc. Also:

To 1 ferry Boat & Riging	05.	00.	00
To 2 ropes	00	06.	00
To a Plush Sadle for a Woman & hackney	03	05.	00

                (continued)

Inventory of Estate of Richard Hutchings (continued)

To 5 books	00	10	00
To 4 Runletts 1 washing Tubb & 1 litle piggin	00	14.	00

Dated 9th Oct. 1712.
Presented by Jane Hutchens and Robert Parsons Exors.

                        signed   Fra Adcocke
                                    James Webb
                                    William Broocke

page 89. Deed of Gift. Jane Hutchings of So. Farn. Par., Essex Co., gives "my children Richard Hutchings John Hutchings and Catherine Hutchings", L 25 Sterl to each child to be delivered at coming of age or marriage. Dated 10 Nov. 1712.
Wit:
James Webb   signed   Jane Hutchings
Jno Williams   her mark
Edwd Adcock
               Rec. 11 Dec. 1712.

page 90. Deed. 10 Dec. 1712. James Halloway of St. Anns Par. Essex Co., planter, sells Nathaniel ffogg of same Par., "Inn holder" (ie inhabitant), for 3000 lb. tobo., 51 acres in St. A. Par. adj land where Halloway now lives, Bates line, etc.
Wit:
Richard Anderson   signed   The marke of
The mark of   James Hollaway
Elizabeth Jones
Salvator Muscoe   Rec. 11 Dec. 1712.

page 92. "An Inventory of the Estate of Mr John Parker Dec'd taken by us the subscribers this 27th day of October x 1712"
Includes:

To 2 lb pickt Cotton	00.	04.	00
To a parcell of Cotton in the Seeds & 2 old basketts	00.	16.	00
To a parcell of old Trumpery	00.	16.	00
To a parcell of old books	00.	10.	00

                (continued)

Inventory of Estate of Mr. John Parker (continued)

To 1 Razor hone old Table and 6 forks	00.	05.	00
To 1 old Table and other Trumpery	01.	05.	00
To 1 Pistoll	00.	02.	06
To 1 Sword belt Cane and 1 old hatt	00.	15.	00

Total amounts to L 75. 05. 00

                                 signed Geo Lloyde
                                            John Graves
                                            Tho Davis

Presented by Martha Parker Admr., 11 Dec. 1712 and recorded.

page 93. Bond. 12 Dec. 1712. William Bourne as Guardian for John Gregory and Sarah Gregory, orphans. L 100 Sterl.
Wit:
Ja Alderson   signed William Bourne
Wm Covington junr   Erasmus x Allen
                                              Wm Grinall

        Rec. 12 Dec. 1712.

page 93. Bond. 12 Dec. 1712. Robert Thomas as Guardian for Elizabeth Thomas, orphan. L 100 Sterl.

Wit: signed Robert Thomas
Ja Alderson   his mark
Wm Covington junr   Thomas Griffin
                                              his mark

        Rec. 12 Dec. 1712.

page 93. Appraisal of the Estate of James Boughan, Dec'd. 10 Aug. 1712.
Includes:

1 large bla Walnut Table and Table cloth	1.	10.	00
a parcell of old books	1.	15.	00
a Silver hilted Sword and belt	2.	15.	00
a Silver headed cane	0.	12.	00
6 forks and a case with them	0.	02.	06

Totals L 226. 02. 09

                              signed   Wm Covington
                                            Ja Fullerton
Given under our hands the   Fran Moore
3d day of Sept 1712

An acco't of Some goods to hand Since the Apprais'l
Includes:

To all his wearing Cloaths given to his brother	— — —
To received of Jos Burgess	100 tobo
To rec'ed of John Harper	810
To a parcell rec'd of Paul Green	200
To a parcell of William Richardson	200
To a parcell of Pierce Gold	200

Add'l Inventory totals 9251 lb. tobo.

                                signed   James Boughan
                                            John Boughan
                                            Benj'a ffisher

Inventory presented 8 Jan'ry 1712 (1712/13) by James Boughan, John Boughan and Benj'a ffisher, Adm'rs.

page 95. Deed. 5 Jan. 1712/13. Richard Jones of So. Farnham Par., planter, sells to Reuben Welch of same Par., merchant, for L 20., two tracts of land of 50 acres each. One lying at head of Piscataway Creek in So. F. Par., adj. land of William Price and being part of a greater tract bought by Richd. Jones of Thos. Johnson. The other 50 acres bounded by a line from a red oak by the creek on Richardson's Island, etc. This last 50 acres Richard Jones had of Richard Taylor in exchange for other land.
Wit:
Isaac Potier   signed   Richard Jones
John x May
John x Nichols   Rec. 8 Jan. 1712/13.

page 97. Deed. 8 Jan. 1712/13. Isaac Potier of So. Farn. Par., Essex Co., weaver, sells to Reuben Welsh of same parish and Co., merchant, 50 acres, which by Indenture dated 9 May 1702 was sold by Thomas Johnson to Henry Johnson and afterwards, on 6 October 1704, assigned to sd. Isaac Potier.
Wit:
Wm Daingerfield   signed   Isaac Potier
Zachary Lewis
Richard Jones   Rec. 8 Jan. 1712/13

page 98. Deed. 8 Jan. 1712/13. Tho. Short, planter, of St. Anns Par., Essex Co., sells Benjamin Martin, planter of same Par. and Co., for 3000 lb. tobo., all that tract of land granted 24 Sept. 1659 to Nathaniel Bentley, in St. A. Par., bounded by John Martins cleared ground, land of William Arnold, etc.
Wit:
Henry Martin   signed   Tho Short
John Martin
John Boughan   Rec. 8 Jan 1712/13

page 99. Bond. L 100 Sterl. Elizabeth Taliaferro as Adm'rx of Est. of James Thelwell deceased (as greatest creditor). Dated 8 Jan. 1712/13.
Wit: signed   Elizabeth Taliaferro
Robert Jones   Rich'd Kemp
Wm Covington jun'r   Thomas Meades

              Rec. 8 Jan. 1712/13

page 99. Will of John Williams of So. Farnham Par., Essex County, planter. Dated 19 October 1712. Probated 11 December 1712.
To grandson Thomas Williams a cow. To beloved daughter fflorandin Marshall a heiffer. To daughter Sarah Twisdale a heiffer. To well beloved son Hugh Williams land in So. Farn. Par. on Rappa. River, he to be Exor.
Wit: signed   John x Williams
George Thomsone
Jane x Huchins
Rich'd x Peirson
           (for Exor's bond see next page)

8-E

page 100. Bond. 8 Jan. 1712/13. L 200. Sterl. Hugh Williams as Exor of Est. of John Williams, deceased.
Wit:
Ja Alderson
Robt. Parker

signed Hugh Williams
John Williams
Dan'l Dobyns

Recorded 8 Jan. 1712/13

page 100. Deed of Gift. William Smith of the Par. of Abington in the County of Gloucester, Gent., gives "for and in consideration of the natural affection and Brotherly love which I have and bear unto my wel beloved brother Augustine Smith of the parish of St Ann in the county of Essex", 920 acres, this land having been patented by William Smith for his brother Augustine, due to his being remote from the Gen'l. Court and he paying expenses. This land lying on branches of Occupation Run and branches of Cockel Shell Creek and bounded by land of Richard Robinson and the line of Mrs Beth Gilson, an Indian Path, etc. Said patent granted 6th April 1712.
Wit: signed Wm Smith
Salvator Muscoe
Abraham Merchant
Isaac Walters   Recorded 12 February 1712/13.

page 101. Power of Atty. 10 Feby. 1712/13. Rebeccah ffisher and Elizabeth ffisher of South Farnham Par., Essex Co., to Mr. John Boughan of So. Farn. Par., to relinquish rights in land sold to Mr. Joseph Smith, merchant and one of her Maj'ty Justices of the Peace of Essex Co., by Jonathan ffisher and Benjamin ffisher son of the said Jonathan ffisher, both of aforesaid parish and county.
Wit:
Ann x Gibins   signed Rebeca fisher
Thomas x Rushell   Elizabeth ffisher

Rec. 12 Feb. 1712/13.

page 101. Deed. 12 Feb. 1712/13. James Boughan Sen'r of So. Farn. Par., planter, son and heir of James Boughan of same Par. and Co., sells John Boughan Senr., of St. Anns Par., planter, for L 50. Sterl., 620 acres granted Richard Holt deceased by patent dated

4 Nov. 1685 and by Richard Holt and William Holt conveyed to the said James Boughan deceased by deed dated 2 Feb. 1705. The land bounded by Kings Swamp below Piscataway Mill, land of Oliver Seager, land formerly owned by Thomas Gaines and John Morraine, Piscataway Creek, etc.

Wit: signed   James Boughan
Dan'll Browne
Tho Ley
Robt Hardee   Rec. 12 Feb. 1712/13

Robert Jones, by letter of attorney from Sarah Boughan wife of James Boughan, relinquishes dower rights to John Boughan. The letter is signed Sarah Boughan and witnessed by Jonathan ffisher and Benj'a ffisher.

page 102. Deed. "Whereas Tobias Ingram formerly of the County of Rappahannock purchased a Tract or Dividend of Land of William Moseley of the County aforesaid, Gent. lying and being in the above County but now Essex County and on the branches of Occupation which said Dividend of Land was to contain 400 acres all of which will appear by a deed of sale from the said William to the said Tobias dated 17th of August 1657 and for as much as the said tract of land is not positively and clearly marked and bounded in the said Deed - - I Edward Moseley of the said county of Essex son and heir of the said William Moseley do hereby these presents settle Establish mark and bound round the aforesaid 400 acres of Land as followeth". Beginning in the fork of Little Occupation and at the Landing of Thomas Ingram Grandson to the aforesaid Tobias and thence Running up the southern branch x thence by the creek up to the Indian Cabin Branch x x to a hickory standing on the main branch of Wassonauson, etc., agreeable to a survey and plat thereof dated 19 March 1686. "and whereas part of the land contained within said bounds was taken up and patented by my said ffather since the said deed was made by him to the said Ingram and knowing that the same was Lawfully purchased and paid for x x I x x confirm unto x x Thomas Ingram, grandson of said Tobias all my x x title x " to the 400 acres. Dated 12 Feb. 1712/13.

Wit: signed   Edwd Moseley
Salvator Muscoe
Ro Brooke junr
Rich'd Anderson Junr

Recorded 12 February 1712/13

page 103. Indenture. 22 Jany 1712/13. Elizabeth Brooks of Essex County, binds over, for a term of 30 years, to Edward Hudson, her daughter ffrances "being a Mulato child". "that she shall not want for such Diet as the said Edward Hudson can afford or other necessaries".
Wit: signed Elizabeth Brooks
Will Young   her mark
John Ragon   Edward Hudson

page 103. Deed of Gift. - February 1712/13. Robert Thomas, planter, of St. Mary's Parish, "for fatherly love and affection which I bear unto my son Robert Thomas", 684 acres 26 perches, lying on main branch of Ware Creek called Mollwebs branch, on the upper side of a patent called Sollomans Garden, on the back part of a patent formerly granted to Prosser and Creighton deceased. Adjs. a corner of the land lately granted to Charles Taliaferro, a branch of Snow Creek, etc. This land granted to Robert Thomas by Sir Edward Nott, Esqr., then Govern'r of this Colony, 2 Nov. 1705.
Wit: signed Robert Thomas
John Bowrne (sic)   his mark
Robt Bowrne
  his mark
              Rec. 12 Feb. 1712/13

page 103. February 9th 1712/13. Inventory of the Estate of John Williams. Includes:
a parcell of old books   0. 5. 0

Totals L 21. 14. 7
                 signed Leo Hill 1712
                           Edw Adcocke
                           Isaac Webb

Presented by Hugh Williams Exor. 12 February 1712/13

page 104. Will of Dan'll Dobyns of Essex County. Dated - Sept. 1712. Probated 12 February 1712/13. "Unto my five sons vizt Richard, Dan'll, Edmund, William and Charles Dobyns" 20 shillings

8-E   40

Will of Dan'll Dobyns (continued)

each to buy them rings.
To daughter Catherine Dobyns a feather bed, etc.
"I give and bequeath unto my three younger sonns that is to say
Griffin, Drury and Isaac Dobyns" L 10. Sterling each when 21.
"that my son Charles Dobyns remaine with his Mother in Law till
Xmas come Two years and that the negro woman Bess remain with my
wife the term of time her master Charles stays"
Balance of Estate to wife Elizabeth, she to be Exor.
Wit:
John Hoskins   signed Danll (Dobyns) Sen'r
  his mark
Thomas ffitsjefres
  his mark
Robt Lumpkin

page 105. Blank space left on page for surveyor's plat. The key
to the plat is entered. Among the items the following:

D is a Red Oak standing by the Main Road that leads to Burnetts
    Rolling house 120 poles from C
E is where the line Intersex Mr John Burnett's Line 9 pole D
M is the Church Road

"The above parcell of land was measured and Laid of and Divided
for Robert Moody and William Crowdas the 29th day of September
1709   John Boughan "

"At a Court held for Essex County the 12th day of March 1712
This survey and plat of Land on the motion of Robert Moodey and
Sarah Crowdas was ordered to be Recorded and is Recorded
                        Test
                            Richard Buckner   Cl Cur "

page 105. Lease and Release. 11 and 12 March 1712/13. Nehemiah
Russell of the parish of Kingston in the County of Gloucester,
planter, sells John Dickinson of the parish of South Farnham in
the County of Essex, Taylor, 192 acres, being part of a patent of
356 acres granted Edward Hudson by patent dated 24 May 1666, in
South Farnham parish, Essex County, bounded by the land of Joseph

Smith and the land of Thomas Day.

Wit: signed N Russell
Homer Roden
John Crow
Evan Davies

Power of Atty. Christian Russell to "my loving friend Mr John Crow" to relinq. dower rights in land sold John Dickinson. Dated 10 March 1712/13.
Wit: signed Christian Russell
N Russell
John Dickinson
Recorded 12 March 1712/13

page 107. Lease and Release. 11 and 12 March 1712/13. William Berry and Margret his wife one of the Daughters and Co-heirs of Enock Doughty deceased of the parish of St Maries in the County of Richmond, planter, sell to Honour Powell of St Anns Par. in Essex Co., planter, 296 acres, part of a patent of 4763 acres granted to Enock Dou'ty on 15 June 1675.
Wit:
John Strang signed William Berry
Thomas Meades Margret Berry
John Boughan
Rec. 12 March 1712/13

page 109. Power of Attorney. 22 October 1712. William Griffin, Gent., of the Town of Salem in the County of Salem to "my trusty and welbeloved friend Colo Richard Covington Gent of the County of Essex" to receive from Timothy Atkinson, late of the Town of Salem in the County of Salem, now living in the County of Essex within the Colony of Virg'a", L 125. 11. 07 , also authority to sell half interest in a water mill called ffoxhills mill conveyed to Griffin by Atkinson by deed dated 21 Oct. 1712.

Wit: signed Wm Griffin
Salvator Muscoe
Wm Covington junr
Recorded 12 March 1712/13

page 109. Agreement. Date omitted. Regards dividing line between "Dividends of Land we now live upon Vizt beginning at a white oak standing in the mouth of old Francis Browns Spring branch which said Tree is a corner Tree to Dan'l Brown Lane that he now lives upon" etc. (may mean 'Dan'l Brown's Lane' or 'Dan'l Brown's Land')
Wit:
James Boughan   signed   Richard Jones
Spilsbee Coleman   John Harper

Date of record omitted.

page 109. Deed. 9 Feb. 1712/13. John Garnet of St. Anns Par., sells William Taylar of same Par., for 3000 lb. tobo., 50 acres bounded by a line beginning at a white oak near Moseley's Quarter x x to a poplar and oak near to a small branch of Gilsons, etc.
Wit:
John x Graves   signed   John Garnet
Thomas x Graves

Ann Garnet, wife to John, relinq. her dower rights.

Recorded 12 March 1712/13

page 111. Deed. Date omitted from record. Plunkett Holt of So. Farn. Par., "son and Devisee of Richard Holt deceased", sells John Boughan, Senr., of St Anns Par., for 1600 lb. tobo., 620 acres granted Richard Holt deceased by patent dated 4 Nov. 1685, begining at Kings Swamp below Piscataway Mill, adj. the land of Oliver Seager, the land of Thomas Gaines and John Morraine, etc.
Wit:
Thomas Bryan   signed   Plunkett Holt
James Edmondson   his mark

Recorded 12 March 1712/13

page 112. Will of Job Virgett. Dated 16 Nov. 1705. Probated 13th March 1712/13. To James Jones wearing apparel. "I give unto my brother Wm Davis one Long Gun and Carbine and my own wearing hatt". To "my Daughter Mary my plantation that I did live upon", also much personal property, also "one Gold Ring that I lent unto

(continued)

8-E

Will of Job Virgett (continued)

Thomas Short which he has not returned as yet and one Gold Ring that my wife has in wearing". Bal of Est to wife Elizabeth, she to be exor.

Wit:
Robt Moseley
Josias Ship

signed Job Virgett
his mark

---

page 112. Will of John Brazer of So. Farnham Par. Dated 23 Oct. 1712. Probated 14 March 1712/13.

To son Richard Brazer all lands
To wife Elizabeth a negro man servant
To son John Brazer a cow calf.
To Son in Law Robert Davis a heifer.
Balance of Est. to be divided betw wife Elizabeth and son Richard, they to be Exors.
"I also will and desire that my son Richard Brazer remain and stay with his Mother in Law till next Christmas come Twelve months"

Wit:
Thomas Russell
  his mark
Ann Gibbons
  her mark
James Edmondson

signed John Brazer
his mark

Bond. 14 March 1712/13. L 300 Sterling. Wm Hudson and Eliza his wife and Richard Brasier Exors of John Brasier deceased.

Wit:
Salvator Muscoe
Ja Alderson

signed Eliza Hudson
her mark
William Hudson
    mark
Rich'd Brasier
James Boughan
Owen Owens
his mark

Recorded 14 March 1712/13

---

page 113. Lease and Release. 16 and 17 January 1712/13. Thomas Tinsley of St Anns Par., sells William Kilpin of Christ Church Par., Middlesex County, 316 acres in St. Anns Par., bounded by a line beginning at a red oak near William Daniel's plantation,

8-E

then crossing the head of Portobago Swamp, etc., to a Gum in Enock Dowtys old Line. The line passing a hickory at Makennys Corner.
Wit: signed   Thomas Tinsley
Will Briant   his mark
  his mark
Thomas Jackson
  his mark   Rec. 9 April 1713.

Sarah Tinsley, wife of Thomas Tinsley, by John Tinsley her atty., relinq. her right of dower. Signed Sarah Tinsley her mark.

page 115. Deed. 8 April 1713. John Ridgdaile, planter, of St Anns Par., Essex Co., and Elizabeth his wife sell Samuel Ellitts of same Par. and Co., for 1500 lb. tobo., 50 acres on S. side of Rappahannock River, in St A. Par., on Popoman Swamp and adj land of Daniell Newell and that of Saml Ellitt.
Wit:
John Andrews   signed   John Ridgdaile
James Hackley   Elizabeth Rigdaile
                                        her mark

Recorded 9 April 1713

page 116. Will of John Prise. Dated 27 Nov. 1709. Probated 9th April 1713. To John Ball "my son in law" plantation, negroes and all other property. He to be Exor.
Wit:
Thomas Harper   signed   John Prise
John Haile   his mark
Nicholas Berrey
    his mark
Margarett hopson
    her mark

Bond. 9th April 1713. L 500 Sterling. John Ball as Exor of John Prise deceased.
Wit: signed   John Ball
Robert Parker   his mark
Robt Jones   James Fullerton
                                           John Haile

Recorded 9th April 1713

8-E

page 116. Bond. 9 April 1713. L 5000. Sterling. Mary Meriwether as Ex'trx. ffrancis Meriwether, deceased.
Wit:
R Buckner
Ja Alderson
        signed Mary Meriwether
               Wm Daingerfield
               Will Young

Rec. 9 Apl. 1713.

page 117. Bond. 9 April 1713. Ann Connaley as Ex'trx of Thomas Connaley, deceased. L 200. Sterling.
Wit:
Robt Parker
R Buckner
        signed Ann Connaley
               her mark
               John Munday
               James Holloway

Rec. 9 Apl. 1713

page 117. Bond. 9 April 1713. L 200. Sterling. Elizabeth Virgett Adm'x Est. of Job Virgett, deceased.
Wit:
Robt Jones
R Buckner
        signed Elizabeth Virgett
               her mark
               Rich'd Long
                 his mark
               Mathew Collins
                 mark

Rec. 9 Apl. 1713

page 117. Will of Thomas Rennolds of Essex Co. Dated 25 Sept.1712. Probated 10 April 1713. To "Brother James Rennolds" 2 negroes. To Charles Waller 700 lb. tobo. Bal. of Est. to be divided betw Brother James, sister Sarah and sister Elizabeth. Bro. Jas. Exor.
Wit:
Charles Waller
Susannah Waller
  her mark
        signed Thomas Rennolds

page 117. Bond. 10 Apl. 1713. L 300 Sterl. James Rennolds as Exor of Est. of Thomas Rennolds, deceased.

Wit: signed
Wm Covington junr   James Rennolds
Ja Alderson   Leo Tarent
                             Robt Brooking

Rec. 10 April 1713.

page 118. Lease and Release. 6 and 7 May 1713. Richard Long, planter, of St Marys Par., Essex Co., sells Nicholas Ware junr of the parish of Stratton Major in the County of King & Queen, 71 acres in St. M. Par., bounded by land of Samuel Elliott, John Buckner, a branch of Golden Vale, land of John Long and Harrison's line.

Wit: signed   Richard Long
Wm Covington junr   his mark
Joseph Edmondson
Ja Alderson
                        Rec. 14 May 1713

page 119. Appraisal of Est of Thomas Rennolds, dec'd., by order of Court dated 10 April 1713.
Includes:

To 1 Clothes and great coat	04. 00. 00	
To 64 yds of Virga Cotton at	06. 00. 00	
To a parcell of old clothes at	02. 10. 00	
To 3 Ells of Garlick holland at	00. 06. 00	
To 1 set of Tinkers Tools at	01. 00. 00	
To 1 Sadle holster pistolls and sword	02. 10. 00	
To 3 books	00. 06. 00	

Totals L 136. 08. 04

                    signed   William Smither
                             Thomas Strechley
                             John Doughity
                             John ffoster

Presented by James Rennolds, Exor., 14th May 1713 and Recorded.

page 120. Inventory of James Thewall's Estate.
Includes:
To a parcell of New Shoe making tools at   01. 08. 00
To a parcell of old Shoe making tools at   00. 06. 00

Total valuation L 16. 14. 06

"Tobacco rec'd of the above Estate
        from Charles Taliaferro   600
        from Robert Slaughter   200
        from Jno Catlett   50

                 signed   Larkin Chew
                         John ffox
                         Richard Johnson
                         Robert Slater
                           his mark

14 May 1713. Presented by Elizabeth Taliaferro Admr.
(Note the two spellings of the name Slaughter in the above entry)

page 121. Appraisal of Est. of Thomas Connaley by order of Court
9th April 1713. Total valuation L 09. 01. 00

                  signed   Edward Moseley
                         Richard Goode
                         Cornelius Sale

Presented by Ann Conneley, Admx., 14 May 1713 and recorded.

page 121. Appraisal of Est. of John Prise by order of Court 9th
April 1713.
Includes:
To 2 Guns at L 1.5 and 1 silver headed cane   02. 00. 00
To 16 1/2 yds of Damask at 2/   01. 13. 00

Total valuation L 252. 03. 07
Appears from inventory to have been a merchant dealing in textiles.

                  signed   Richard Dudley
                         John   x   Gatewood
                         Alexander   x   How

14 May 1713. Presented by John Ball Exor., and recorded.

page 122. Bond. 14 May 1713. L 1000 Sterling. "Whereas the above bound Joseph Smith has obtained a Comission for the office of Sheriff of Essex County".
Wit:
Ja Alderson
Leo Tarent

signed Joseph Smith
        ffrancis Gouldman
        Richard Buckner

Recorded 14 May 1713

page 122. Appraisal of Est. of John Brasier Dec'd., by order of Court dated 14 March 1712/13. Total valuation L 78. 01. 01. Submitted by Eliza Brasier Extrix.

signed Wm Johnson
        Benj'a ffisher
        P Godfrey

Rec. 14 May 1713.

page 123. "Pursuant to Order of Essex County Court I went upon the Land of Joseph Baker and in presence of Erasmus Allen laid out the Road of Thomas Wheeler in the North Side of his corn field upon the Levill by the house where Richard Gatewood now lives into the main road   Given under my hand this 14th of May 1713

Wm Daingerfield

Truly Recorded
        Test
              Richard Buckner   Cl Cur "

page 123. Lease and Release. 9 and 10 June 1713. "John Rackley of the parish of South farnham in the county of Essex within the Colony of Virginia Son and heir apparent of John Rackley late of the aforesd p'ish County and Colony Dec'd" sells Wm Grinall, planter, of same Par. and Co., a plantation of 180 acres, "given to my ffather John Rackley Dec'd by a Certain Will of Anthony Norths Dec'd dated the three and Twentieth day of August one

Thousand six hundred Eighty and four" on S. side of Rappa about 2 miles above "hobs his hole".
Wit:
Erasmus Allen   signed John x Rackley
Ro Brooke Junr
Salvator Muscoe
            Rec 11 June 1713.

page. Richard Procter records mark for cattle. 1712.
    Joanna Procter records her mark for cattle, 1712.

page 125. Lease and Release. 9 and 10 June 1713. Nathaniel Vickers, planter, of St. Marys Par., Essex Co., sells Andrew Harrison the younger, planter, of the same Par. and Co., 100 acres in St. Marys Par., adj. land of Richard Long where he now lives, Edward Evans corn field, etc.
Wit:
Richard x Long   signed Nathaniel Vickers
Edward x Evans
Augt Smith
       Rec. 11 June 1713.

page 127. Lease and Release. 9 and 10 June 1713. Andrew Harrison the younger, planter, of St Marys Par., Essex Co., sells Nath'll Vickers of same Par., 200 acres, adj. land of Mr. Buckner and that of Richard Long.
Wit: signed Andrew Harrison
Richard x Long
Edward x Evans
Augt Smith   Rec. 11 June 1713.

page 129. "An account of some more of the Estate of Richard Wilton Dec'd vizt To two Doe skins, To 1 Spinning Wheele To 1 pr of shot and bullet mools
Presented by Richard Wilton Admr of Richard Wilton dec'd and is Recorded
      Test Richard Buckner Cl Cur "

page 129. Power of Atty. 6 Feb. 1712/13. George Mason of the "Citty of Bristoll", merchant, to "the Hon'ble Colonell William ffitzhugh in Potomack River" to collect from Col. George Mason in Virga., money, goods, wares etc.
Wit:
Robert Boyd   signed   Geo Mason
Tho Mackey

Proved by oaths of witnesses in Essex Court 11 June 1713 and recorded.

page 130. Deed. 12 March 1712/13. Morgan Swyney and Ann his wife and Henry Purkins and Tabitha his wife all of Essex Co., sell to Alexander Graves of Middlesex Co., for 4200 lb. tobo., 200 acres, now lived on by Swyney and Purkins, adj. land of Thomas Crow, land of William Chance, land of William Geffereys and the land of Dan'l Dobyns.
Wit: signed   Morgan Swiney
Nicho Smith Junr   his mark
Jno Gibson   Ann Swiney
Benj'a ffisher   her mark
                                     Henry Purkins
                                     Tabitha Purkins
                                     her mark

Rec. 11 June 1713.

page 131. Lease and Release. 28 and 29 May 1713. Larkin Chew, Gent. of Essex Co., sells "the Right honourable George Earle of Orkney Her Majestys Lieutenant Governor Generall of the Colony and Dominion of Virg'a", for fifteen pounds Sterling, 1/16 part of a certain Tract of Land containing 4020 acres in St. Mary's Par. in Essex Co., on the south side of the South River of Rappa. River and on a great swamp of the said River, granted to the said Larkin Chew by patent dated 2 May 1713.
Wit:
Jer Clowder   signed   Larkin Chew
Wil Robertson
Richard Buckner

Hannah Chew, wife of Larkin Chew, relinq. her dower rights.

8-E

page 133. Lease and Release. 28 and 29 May 1713. Larkin Chew, Gent., sells "the hon'ble Alexander Spotswood Esq'r Lieutenant Governor and Com'ander in Chief of the Colony and Dominion of Virg'a", for L 50. Sterl., 1/4 part of 4020 acres - see foregoing Lease and Release. Signature and witnesses as before.

page 135. Lease and Release. Larkin Chew, Gent., sells "Christopher de Graffenried Esq'r otherwise called Christopher Baron de Graffenried of the Province of North Carolina", for L 15. Sterl., 1/16 part of 4020 acres. Same date, signature and witnesses as foregoing.

page 137. Lease and Release. 28 and 29 May 1713. Larkin Chew, Gent., sells William Robertson, Gent., of James City Co., for L. 15 Sterl., 1/16 part of 4020 acres. See foregoing entries.
Wit:
Jer Clowder   signed Larkin Chew
Richard Buckner
Jos Davenporte

page 139. Lease and Release. 28 and 29 May 1713. Larkin Chew, Gent., sells Richard Buckner, Gent., of Essex Co., for L 15. Sterling, 1/16 part of 4020 acres, as above.
Wit:
Jer Clowder   signed Larkin Chew
H Bowcocke
Wil Robertson

page 141. Lease and Release. 11 and 12 June 1713. Larkin Chew sells Richard Buckner, for L 8. Sterl., 1/32 part of 4020 acres, as above
Wit:
Wm Woodford   signed Larkin Chew
Reub'n Welch
R Beverley   Rec. 12 June 1713.

page 142. Lease and Release. 8 and 9 June 1713. Larkin Chew of Essex County sells Gawin Corbin of King and Queen County, for

L 45. Sterling, 3/16 part of 4020 acres, as above.
Wit:
Jno Tayloe   signed   Larkin Chew
Tho Newman
Nath ffogg

                      Recorded 13 August 1713.

page 144. Lease and Release. 1 and 2 June 1713. Larkin Chew of Essex Co., Gentleman, sells Jeremiah Clowder of King and Queen Co., Gentleman, for L 15. Sterl., 1/16 part of 4020 acres, as above.
Wit: signed   Larkin Chew
Wm Roy
Jno Roy
Robert x Shepard   Recorded 13 August 1713.

page 146. Deed of Gift. Edward and Richard Booker of Essex Co., give to "our welbeloved Brother Edmund Booker", 100 acres, upon head of Portobacco Swamp, adj. land of Richard Booker and the land of Edward Booker. Dated 8 July 1713.
Wit:
Tho Turner   signed   Edw'd Booker
Thomas Robins   Rich'd Booker
  his mark
                      Recorded 13 Aug. 1713.

page 147. Deed. 27 April 1713. Thomas Short of St Anns Par., Essex Co., planter, sells Jeremiah Biswell of same Par. and Co., planter, for 3000 lb. tobo., 100 acres in St. Anns Par., adj land of Charles Brown and the land of Thomas Short.
Wit:
Thomas ffenwick   signed   Thomas Short
Thomas Shortt Junr
John Boughan

Abigall Short, wife to Thomas Short, relinq. dower rights.

                      Recorded 13 Aug. 1713.

page 148. Lease and Release. 7 and 8 July 1713. Thomas Short, planter, of St Anns Par., Essex Co., sells Thomas ffenwick of the same Par. and Co., planter, 100 acres in St. A. Par., adj land of Stark, line crossing main Run of Occupation, the land of Pannill, the land of Blackburn and that of Charles Brown.
Wit:
Samll Stallord   signed   Thomas Short
Thomas Short junr
William x Webster

Abigall Short, the wife of Thos. Short, relinq. dower rights.

Rec. 13 Aug. 1713.

page 150. Deed. 6 April 1713. Jeremiah Beswell sells Charles ffarrell, for 3000 lb. tobo., 1/2 of that tract of land "whereon John Spires now liveth", 80 acres which sd Beswell formerly purchased of sd Spires, on east branch of Occupation Creek and adj. land of Capt. Edward Rowzee.
Wit:
Thomas Ingram   signed   Jeremiah Biswell
Charles hill   (sic)
Nicholas Morane

Mary Biswell, wife to Jeremiah, relinq. dower rights.

Rec. 13 Aug. 1713.

page 151. Bond. 13 Aug. 1713. L 300. Sterl. John Battaile as Guardian of Lawrence Battaile
Wit: signed   John Battaile
Augt Smith   Charles Taliaferro
Robt Jones
                 Rec. 13 Aug. 1713.

page 151. Will of Rees Evans of Essex Co. Dated 31 Oct. 1712. Probated 13 Aug. 1713. To daughter Elizabeth, a negro slave. To son John, land and slaves. To daughter Mary, 2 slaves. To son, land "I now live on" adj. to Golden Vale Creek. To son Edward and wife Elizabeth, bal of Est., they to be exors.
Wit:
John Catlett   signed   Rees Evans
Henry Machon

page 152. Bond. 13 Aug. 1713. L 500 Sterl. Edward Evans and Elizabeth Evans as exors. of est. of Rees Evans deceased.
Wit:
Augt Smith
Robt Jones

signed   Edward Evans
         his sign
         Eliza Evans
         sign
         Charles Taliaferro
         Richard Johnson

Rec. 13 Augt. 1713.

page 152. Will of Christian Johnson. Dated 8 Aug. 1712. Probated 13 Aug. 1713. To two sons John Bourn and Robert Bourn L 12. each. Bal. of Est. to "welbeloved son" Peter Bourn, he to be exor.
Wit:
Hen Mackie
Richard Johnson
John Broadley.

signed   Christian Jonson

Exor's Bond. 13 Aug. 1713. L 300. Sterl. Peter Bourne as exor of Est. of Christian Johnson, deceased.
Wit:
Ja Alderson
Robt Jones

signed   Peter Bourne
         Charles Taliaferro
         Richard Johnson

page 153. Bond. 13 Aug. 1713. L 500. Sterl. Eliza Dobyns as Extrx of Daniel Dobyns, deceased.
Wit:
ffra Gouldman
Ja Alderson

signed   Eliza Dobyns
         Bonj'a ffisher
         Wm Cheney

Rec. 13 Aug. 1713.

page 153. Will of Andrew Dudding, planter, of South Farnham Par. To three God children Thomas Brooks son of Richard Brooks, William Cheney the son of John Cheney and Susanna Dike daughter of John Dike, 20 shillings Sterl and 200 lb. tobo. each. To Paul Groen another God child L 12. To Robert Parsons, no relationship shown,

Will of Andrew Dudding (continued)

500 lb. tobacco. To Mr Dan'l Dobyns Senr one shilling. To the children of the said Mr Dan'l Dobyns, vizt, Richard, Daniel, Elizabeth, Catherine, William and Charles Dobyns, each of them one shilling. Plantation "whereon I now live", 200 acres, etc., to "my housekeeper Mary Richards", also to her 30 acres bought of George Kilman, also balance of estate. Dated 18 Feb. 1709/10.
Wit:
George Thompson   signed   Andrew Dudding
John Dickinson   his mark
Jno Loase

Proved 13 Aug. 1713 by oaths of Mary Richards and of George Thompson and of John Lease.

Bond. 13 Aug. 1713. L 300. Sterl. Mary Richards Extrx of Est. of Andrew Dudding.
Wit: signed   Mary x Richards
Robert Jones   Ja Alderson
James Breckin   John x Lacey

Recorded 13 August 1713.

page 154. Will of Mary Welsh. Dated 14 April 1713. Probated 13 August 1713. To daughter Mary Connarnell one shilling. Balance of estate to "my loving son John Robards", he to be exor.
Wit:
Thomas Gorbill   signed   Mary x Welsh
Mary Gorbill
Charles Waller

Bond. 13 Aug. 1713. L 200. John Robards as exor of est. of Mary Welsh dec'd.
Wit: signed   John Robards
Ja Alderson   Charles Waller
Benja ffisher   Tho Graves (mark)

Recorded 13 August 1713.

page 155. Will of Samuel Thacker of Essex Co. Dated 16 Dec. 1712. Probated 9 October 1713. To Robert Brooke a gold ring of 20 shillings price. To his son Robert Brooke a ring of the same value. To Mary Brooke daughter of Robert Brooke "my God Daughter" all land and plantation at the Range, etc., "to be Delivered to her

Will of Samuel Thacker (continued)

at her day of marriage or my wifes Death". To "my serv't John Glany" one year of his time. To Eleanor Merritt, if she stay her time of service, a cow and calf. Balance of Estate to wife, she to be exor.

Wit:
Geo McCall
Martha Parker
Ro Brooke

signed Sam Thacker

9 Oct. 1713. This will proved by oath of Mary Thacker Executrix herein named, etc.

page 155. Will of Thomas Harwar. Dated 25 May 1713. Probated 8 Oct. 1713. "Thomas Harwar of the County of Essex in the Colony of Virg'a, Gent being sick and weak x x". "that if the child which my wife now goes with x x prove to be a boy that then I give and Devise to the said child all my Lands, Tenements and hereditam'ts to him and his heirs forever". "But if it prove to be a Girl, then it is my Desire that then my Lands and Tenem'ts be equally Devided between my Two Daughters and the said Girl that is to be born x x". Wife to have her residence in "my now dwelling house" during her natural life, also a fourth or child's part of Est.

To Richard Moore a horse called Button
To Susanna Dicke a gold ring of ten shillings price and a negro
  slave.
To John Vass a gold ring of ten shillings price.
To "my welbeloved friends Mr Leonard Hill and Mr Willoughby
  Allerton each of them a ring of Ten shillings price"
Daughters to be paid their portions at 16 or day of marriage.
"My Dear Wife and my Good friends Mr Willoughby Allerton and Mr
  Leonard Hill Exor's x x".

Wit:
William Wayd
Thomas Blatt
John Dike
Jno Vass

signed Tho. Harwar

8 October 1713. Proved by oaths of Elizabeth Harwar and Leonard Hill Two of exors, etc.

page 156. Bond. 8 Oct. 1713. L 2000. Sterling. Eliz'a Harwar and Leonard Hill as Exors of the Est. of Thomas Harwar, dec'd.

Wit:
Daniel Hayes
Ja Alderson

signed Elisa Harwar
Leo Hill 1713
Rich'd Covington
James Edmondson

Rec. 8 Oct. 1713.

page 156. Lease and Release. 5 and 6 Aug. 1713. Timothy Hay, late of the County of Essex, planter, sells Timothy Conner of the County of King and Queen, planter, 350 acres, "being in the County of Essex in the fforest between Burtons Range and Portobago path"
Wit:
Richd Gass
James x Colings
Thomas Bates
Alexander Cambwell

signed Timothy x Hay

Rec. 8 Oct. 1713.

page 158. Lease and Release. 6 and 7 Oct. 1713. Robert Ransone of the Par. of St. Stevens in the county of King and Queen, planter, and ffrances his wife, sell Joseph Brooks of the Par. of Kingstone in the county of Gloucester, planter, 436 acres in South Farnham Par., Essex Co., upon Rappahannock River and Thomas' Creek, for L. 83.
Wit:
Will Young
Reub'n Welsh
Richard Carter

signed Robert Ransone
ffrances Ransone

Rec. 8 Oct. 1713.

page 159. Inventory of the Est. of Job Virgett, Dec'd., taken 13 May 1713.
Includes:

2 bibles and other old books	00.	08.	00
9 hogs at 7/ a piece	03.	03.	00
5 more hogs not soon of the same age	--	--	--
one old chest and pr of lether briches	00.	12.	00
6 old chair frames and old coat and Large briches	-	-	-

Total not shown. Approx. L 60.

signed Nicholas Coplin
Ralph Rowzee
Sam'll Ellitts

Presented by Elizabeth Virgett 8 October 1713.

page 160. Bond. 10 Oct. 1713. L 72. Sterl. ffrancis Gouldman and Rich'd Buckner to James Brechin, clerk. Judgement being this day in Essex Court to Rev. Brechin agt. Martha Gouldman and ffrancis Gouldman, Executors of Edward Gouldman deceased in a suit in

8-E

Chancery for L 36. 00. 05 Sterling, an appeal being made to next Court, etc.
Wit: signed   ffrancis Gouldman
Ja Alderson   Rich'd Buckner
Zach Lewis
                    Rec. 10 Oct. 1713.

page 161. Deed of Gift. Vincent Vass, planter, of South Farnham Par., gives for "that entire love and tender regard I have for my only Son John Vass of the said parish x x", the plantation whereon he "now liveth" in So. F. Par., with 2 negroes, stock, etc.
Wit: signed   Vincent Vass
Lewis Latane   his mark
William Waye
                    Rec. 12 Nov. 1713.

page 161. Deed. 11 Nov. 1713. James Bidlecom of Richmond County and Elizabeth his wife Daughter heir apparent of Thomas Kirk, deceased, sell to Charles Brown of Essex Co., for 1400 lb. tobo., - acres in Essex Co., originally granted to James Coghill 24th March 1664/5 and by Coghill assigned to afsd Thomas Kirk.
Wit:
Mathew Collins   signed   James Bidlecom
William Brown   his mark
                                           Elizabeth Bidlecom
                                           her mark

                    Rec. 12 Nov. 1713.

page 162. Bond. 14 January 1713/14. 34214 pounds of tobacco. Joseph Smith. "Whereas the Court of the aforesaid County of Essex hath thought fit to intrust the above bound Joseph Smith Gentleman with the collection of seventeen thousand one hundred and seven pounds of Tobo being the whole County Levy of Essex aforesd for this present year x x "
Wit:
Ja Alderson   signed   Joseph Smith
Robt Jones   Rich'd Buckner

                    Rec. 14 Janry 1713/14.

page 162. Deed of Gift. 8 Dec. 1713. Richard Dobyns gives Daniel Dobyns "for x natural Affection and brotherly love which I have and bear unto my wel beloved brother Daniel Dobyns of the aforesaid parish and County", 50 acres, part of the tract "whereon I now dwell".
Wit: signed   Rich'd R Dobyns
Joseph Williams   sign
Henry Adcocke
John Spann

Elizabeth Dobyns, wife to Richard, relinq. dower rights.

Rec. 14 January 1713/14.

page 163. Deed of Gift. 13 Jan. 1713/14. John Williams, planter, of Essex Co., for "the affection that I do bear to Henry Hudson of the same county", gives land, acerage not shown, on So. side of Rappahannock River.
No witnesses   signed   John Williams
shown on record.
                Recorded 14 January 1713/14.

"Know ye that I the said Henry Hudson do oblige my Self my heirs Exor's or Adm'rs from keeping any more than five hoggs and not to keep any piggs on the said Land that is above Two months old Given under my hand the day and year above written
                                Henry Hudson
               Truly Recorded
                    Test
                          Richard Buckner Cl Cur"

page 163. Lease and Release. 12 Jany. 1713/14.(only one date). Samll Prosser of St. Mary's Par., sells Gabriel Long, planter of same Par., for 1300 lb. tobo., 53 acres in St. Mary's Par., on both sides of the Main Run of Golden Vale Creek, etc.
Wit:
Larkin Chew   signed   Samll Prosser
John Sutton
John Evans

                Recorded 14 Jan. 1713/14

page 165. "Tobacco that I have recieved belonging to Robert Mills Estate since the appraisal Twelve hundred and Eighty and likewise young hogg near two year old Chopping knife"

                    signed Henry Byrom

At a Court held for Essex the 14th day of Jan'ry 1713 presented by Henry Byrom Exor of the last will of Robert Mills dec'd and is Recorded

                    Test
                      Richard Buckner Cl Cur

page 165. Lease and Release. 11 and 12 Jan'ry 1713/14. Sam'll Prosser of St. Mary's Par., sells Robert Kay jun'r of same parish, - - acres, "formerly Granted to my Grandfather Jno Prosser", on the upper side of a creek known by the name of Golden Vale and adj. land of Mr. Wm Stanard and that of Robert Kay Senr.
Wit:
William Stemson   signed Samll Prosser
Jno Roy
Robt Parker
                Rec. 14 Jan. 1713/14

page 166. Simon Beckham records mark for cattle. No date by entry but is of 14 Jany. 1713/14.

page 166. Deed of Gift. 14 October 1713. Elizabeth Wheeler of Middlesex County gives to Katherine Midleton, daughter of Pursilla Midleton of Essex County, a heifer.
Wit:
William Daniell   signed Elizabeth Whealer
Mary Rice   (sign)
  sign

                Rec. 14 Jan. 1713/14

page 166. Will of George Lloyd of St. Anns Par. Dated 19 Dec. 1713 Probated 14 Jan. 1713/4.

To son Samuel Loyd, 200 acres out of a tract purchased from Mr. ffrancis Meriwether, to include plantation "whereon I now live", adj. Brices Swamp. He failing in heirs to dau. Anne Loyd. That son be of age at 18 if his mother marry, if she does not marry then at 21.

To dau. Anne Loyd, 100 acres purchased from ffrancis Graves adj. Brices Swamp.

To dau Eliza Loyd, 100 acres purchased from Thomas Merritt adj. Brices Swamp.

To dau. Martha Loyd all land on the upper side of Brices Swamp excepting plantation purchased from Thomas ffarmer.

To son in law John Diskin 100 acres in So. Farn. Par. purchased from William Read and Elinor his wife, to be laid off at the charge of Capt. William Covington. Also a colt had from Paul Pitman.

To daughter in law Mary Diskin 50 acres, being the plantation purchased from Thomas ffarmer.

To son in law Daniel Diskin 2000 lb. tobo. for his education.

To wife Johanna Loyd various personal items.

Balance of Estate to be divided betw. wife and children.

Exors, wife Johanna, Salvator Muscoe, Mr James Alderson and Mr Robert Beverley.

Wit:
Salvator Muscoe   signed   George Lloyd
Thomas Munday
Arth Bowers

Bond. 14 Jan. 1713/14. L 1000. Sterling. Joanna Loyd as Admr. of Est. of George Loyd, Dec'd.
Wit: signed   Joanna Loyd
Robt Jones   her mark
Ja Alderson   James Boughan
                                  James Edmondson
                                  Fran Moore
                                  Arth Bowers

Recorded 14 Janry 1713/14

page 167. "To one young mare 2 years old to be added to the Estate of Thomas Sanders Dec'd this 15th Day of Jan'ry 1714
per me
Richard Hill

Truly Recorded
Test
Richard Buckner   Cl Cur   "

page 168. Deed. 14 Jan. 1713/14. James Boughan, Senr., planter, of South Farnham Par., son and heir of James Boughan of same Par., deceased, sells Henry Boughan, planter, of the same Par., all rights in - acres of land formerly in co-partnership between Thomas Harper and his grandfather James Boughan, both deceased, and formerly given by a Deed under the hand of his father James Boughan to John Boughan, Henry Boughan and Alexander Boughan, dated 29th March 1678, the original patent dated 8 Oct. 1672.
Wit:
James Edmondson   signed   James Boughan
Jos Baker
                 Recorded   14 Jan. 1713/14

page 168. Will of John Webb, of South Farnham Par., Essex Co. Dated 7 Dec. 1712. Proved 15 Jany 1713/14.
"I give unto John Webb als Montague" a cow. Balance of Estate to be divided betw. wife Elizabeth and John Webb als Montague. Gun to John Webb als Montague. "and in case my wife marrys again I leave my wife one Cow more than John Montague shall have in his share of the Estate, my desire is that Jno Webb als Montague do live with my wife till he arrives to the age of Twenty one years (if she does not marry) but if she marrys he to be at liberty, if my wife marrys before Jno Webb als Montague arrives to the age of Twenty one years then the Estate to be Equally Divided but not till then otherwise".
Exors wife and John Webb als Montague.
Wit:
Wm Hudson   signed   John Webb
Joseph Anderson   his mark
Robert R Webbs mark

At a Court held for Essex County 11 day of March 1713 (1713/14) "Eliza Webb one of the Exors within mentioned Giving Bond with Security Certificate is Granted her and Jno Webb als Montague for obtaining a probate thereof in due form
                     Test
                         Richard Buckner   Cl Cur.

page 169. Lease and Release. 13 and 14 Janry 1713/14. William Neale, planter, of So. Farn. Par., sells William Johnson, planter, of the same Par., 100 acres in So. F. Par., a part of 600 acres formerly granted to Wm. Johnson 6 Oct. 1656, on the N.W. side of Piscataway Creek, along the line of Robert Youngs land, now

called and known by the name of Argill Blackstons line to a corner of John Picketts land and Wm Johnsons land and from "thence along the said Johnsons land by the side of a White Oak Swamp untill it comes to the line of Henry Picket dec'd which was formerly a division between Henry Picket and Ralph Neale the father of William Neale aforesd".
Wit:
Jno Gaines
Wm Smith
John Chamberline

signed William Neale
his mark

Rec. 14 Jan. 1713/14.

page 170. Lease and Release. 10 and 11 Dec. 1713. Thomas Winslow, "Taylor", of St. A. Par., sells William Mackenny, planter, of same Par., 100 acres, part of a tract of 200 acres purchased by Thomas Munday of Thomas Moncaster of Charles County, Maryland, by Deed dated 5 Aug. 1700, and purchased from Munday by Tho.Winslow on 11 Sept. 1700.
Wit:
John Boughan
James Boughan
Henry Byrom

signed Thomas Winslow

Rec. 15 Jan. 1713/14

page 172. Lease and Release. 2 Feb. 1713/14. Larkin Chew, Gent., of Essex Co., sells Jeremiah Clowder, Gent., of King and Queen Co., 1/32 part of 4020 acres in St. Mary's Par., patented 2 May 1713, etc., for L 7. 10. 00
Wit:
Joseph Smith
Jno Roy
James Edmundson

signed Larkin Chew

Rec. 11 Feb. 1713/14

page 174. Deed. 11 Feb. 1713/14. Henry Long and Christian his wife, of Hanover Par., Richmond County, one of the Daughters and Co heirs of Vallentine Allen dec'd sell Richard Edwards of St Anns Parish, planter, for 2000 lb. tobo., 60 acres being part of 3000 acres granted Thomas Page, etc., in St. Anns Par., adj. land of Capt. Hawkins, Popoman Swamp.

Wit:
John Boughan   signed Henry Long
William Stemson   Christian x Long

Rec. 11 Feb. 1713/14

---

page 176. Lease and Release. 20 and 21 Nov. 1713. John Powell, planter, of Essex Co., sells Michael Lawless, planter, of Essex Co., 158 acres, adj. land of Richard Long and that of Thomas Powell

Wit: signed John Powell
Augt Smith   his mark
Jno Taliaferro
Jno Battaile

Jane Powell wife to John Powell relinq. dower rights.

Rec. 11 Feb. 1713/14

---

page 177. Bond. 10 Feb. 1713/14. L 50. John Rotterford of St Anns Par. to Wm Price. Regarding division of land in dispute, said land on west side of Cockell Creek and near Browns Mill. Adjoins Brown's Mill Dam and the land of Henrick Lucas.

Wit:
John Hawkins   signed John J Rotterford
John Wridings   His Mark

Bond as above William Price to John Rotterford

Recorded 11 Feb. 1713/14

Inventory of Estate of Daniel Dobyns taken by order of Court 14 Jan. 1713/14.

Includes:
To a warming pan some books and a looking glass   02. 01. 00
To a Sadle and bridle pistols and Holster and
    Sword   01. 15. 00
To 4 silver spoons   02. 00. 00

8-E   65

Inventory of the Estate of Daniel Dobyns (continued)

To a Silver Tobo box   01. 10. 00
To a old sword   00. 00. 06

Total approx. L 80.
                        signed   Nicho's Smith Junr
                                 James Edmundson
                                 Isaac Webb

Presented by Elizabeth Dobyns, Exor. 11 Feb. 1713/14.

page 179. Lease and Release. 11 Jan'ry 1713/14 (only one date shown) Nathaniel Vickers, planter, of St. Marys Par. sells Andrew Harrison the younger, planter, of same Par., 100 acres, bounded: beginning at the mouth of John Catlett Junr Spring branch x to Edward Evans line x over the top of a hill where Robert Waite did design to build his house x to land w'ch Thomas Hilliard lives on x to Golden Vale Run x x.
Wit:
Robert Jones   signed   Nathaniel N Vickers
Robert Parker   sign

                Rec. 11 Feb. 1713/14

page 180. Lease and Release. 8 and 9 Feb. 1713/14. Andrew Harrison, Junr., of St. Marys Par., sells Nathaniel Vickers of same Par., 100 acres being part of a patent granted John Prosser, dec'd., on Golden Vale Creek, adj. the land of Richard Long, etc.
Wit:
Robert Jones   signed   Andrew Harrison
Robert Parker
                Rec. 11 Feb. 1713/14

Elizabeth Harrison, wife of Andrew Harrison, by John Battaile her attorney, relinq. her dower rights.
Wit:
Jno Roy   signed   Elizabeth x Harrison
Michael Lawless
                Rec. 11 Feb. 1713/14

page 182. "An Inventory and appraisment of the Estate of Francis Meriwether Deceased"
This is a very long inventory. The following items are included:

1	paper book bound	00.	5.	00
28	Law books	5.	2.	6
7	Folio books	1.	10.	0
32	other books Severall Sorts	0.	11.	0
3	New Bibles	0.	12.	0
3	Old bibles 1 old Com'on Prayer 1 old Duty of Man	0.	2.	6
1	Sett of Surveyors Instruments	2.	-	-
1	horizantal Sun Dyall	-	3.	6
1	pr old Money Scales and weights 2 pr Do Stillards	-	2.	-
4	old Razors 2 Strops and 4 hones	-	5.	-
3	old snuff boxes 1 old Inkhorn 1 paper Ink powder	-	1.	1
12	black haft knives 12 forks and box	-	5.	-
1	parcel of Phisick	-	12.	-
4	pr plane shoes 3/	-	12.	-
a parcel of silk fringe		-	10.	-
14	pr Mens Wash Gloves	-	14.	-
3/9 1 Spice of Severall Sorts		-	10.	-
1	Ivory comb	-	-	10
1	large ovall Table	-	18.	-
1	small Do	-	8.	-
12	Rush: Leather Chairs 8/	4.	16.	-
1	large looking glass	1.	4.	-
1	Picture	-	10.	-
1	old chest	-	4.	-
1	chest of Drawers Japan'd	5.	-	-
1	ovall Table Dressing and powder boxes 2 looking glasses	3.	6.	-
1	Easy Chair and Cusheon	2.	-	-
6	low Rush. leather chairs 7/	2.	2.	-
6	Rush Leather Chairs	1.	16.	-
1	Small Table 2 old cane chairs	0.	10.	-
1	Rush Leather Trunk	0.	16.	-
8	horses	23.	15.	-
8	Mares	16.	-	-
6	colts	6.	-	-
5	bulls 27/6	6.	17.	6

Negroes 14 Men
         12 Women
         15 boys
         12 girls   1046.   -   -

Jane Slaughter an Indented Servt having
    3 yrs 10 months to serve   8.   -   -
Isabella Housing the same   8.   -   -

8-E

The Inventory of Francis Meriwether (continued)

161 oz 11 pwt of plate 5/	40.	7.	9
1 Doz table cloth	-	4.	-
6 Diaper Do 5/	1.	10.	-
1 old Camblett Cloak	-	10.	-
1 old serge Coat Wascoat and Breeches	1.	5.	-
1 Silk Drugget Do	4.	-	-
1 old cloth Wascoat	-	10.	-
1 old silk Do	-	10.	-
1 pr old Plush Breeches	-	4.	-
1 pr old serge Do	-	2.	6
a Ticken Wastcoat and 2 pr Breeches	1.	-	-
1 old fflannel 1 Do Dimo Wastcoat	0.	4.	0
3 pr worsted 4 pr thred stock's	-	12.	6
1 Periwig	1.	15.	-
1 Do	1.	-	-
3 old hats	-	12.	-
Cash	3.	4.	-
4 Gold Rings qt 13 ow a 4/	2.	12.	-
1 Bell Metal Skillett	-	5.	-
6 old knives 3 forks	-	2.	-
14 patty pans	-	2.	4
6 Biskett Do	-	3.	-
4 Quart Bottles empty	-	-	8
3 Wheel barrows	-	7.	6
1 pr Silver shoe buckles	-	6.	-
6 Muslin Neckcloths 4/	1.	4.	-
63 bushels salt 3/6	7.	17.	6
1 spring lock	-	1.	6
Some oyl and Colours	-	5.	-
a parcel of Cotton in the Seed	-	10.	-

Total valuation of inventory L 1909. 5. 11 1/2, the appraisors having first set apart the widow's dower. Certain items in list are shown as being at John Moody's Quarter.

signed 27 Jan. 1713/14.

Leo Hill   1713
Reubn Welsh
Ja Edmondson

Presented by Mary Meriwether, Admr. Est. of ffrancis Meriwether, Dec'd., 11 February 1713/14

page 188. Add'l items amounting to L 6. 3. 11 submitted.

page 188. Appraisal of Est. of Mary Welsh, Dec'd., by order of Court dated 13 Aug. 1713. Total valuation L 18. 18. 2

        signed Charles Waller
             John Mackenny
             Wm Gordin his mark

Presented by John Robards Exor of Mary Welch 11 Feb. 1713/14 and is Recorded.

page 189. Appraisal of Est. of Andrew Dudding, Dec'd., made by order of Court 13 August 1713, which order being renewed 14 Jany 1713/14, the subscribers being first sworn before Capt. William Young. Total approx. L 40.

        signed James Edmondson
             James Webb
             Nicholas Smith junr

Presented by Mary Richards Executrix of Andrew Dudding 11th Feb. 1713/14.

page 190. Deed. 11 Feb. 1713/14. William Brown, planter, of St. Anns Par., sells Samuel Stallord, planter, of same Par., for 1800 lb. tobo., 60 acres adj. land of Capt John Hawkins, Popoman Swamp and the land of Robert Parker.
Wit:
Jno Vawter   signed William Brown
Thomas ffenwicke
John Wriding
       Rec. 11 Feb. 1713/14

page 190. Deed. 6 Feb. 1713/14. John Ridgdaill, planter, of St. A. Par., sells Jno ffoster, planter, of same Par., for L 35., 50 acres, being part of a tract belonging to John Andrews in St. A. Par., adj land of Mess Nowell, Samuel Elletts, Jno Anderson, Abner Gray and of Major Robinson. The name also appears as Ridgall in the entry.
Wit: signed John Ridgdaile
John Boughan
John Butler
Robert x ffoster
       Recorded 11 Feb. 1713/14

page 192. Deed. 6 Feb. 1713/14. John Butler, planter, of St. A. Par., sells Robert ffoster, planter, of same Par., for 9000 lb. tobo., 100 acres, being part of a patent of 600 acres granted to Capt. Israel Linch, 14 Sept. 1650 and granted Richard Coleman the same day and year, adj. land of Thomas Loy, land of Robert Biswell, etc.

Wit:
John Boughan   signed John Butler
john ffoster his mark
John Ridgdaile

Agnis Butler, wife to John Butler, relinq dower rights by Robert Jones her attorney.
         Rec. 11 Feb. 1713/14

page 193. Deed. 11 Feb. 1713/14. Elias Blackburn, planter, of St. Anns Par., sells John Butler, planter, of same Par., for 8000 lb. tobo., 116 acres, part of a patent of 600 acres granted Captain Israel Linch 14 Sept. 1650 and granted to Richd Coleman the same day and year, on West side of Colemans Creek at the southside of a Branch called the Schoolhouse Branch, etc.

Wit:
John Boughan   signed Elias Blackburn
Thos Ley
James Cocker his mark

Martha Blackburn, wife to Elias, relinq. dower rights.
         Rec. 11 Feb. 1713/14

page 195. Power of Atty. 10 Feb. 1713/14. Mrs. Martha Blackborn to John Boughan.
Wit: signed Martha Blackburn
Francis Gipson his mark   her mark
James Cocker his mark

         Rec. 11 Feb. 1713/14

page 195. Award. John Boughan, John Hawkins and Samuel Stallord of Essex Co., award there is no cause for action in suit depending in Essex Court betw. Capt. Lawrence Smith of York Co. of one part and John Willard and Ann Phillips of Essex Co. of the other part, concerning land in Essex Co. Lawrence Smith represented by Augustine Smith his attorney. This land adj that of Mr Daniel Gaines and Peter Cornwell, Cattail Branch, a corner tree of Pain, Page and Cornwell, Job Spearman and John Willard.

         Rec. 11 Feb. 1713/14.

page 196. Deed. 15 Jan. 1713/14. Richd Covington of St Anns Par. and James Boughan of So. Farnham Par., son and heir of Major James Boughan late of said Par., deceased, sell to Thomas Gouldman and Edward Gouldman sons and Devisees of Edward Gouldman late of St. Anns Par., deceased, land, acerage not shown, "Whereas the said Edward Gouldman by purchase from one William Williams a certain parcel of land granted to Collo Richard Covington ; Major James Boughan and the sd William Williams, by Patent Dated the 25 day of Aprill 1704", in St Anns Par. This land formerly granted to Thomas Pannell Dec'd by Patent 4 Nov. 1673, and afterwards granted to Covington, Boughan and Williams, having been lost by Pannell for want of seating. The land was partitioned between the said Collo Richard Covington of the first part, and Major James Boughan, Benjamin ffisher and James Boughan Junr. of the second part, and the said Edward Gouldman (who had purchased Williams' share) of the third part, by deed the 9th August 1708, recorded 10 Aug. 1708 in Essex Court.

And whereas Collo Richard Covington and Major James Boughan, by deed, 11 Aug. 1707, between William Pannell, son and heir of the said Thomas Pannell, deceased: Francis Stone and Mary his wife Daughter of the said Thomas Pannell, of the one part, and Richard Covington and James Boughan of the other part, for L 39., did purchase the interest of Wm Pannell, Francis and Mary Stone.
Wit:
Zachary Lewis   signed   Richard Covington
Will'm Todd   James Boughan

Recorded 11 Feb. 1713/14

page 197. Deed. Dated 9 Jan. 1713/14. James Boughan of So. Farn. Par., sells Martin Nalle of same Par., for 7000 lb. tobo., 194 acres. "the ninety four being entered for Queens Land by the said James Boughan last yeare", the other 100 acres inherited by James Boughan from his father. Adj. a swamp formerly called Gregorys Swamp, near line of Joseph Baker's land, the main road "that leadeth from Piscataway Ferry to the old mill", also adj. Martin Nalle's tobacco ground.
Wit:
Jos Baker   signed   James Boughan
Joshua Rycraft
   his mark
                      Recorded 11 Feb. 1713/14

page 199. Appraisal of the Est. of Mr. George Loyde deceased submitted by Johannah Loyde Adm'r taken 5 Feb. 1713/14 by order of Court dated 14 Jan. 1713/14.

Includes:

To	1 silver hilted Sword 1 steel hilted Sword	02.	15.	00
To	1 case Pistols 2 sets Holsters 2 Breast plates	01.	15.	00
To	8 small pictures in Frames	-	04.	-
To	a parcell of old Books	-	10.	-
To	1 ole Lignum vite Punch Bowle	-	03.	-
To	1 Silver Ladle	-	15.	-
To	3 Common Prayer Books and 1 Letter Case	-	06.	-
To	1 Silk hankerchief 1 pr Gloves and Gartering Stuff	-	05.	-
To	2 old Ivory Combs and 3 horn combs	-	01.	-
To	6 packs cards	-	01.	-
To	4 brass Candlesticks 2 brass ladles Snuffers and snuff Dish	-	12.	-
To	3 Guns	-	22.	-
To	5 old Iron Candlesticks	-	02.	-
To	3 old Side Saddles	-	5.	-
To	6 1/2 Dozen spoons	-	13.	-
To	2 Dozen plates	1.	-	-
To	1 Bason and 3 Porrengers	-	05.	-
To	a quantity of snuff in a Bottle and paper	-	02.	06
To	1 pr Lether Breeches	-	10.	-
To	1 fine Druggett Sute of Cloaths	3.	10.	-
To	1 great broad Cloath Coat	1.	09.	-
To	1 pr old Boots 1 pr mens shoos	-	09.	-
To	2 pr old shooes 1 old Hatt	-	03.	06
To	25 lb Shott	-	03.	06
To	4 chair cushons	-	08.	-
To	4 old shirts 1 pr stockings	-	08.	-
To	2 old spining wheels	-	08.	-
To	Cash	04.	04.	-
To	2 Gallon Runlets	-	03.	-
To	1 Cheese plate 1 pewter Dish	-	05.	-
To	2 of this Country Cloath waistcoats	-	01.	-

Total valuation of Estate L 254. 06. 09

Signed   The mark of
         Johannah Loyed

                    signed   Richd Covington
                             Tho Winslow
                             Ro Brooke Junr
                             Robert Jones

Appraisal sworn before Leo Tarent

page 202. Bond. L 200. Sterl. 12 Feb. 1713/14. Elizabeth Newton, Extrix., Henry Newton, deceased.
Wit:
Ja Alderson
Robert Jones

signed Eliz x Newton
John Strang
Thomas x Davis

Rec. 12 Feb. 1713/14.

page 202. Appraisal of Est. of Rees Eveins, late of Essex Co., Dec'd, by order of Court dated 12 Feb. 1713/14. Principally slaves and stock. Totals L 245. 03. 8 1/2

signed Law Taliaferro
John Catlett Junr
Robert Kay

Presented by Elizabeth Evans and Edward Evans Exorx. 11 Mar. 1713/14

page 203. Appraisal of Est. of Mr. Thomas Harwar, deceased, by order of Court 8 Oct. 1713. Sworn before Mr. Henry Robinson, one of her Majestys Justices.

Includes:
12 Negroes
To a set Pistols Holsters and Silver hafted sword 04. 10. 00
To a parsell of Books   01. 10. 00
To 53 oz Silver   13. 05. 00
To Cash   06. 04. 02
To 3 Gold Rings   01. 15. 00
To a Watch   06. 00. 00
To a Silver Pipe Stopper   00. 02. 06
To a hatt and 3 Wiggs   01. 02. 00
To an Inkhorne and Penknife Seal and Case Rasors 00. 15. 00
To a Druggett Sute Cloaths   03. 00. 20
To a boat   02. 10. 00
To 1/2 Doz knives and forks   00. 04. 00
To 5 new England Bucketts   00. 06. 00

The above is from a long inventory not added up. Total approx. L 1000.

signed Nicholas Smith Junr
James Webb
Fran: Moore

Presented by Elizabeth Harwar and Leonard Hill Exors. 11 Mar. 1713/14.

page 206. Lease and Release. 9 and 10 March 1713/14. Henry Steevens of Abington parish in Gloucester County, Planter, sells to Robert Thomas Junr., Planter, of St. Marys Par., for L 60., for 159 acres in St. Mary's Par.
Wit:
George Moore   signed Henry Stevens
Edward Steevens Junr
John Stevens

Rebecca Stevens, wife of Henry, relinq. her dower rights through William Smith, her attorney.

     Recorded 11 March 1713/14

page 208. Lease and Release. 9 and 10 March 1713/14. Robt. Thomas, Junr., of St. Marys Par., sells Henry Stevens of Abingdon Par., Glo'cester Co., for L 60., 500 acres in St. Marys Par.
Wit:
Geo Moore   signed Robert Thomas Junr
Edward Stevens Junr
John Stevens

Sarah Thomas, wife of Robert, relinq. her dower rights by Charles Taliaferro, her attorney. Power of Atty witnessed by Augt Smith and Robert Parker.
    Rec. 11 March 1713/14

page 210. Lease and Release. 9 and 10 March 1713/14. Charles Waller of So. Farn. Par., Essex Co., sells Edward Waller of the Par. of Stratton Major in the County of King and Queen, 200 acres, being part of 400 acres, which belonged to Charles Waller, which he purchased of Mr. William Upshaw, it being part of a patent that belonged to Harry Beverley, lying in Essex County, on N. side of Hoskins Swamp, adj. Thrashleys Line near his plantation there.
Wit:
Thomas Streshley   signed Charles Waller
 his mark
William ffletcher
 his mark

Susanna Waller, wife to Charles, relinq. her dower rights.

    Rec. 11 March 1713/14

page 211. Lease and Release. 8 and 9 March 1713/14. William Smith of the parish of Abington in the county of Gloster Gent (sic) sells Lawrence Taliaferro of St Marys Par., Gent., for L 96. Sterling and 3000 lb. tobo., 700 acres on S. side of Rappa., bounded by "a Line of Massaponax Patent", Massaponax Swamp, near the Round Marsh, the river bank, etc.
Wit:
Aug't Smith   signed William Smith
Cha's Taliaferro
J White
                   Rec. 11 March 1713/14

page 214. Lease and Release. 9 and 10 March 1713/14. William Smith of Abington Par. Gloucester Co., Gent., sells to Charles Taliaferro of St. Marys Par. Essex Co., Gent., for L 30. Sterling, 420 acres in St M. Par. Description of property incomplete. 200 acres thereof by deed dated 10 Apl 1708. On Rappa. River at the mouth of Haysell run, etc.
Wit:
Aug't Smith   signed William Smith
Richard Johnson
Wm Marchant
                   Rec. 11 March 1713/14

page 214. Will of Wm Dier of Essex Co., planter. Dated 20 Janry 1713/14. Prob. 11 March 1713/14.
To Grand daughter Alice Evis, Cattle and 1800 lb. tobo. due from Andrew Priccet, also rents to be received from James Douchberry, also various personal possessions including "one small box which was her mothers" x x "all this to be full satisfaction for what was left the said Alice Evis by her ffather". To be paid at 21 or marriage. Son John Dier sole exor.
Wit:
Thomas Lambert   signed William Dier
Elizabeth Jones her mark   His Mark
Mary Evans her mark

page 216. Bond. 11 March 1713/14. L 300. Sterl. John Dyer Exor of William Dyer deceased.
Wit: signed John Dyer
Robt Jones   Wm Winston
Ja Alderson   Henry Byrom
                   Rec. 11 March 1713/14.

page 216. Estate of Henry Newton, deceased.
Includes:

To	2 doz Spoons at	00.	05.	00
To	1 Sute of Mens Cloths	05.	00.	00
To	1 Sute do	03.	00.	00
To	1 Gunn at	00.	16.	00
To	4 pales and 1 piggin	00.	13.	00
To	2 pewter bottles and 1 pint pott	00.	04.	00
To	1 old Bible and 2 old books	00.	03.	00

Total valuation L 105. 14. 07

Presented by Eliza Newton, Extrx., 11 March 1713/14 and is Recorded.

       signed Nathaniel ffogg
           John Miller his mark
           Cornelius Sale
           Eliza Newton her mark.

page 217. Deed. 3 Feb. 1713/14. "Nathaniel Burwell of the County of Gloster in Virga (Exor of Lewis Burwell Deceased, who was Executor of John Fry sometime since of King and Queen County Deceased)", sells to John Ambrose, 400 acres, sold by the said Fry to the said John Ambrose's Father, in Essex Co., adj. land of Jonathan Hide, "and bounded with the outside line of the Grand Patent of ffive Thousand acres which did belong to Mr Fry and so according to the marked line as Mr Thomas Todd has Laid it"
Wit:
William Stokes   signed N Burwell
 his mark
Robert Crokett

Rich'd Buckner, by Letter of Atty., from Nathaniel Burwell acks. this Deed.

page 218. "John Ambrose the Bearer hereof brought me a Sort of a Paper ready writ to Convey my Right and title of four hundred acres of Land his Father bought of John Fry to him. Fry died before he conveyed it and so did my Father who was ffrys Exor and therefore he apply'd himself to me for my Title x x x I am in hopes the Punishment you might justly Expect from yo'r County People for misplacing your Warehouse is over and that you are better Reconciled to them I am
         Yo'r Humble Serv't
         N Burwell
Glo'ster. ffebr'y the 23 1713 "

8-E

page 218. Deed. 24 Feb. 1713/14. John Ambrose of Richmond Co., sells William Hall, 200 acres in Essex Co., being half of 400 acres from Major Burwell.
Wit:
Wm Stoakes   signed   John Ambrose
  his mark
John Orphen   Rec. 11 March 1713/14

page 218. Will of Henry Newton of St. Anns Par., Essex Co., dated 15 October 1712. Probated 12 Feb. 1713/14.
To son Thomas Newton, 195 acres, the line beginning at a School house, running along the Church road and upon the Top of the brink of the hills at my son Henrys. He failing in heirs this land to "my Grandson the son of Henry Newton x x and if the said Henry Newton shall die without heirs to the Grandson David ffalconer"
To wife Elizabeth, plantation, 150 acres "whereon I now live as long as she keeps a widow". If she marry to son Henry Newton, he failing in heirs to David ffalconer.
To son Henry Newton, 2 cows.
To dau. Martha Newton, 3 ewes.
Bal. of Est. to wife Eliza Newton, to son Thomas Newton and dau. Martha Newton to be equally divided. Wife exor.
Wit:
Rich'd Wilton   signed   Henry Newton
Andrew Micall   his mark
  his mark

page 219. Bond. 11 March 1713/14. Elizabeth Webb Executrix Est. John Webb deceased. L 200. Sterling.
Wit:
Ja Alderson   signed   Eliza E Webb
Wm Winston   mark
                                          Benj'a ffisher
                                          Rich'd Webb
                                          his mark

                      Rec. 11 March 1713/14

page 220. Bond. 11 March 1713/14. L 500. Sterl. John Billups and Dorothy his wife admr. of Est. of Henry Awbrey deceased.
Wit:
Robert Jones   signed   Jno Billups
Ja Alderson   James Boughan
                                          John Boughan
                      Rec. 11 Mar. 1713/14.

page 220. Bond. 11 March 1713/14. L 500. Sterl. John Billups and Dorathy his wife Admr. Est. Mary Avery, deceased.
Wit:
Robert Jones   signed   Jno Billups
Ja Alderson   James Boughan
                                 John Boughan

              Rec. 11 March 1713/14

page 221. Lease and Release. 17 and 18 Feb. 1713/14. Peter Mason of St Johns Par. King William Co., sells Edward Smart of Essex Co. for 1600 lb tobo., 50 acres in Essex Co., at head of Dragon Swamp.
Wit:
John Dickinson   signed   Peter Mason
frances - a -
Ephriam Paget

Power of Atty. fflower Mason, wife of Peter Mason, to "Trusty and welbeloved friend Edward Smith", to relinq. dower rights.
Wit:
Jo Bickley   signed   fflower   F   Mason
William Robertson   (mark)
    (mark)
              Rec. 11 March 1713/14

page 225. Will of John Garnet. Dated 7 Oct. 1713. Prob. 11 March 1713/14.
To 3 sons James, John and Anthony Garnet, 150 acres to be equally divided when they are 21. When Eldest son James Garnet is 21 he to take his part, the other 100 acres to be in hands of Thomas Garnett and William Taylor until the other two sons come of age. Bal. of Estate to wife Ann Garnet, she exor.
Wit:
George Murrell   signed   John Garnet
Nicholas ffaulconer
Edwd Coffee

page 225. Deed. 8 April 1714. "Leonard Tarent of the County of Essex Gentleman and Mary his wife legatee in the Last will and Testam't of Sam'll Thacker formerly of the said County Dec'd" sell James Edmondson of Essex Co., Gent., for L 45., 150 acres formerly belonging to William Williams and given by the sd Samll Thacker by his last will and Testam't to Mary Brooke now the wife of the sd Leonard Tarent, in Essex Co., being part of Buttons Range patent, adj. land of Wm Howlett, land of Makum Wright (Mottrom Wright - this may give us the correct pronunciation of the hard drinking and important old Col. John Mottrom's name)

Wit:
Richard Jones
Ja Alderson
Ann Alderson

signed Leo Tarent
       Mary Tarent

Ack. by Leonard Tarent and Mary his wife to James Edmondson in Essex County Court the Eighth day of Aprill 1714 and is Recorded.

Wit:
Wm Raines
Timo Sallavand

page 227. Bond. 8 Apl. 1714. 10,000 lb tobo., Joanna Loyd to keep an ordinary at her house near the Court House.

Wit:
Zach Lewis
Benj'a ffisher

signed Joanna E Loyd
          mark
   Rich'd Covington
   Ja Alderson

Rec. 8 Apl. 1714.

page 227. Lease and Release. 5 and 7 April 1714. James Samuel, planter, and Sarah his wife of Essex Co., sell Paul Micou, Chirurgeon, of the same Co., 75 acres, for L 20. Sterling, being 1/2 of a tract given by Warwick Gray in his last will to Sarah Samuel and William Gray to be equally divided betw them, in St. Anns Par., on Rappa River, adjoining the land of Silvester Thacker

Wit:
Wm Daingerfield
Leo Tarent

signed James Samuel
      The mark of
      Sarai Samuel

Rec. 7 April 1714.

page 229. Appraisal of Est. of John Webb, deceased, taken by order of Court, 11 March 1713/14, presented by Elizabeth Webb, Extrix., and sworn to before "one of her Maj'ts Justices of the peace Capt William Young".
Includes:
To one Sword and old Iron Lumber   00. 04. 00
To horse whip and pepper box and 2 books   00. 13. 00

Total valuation L 29. 09. 04

Wit: signed Vincent x Godfrey Pile
Mr Benj'a ffisher   Henry x Woodnot
                                 Owen x Owens

Rec. 8 April 1714.

page 229. Deed. 3 Apl. 1714. John Willard of St. A. Par. sells James Landrum of same Par., for 600 lb. tobo., 15 acres on S. side of Rappa. River, upon the branches of Blackborn's Creek, adj. the land of James Landrum, and that of John Williams.
Wit:
Jno Vawter   signed John x Willard
Samuel Landrum
William Brown

Sarah Willard, wife of John, relinq. dower rights.

Rec. 8 Apl 1714.

page 230. Deed. 20 March 1713/14. William Brown of St. Anns Par., sells John Willard of same Par., for 3500 lb. tobo., land, acerage not shown, on S. side Rappa. River, adj. land of Martin Willard, James Landrum and John Pitts old field.
Wit:
Samll Stallord   signed William Brown
Joseph Rowlson
John Rouse

Rec. 8 Apl. 1714.

page 231. Deed. 20 March 1713/14. William Brown of St. Anns Par., sells Martin Willard of same Par., for 1500 lb. tobo. a tract of land, acerage not shown, on S. side Rappa. River, "upon the branches of Lucas his Creek" and adj. land of John Martin, William Beasley and John Williams
Wit:
Saml Stallord   signed   William Brown
Joseph Rowlson
John Rouse
                Rec. 8 Apl. 1714.

page 233. Will of Thomas Ingram of St. Ann's Parish. Dated 19th 1715 (doubtless an error and should be 1713). Probated 8 Apl. 1714. To two sons Tobias and Thomas Ingram all land in St Anns Par. Eldest son, Tobias Ingram, to have in his part the plantation "I now live on".
To wife Martha Ingram, tract of land in Richmond County, in St. Marys Parish, adj land of Henry Berry and that of Robert Peck, also balance of estate, she exor.
Wit:
Ro Brooke Junr   signed   Thomas Ingram
John x Sorrell

page 233. Bond. 8 Apl. 1714. L 300. Sterling. Martha Ingram Extx. Thomas Ingram, deceased.
Wit:
Robert Jones   signed   Martha x Ingram
Ja Alderson   John Hawkins
                                 Ro Brooke jun'r
               Rec. 8 April 1714.

page 233. 14 December 1713. John Smith of St. Anns Par. makes over all his property "whatsoever from the beginning of the world until the day of the date hereof", to Ephriam Paget.
Wit:
Salvator Muscoe   signed   John Smith
Nath'll ffogg
Tho: Winslow

               Rec. 8 April 1714.

page 234. Will of Abraham Stapp of Essex Co. Dated 20 Oct. 1710.
Probated 8 April 1714.
To son Abraham Stapp all land on N. side of Road of "my now
dwelling plantation". To son William all land on S. side of road.
To son Jacob Stapp upper part of land bought of Edward Moseley and
to son Joshua Stapp the lower part bordering on Mr. Robt. Brooke.
To young sons Joseph Stapp and James Stapp 25 acres each of lower
land. Jacob and Joshua to buy them 100 acres each elsewhere.
To wife Dorothy all property during lifetime. To dau. Ruth Stapp
cattle, etc. To two daus. Rebecca and Martha Stapp a shilling each.
Wit:
Robert Moss   signed Abraham Stapp
Peter Hollon
Will Harte his mark

page 234. Bond. 8 Apl. 1714. L 300. Sterling. Dorothy Step (sic)
Extx. Abra Step.
Wit: signed Dorathy Stapp
John Pickett   Dan'll Hayes
Daniel Brown   John Hart

            Rec. 8 Apl 1714.

page 234. Bond. 8 Apl. 1714. L 100. Sterl. Ann Coleman Extrx Est.
of Robt. Coleman, deceased.
Wit: signed Ann Coleman
Thos Hemman   Edward Coleman
Ja Alderson   Daniel Brown
                                       John Pickett
            Rec. 8 Apl. 1714.

page 235. Bond. 8 Apl. 1714. L 300. Sterling. Henry Berry Admr of
William Harper, deceased.
Wit: signed Henry Berry
Robert Jones   Ro Brooke junr
Richard Gatewood.   Robt Parker
            Rec. 8 Apl. 1714.

page 235. Release. 7 April 1714. Thomas Merrit of St. A. Par.,
planter, of one part and John Bates and Phebe his wife of same Par.
of the other part. For 2000 lb. tobo. release 25 acres according
to a deed 8 February 1709/10.
Wit: signed Thomas x Merrit
Nathaniel ffogg
John Strang   Rec. 8 Apl. 1714.

page 236. Lease and Release. 10 and 11 Dec. 1713. John Smith, planter of St. A. Par., sells Ephriam Paget and Mary his wife of same Par., for 5000 lb. tobo., tract of land where Thos Con'oly lived and also 115 acres in St A. Par., on the Main Swamp of Brices, etc.
Wit: signed John Smith
Nath'll ffogg
Tho Winslow   Rec 9 Apl. 1714.

page 238. Deed. 12 May 1714. Thomas Dickinson of Essex Co., sells John Reynolds of same Co., for 2000 lb. tobo., 50 acres, part of a parcel of land the sd Dickinson bought of Richard Waklin, being part of a Dividend of 1000 acres formerly Granted to Edw. Merrit and William Waklin by patent dated 26 Apl. 1704.
Wit:
Sam'l Bizwell   signed Thomas Dickinson
William Tharp

Ealse Dickisson, wife to Thomas, relinq. her dower rights.

"x x delivered by turf and twigg by x Thomas Dickinson unto within mentioned John Reynolds son of William Reynolds x x"
        signed Thomas Do'eson

    Recorded 13 May 1714.

page 239. Bond. 13 May 1714. L 200. Sterl. Cary Caston Admr. Est. of Class Caston, deceased.
Wit: signed Cary Caston
Robert Jones   Wm Dunn
Ja Alderson   Henry Purkins

    Recorded 13 May 1714.

page 240. Lease and Release. 26 and 28 April 1714. Phillip Graffort, mariner, and Pollatia his wife of St. Pauls Parish in the County of Stafford in the Colony of Virginia, sell Mr. Lawrence Taliaferro, Gent., of St. Marys Par., Essex Co., 1/3 part of a tract of land lying in the forest in Essex County, part of a Dividend formerly granted Mr Enoch Doughty by patent dated 15 June 1675 of 4763 acres, bounded according to patent, which 1/3 was formerly in lawful possession of William Berry of Richmond Co., who conveyed it in fee simple to Benjamin Newton of Stafford County by deed dated 11 April 1690, which land Benj. Newton by his will dated 3 January 1709 gave the tract of land to his daughter Pollatia now the wife of Phillip Graffort.

Wit:
Leon'd Tarent
Roub'n Welsh
Cha. Taliaferro

signed Phillip Graffort
Pellatia Graffort

Rec. 13 May 1714.

page 241. Deed. 23 March 1713/14. John Taylor, planter, of Hanover Par. Richmond Co., sells Daniel Smith, planter, of St. A. Par., Essex Co., for 2000 lb Tobo., 100 acres, part of a patent of 4000 acres granted to Thomas Meadar and Henry Petrus, in St. A. Par., adj. land of George Loyd.

Wit:
Thomas Spiers
ffra Smith

signed John Taylor

Mary Taylor, wife to John, relinq. dower rights by Robert Parker her attorney.

Rec. 13 May 1714.

page 242. Taylor's bond to Smith witnessed by Sam'll Bizwell and Henry Long.
Mary Taylor's Power of Atty to Robt. Parker witnessed by Jno Taylor and Henry Long.

page 243. Appraisal of Est of Thomas Ingram, Dec'd. by order of Court dated 8 Apl. 1714. Presented by Martha Ingram, Extx.
Includes:

To 1 gold ring and 1 brass Do	0. 10. 0	
To 2 silver shirt buckles 1 silver chain 1 money Purse and box	0. 01. 6	
To 1 silver bodkib	0. 02. 0	

Total valuation L 24. 08. 11

signed Edwd Moseley
Jeremiah Biswell
Jno Cooke his mark

Recorded 13 May 1714.

8-E   84

page 243. Appraisal of Est. of Abraham Stepp Dec'd by order of
Court 8 Apl. 1714.
Includes:
To 3 doz and 5 spoons   00. 08. 06
To 1 old gold ring   00. 06. 00
To a Small parcell of truck   00. 06. 04
To 1 old Bible and a small parcel of books   00. 13. 00
To a parcell of Damnified Paper   00. 01. 00
To 10 Goose and 8 Goslings   00. 19. 00
To 250 gallons of Cyder   04. 03. 04
To 3 hides in Tann not seen   -   -   -

Total valuation L 91. 13. 07
                                signed   Edwd Moseley
                                         Cornelius Sale
                                         John ffoster
                                              his mark

Presented by Dorothy Stepp Extrx.

                    Recorded 13 May 1714.

Note: Alas ! - the goose who wrote the small parcel of books must
also have known of their valuation.   B. F.

page 244. Will of Robert Moss of Essex County. Dated 1 Nov. 1713.
Probated 13 May 1714.
Personal Est. to be divided equally among wife and children. Land
equally among sons, wife to have 1/3 during life. Refers to "wel-
beloved Wife Martha Moss and my Children named Thomas, William,
Richard, John, Robert, Ann and ffrances Moss". Wife and eldest son
Thomas to be Exors.
Wit: signed   Robert Moss
William Brockenbrough
New. Brockenbrough
James Jugo

page 244. Bond. 13 May 1714. L 200. Sterl. Wm. Price Admr Est of
Isaac Potier, deceased.
Wit: signed   William W Price
Ja Alderson   mark
Wm West   Jno Pickett
                                         Benja ffisher

                    Rec. 13 May 1714.

page 245. Will of James ffullerton. Dated 10 Dec. 1713. Probated 13 May 1714.
To son James ffullerton all land and plantations, he failing in heirs to be divided equally among his five daughters.
Personal estate to be divided equally betw wife and children at age or day of marriage.
Exors wife 'Coson' James Griffin and Mr. William Johnson. If wife remarry her exorship to be discontinued.
Wit:
The mark of   signed   James ffullerton
William Dyer
The mark of
William Comton
Erasmus Allen

Bond. 13 May 1714. L 1500. Sterling. Sarah ffullerton and James Griffin as Exors of James ffullerton, deceased.
Wit:
Ja Alderson   signed   Sarah ffullerton
R Buckner   James Griffing
                                        Jno Picket
                                        John Hailes
                                        William Picket

Rec. 13 May 1714.

page 246. Power of Atty. No date. Sarah Boughan to Mr Robert Jones to ack. Right of Dower, 190 acres of land, to Martin Naul.
Wit:
Richard Jones   signed   Sarah Boughan
Henry Browne   her mark

Rec. 13 May 1714.

page 246. Will of John Boulware. Dated 5 April 1714. Prob. 13 May 1714.
To son John Boulware the land "whereon I now live", he failing in heirs to daughter Mary Boulware.
To daughter Elizabeth Boulware plantation where James Allin now lives, she failing in heirs to Susanna Boulware.
To daughter Susanna Boulware land "which my brother William Boulware did purchase of John Hackley", she failing in heirs to son John Boulware.
To son John plantation where Richard Matthew now lives, he failing

Will of John Boulware (continued)

in heirs to daughter Mary.
Richard Mathews and his wife frances Mathews to have priveledges according to their lease.
To son John, 2 guns, pistols, sword, etc.
To daughter Mary a gold ring with a stone therein
To daughters Elizabeth and Susanna each a hoop gold ring
Wife's clothing to daughters
To Rebecca Rowzee 600 lb tobo.
"My personal Estate I give to be Equally Divided amongst all my children and Eliza Mathews instead of what I received of Richard Mathews for her maintenance". Children to be of age at 16.
Exors George Berry and Sam'll Stallord. "That George Berry dwell on my plantation untill my son John Boulware be of age"
Wit:
Stephen Chenault   signed   John Boulware
  his mark
James Allin (mark)
Rebecca Rowzee her mark.

page 247. Appraisal of Est. of Wm. Dier, deceased, made 1 May 1714 by order of Court dated 8 Apl. 1714.
Includes
To his wearing apparell   2. 15. 00
Total valuation approx. L 30.

                         signed   Henry Byrom
                                 William x Grenell
                                 Thomas   x   Evans

Presented 13 May 1714 by John Dyer Exor of William Dyer deceased and recorded.

page 247. Land Grant. Nathaniel Bacon Esq., "President of their Maj'ties Council of State of Virginia" to Mr Robert Yard and Mr John Waters, 179 acres in Rappahannock County, on S. side of Rappa River, adj land of Mrs Eliz'a Cox and Leonard Chamberlain, Hoskins Creek, land of Thomas Petties, land of Thomas Green, Piscataway Creek, land given by Mr John Cox to Henry White. This land due for importation of four persons. Dated 21 April 1690.
                         signed   Nathaniel Bacon Pr
                                William Cole Sec'r

page 248. Assignment of above by Robert Yard of the County of

Gloster Gent'l, for L 10. Sterl., to Thomas Edmondson of Essex Co.
Dated 12 August 1696.
Wit: signed   Robert Yard
John Griffing
Robt Halsey
James Boughan

page 248. Ack in Essex Co Court, 10 Sept 1696 by James Taylor,
according to a Letter of Attorney from Robert Yard.
                Test   Francis Meriwether   Cl Cur

page 248. Assignment of above land to Colo John Smith Esqr., 3rd
Sept. 1713.
Wit: signed   Tho Edmondson
Jos Baker
Chr Beverley
Benj'a ffisher

Ack and Rec. 13 May 1714.
                Test   Richard Buckner   Cl Cur

page 248. Will of Richard Kemp of St Anns Par. Date omitted in
records. Probated 13 May 1714.
To son Richard Kemp all land. 4 negroes.
To daughter Ann Taliaferro, 4 negroes, cattle, a large looking
    glass
To daughter Rachel Gatwood (sic) 5 negroes, cattle, a large looking
    glass.
To wife Elinor 4 negroes.
To Eliza Minor, Joan Guttrey, Mary Nall (this name is possibly
    Mary Hall) Catherine Talburt, 600 lb tobo each.
Money in hands of Colo Robert Carter to be equally divided betw.
    son Richard Kemp and two daus. Ann Taliaferro and Rachell
    Gatwood
Balance of estate to be divided betw son Richard and wife Elinor.
Exors son Richard, "my two Sons in Law Charles Taliaferro and
    Richard Gatewood", and wife Elinor.
Wit:
Thomas Ramsey   signed   Rich'd Kemp
Rob't Biswell
ffrancis Abbott
Eliza Abbott

page 249. Bond. L 1000. Sterling. 13 May 1714.
Richard Kemp, Charles Taliaferro and Richard Gatewood Exors of the

Estate of Richard Kemp, deceased.
Wit:
Ja Alderson
Jos Baker

signed Richard Kemp
Charles Taliaferro
Richard Gatewood
John Boughan
Tho x Griffin

Recorded 13 May 1714.

page 249. Lease and Release. Both Indentures dated 13 May 1714. Daniel Brown of So. Farn. Par., sells William Covington and Ann his wife, of the same Par., 100 acres in So Farn Par., on south side of Piscataway Creek, adj. land of Thomas Jenkins. This sale is made in consideration of L 13. paid by Mr Robert Coleman late deceased.
Wit:
George Trible
Edward Price

signed Dan'll Brown

Rec. 13 May 1714.

page 250. Deed. 8 April 1714. Thomas Tinsley, planter of Essex county, sells Leonard Tarent, for L 13. Sterl., and 1500 lb. tobo. 1100 acres Granted to John May on 20th October 1709 (or 1704) and by him sold to Thomas Tinsley. The said Tinsley having made several sales out of the tract, to wit: to Thomas Sneed 150 acres, to Cornelius Vaughan 150 acres, to Thomas Bell 125 acres, to John Mackenny 100 acres, the remainder being 500 and some acres in St Anns Par., adj the land of John Coleman, John Mackenny, Thos. Bell etc.
Wit:
Law Taliaferro
Samuel Hawes

signed Thomas x Tinsley

Recorded 10 June 1714.

page 252. Will of John Williams of St Anns Par. Dated 23 February 1713/14. Probated 10 June 1714.
To Son in Law Joseph Lemon and his wife Margaret the plantation 'whereon I live' with all appurtenances.

(continued)

The Will of John Williams (continued)

To Grandson John Boulware, son of John and Susanna Boulware, 100 acres, in the forest where my Son in Law Jo. Lemon now lives, also a mare and "my little gun".
To grand-daughter Eliza Boulware the daughter of John Boulware and Susanna his wife a cow calf.
To grand-daughter Mary Boulware a cow calf, 100 acres of land in the forest.
To Eliz'a Williams Daughter of Marg't Lemon all my Plantation where Robert Biswell Senior now lives, with 100 acres thereto adjoining, she failing in heirs to Joseph Lemon and Margaret his wife.
To grandsons John Lemon and Joseph Lemon each a gun.
Bal of Est to be equally divided betw the 4 children of Susanna Boulware and the 4 children of Marg't Lemon.
Exors Sons in Law John Boulware and Joseph Lemon
Wit:
Stephen Chenault   signed   John W Williams
Susanna Cook her mark   mark
James Allin

Will probated by Joseph Lemon, one of the exors, he giving bond with security. 12 August 1714.

page 253. Deed. 20 Apl 1713. John Bates of St Anns Par., sells Nath'll Fogg of the same Par., for 2500 lb tobo., 25 acres part of a tract of land adj the land of Peter Winnam, etc.
Wit:
James Boughan   signed   Jno Bates
William Jordan

Possession given 20 April 1713 by Turf and Twigg
Wit: signed   John Bates
Jacob Divilliard
Richard Hollaway
   his mark   Recorded 10 June 1714.

page 254. Deed. 9 June 1713. John Spiers (Spicer) of St. A. Par., sells Richard Guggey of Essex Co., for 3100 lb. tobo., plantation whereon Spicer now lives, 80 acres, on S side of Occupation Run, adj land of Capt. Edward Rowzee, land sold by Spicer to Jeremiah Biswell and now in possession of Charles Farrell, the land of

8-E

Maj'r Edward Moseley, the land of Bouler (Boulware).
Wit:
Robert Jones   signed   John Spicer
Saml1 Prosser
                    Rec. 10 June 1714.

page 255. Deed of Gift. 10 June 1714. Charles Brown and Susanna his wife give to their two sons, William and Edward Brown, 100 acres each, on S side Rappa River, being part of a patent formerly granted by Sir William Berkeley to James Brown. The sd land lyeth on Cockell Shell Creek in Essex County. They failing in heirs to "our son Charles".
Wit: signed   Charles Brown
Samuel Johnson   Susanna x Brown
Robt. Cooke
                    Rec. 10 June 1714.

page 255. Will of Rebecca Tomlin of St. Anns Parish, Essex Co. Dated 25 Nov. 1709. Probated 10 June 1714.
To the four children of "my Deceased Daughter Rebecca Rowzee" 12 young cattle.
To Mary Smith a heiffer. To William Smith a feather bed. To Francis Gouldman Junr a feather bed and other household goods. Also 6 head cattle.
To Thomas Gouldman household goods and 6 head cattle.
To "my Daughter Martha Gouldman" household furniture and crop. To Jane Blundel 9 1/4 yards of serge. To George Goudye cattle when he is 21.
To daughter Martha Gouldman negroes and a servant man named Daniel Kelly.
To ffrancis Gouldman a white servant named John Nowland.
To daughter Martha Gouldman, crop of tobo and hogs due from Arthur Mackdaniell.
To Lancelot Tomlin proceeds of Tobacco shipped to Great Britain, Exors to keep this till he is 21, he dying before then "to my said Daughter".
To daughter Martha Gouldman balance of cattle, etc., she to be Exor.
Wit:
fra Gouldman   signed   Rebecca Tomlin
Ann Smith her mark   her mark
James Stark his mark

"At a Court for Essex County the 10th day of June 1714
This will was proved by the oaths of William Winston and Martha his wife Extrx Therein named and by the oaths of ffrancis Gouldman

Will of Mrs. Rebecca Tomlin (continued)

and Ann Smith two of the witnesses hereto and is Recorded
        Test
         Richard Buckner Cl Cur "

Bond. 10 June 1714. L 1000. Sterling. William Winston and Martha his wife late Martha Gouldman, as Exors of the est. of Rebecca Tomlin, deceased.
Wit: signed Wm Winston
Robert Jones   Martha Winston
Ja. Alderson   Ralph Rowzee
           Peter Byrom

     Recorded 10 June 1714.

page 256. Appraisal of Est. of James Fullerton, deceased, taken by order of Court 3 June 1714.
Includes:

To	6 negro men at 30 pounds apiece named Tom, Jack, Sam, Dick, Mingo and Guy	180. 00. 0	
To	1 Indian boy Twenty pounds	20. 00. 0	
To	2 negro women at 20 pounds a piece named Sue and Doll	40. 00. 0	
To	1 negro woman and Mulato at 26 a piece named Jeny and Nan	52. 00. 0	
To	1 negro child named Judy	05. 00. 0	
To	1 white Serv man having 8 months to serve named William Dier	03. 00. 0	
To	54 pound of new pewter at 9 d per pound	02. 00. 6	
To	33 pounds of old pewter at 7 d per lb	01. 02. 0	
To	3 doz: and 4 new spoons at 2 d a doz	00. 06. 8	
To	1 case of Knives and forks	00. 06. 0	
To	a Sword pistols and holsters	01. 15. 0	
To	1 p'r of old boots	00. 05. 0	
To	1 fine hatt and 1 pr Gloves	00. 11. 0	
To	Sagaty Coat and Damask Jacket	02. 10. 0	
To	1 Bible 1 Sermon book 1 primer	00. 10. 0	
To	10 yds and 1/4 of Irish Linen at 2 s	01. 01. 0	
To	7 sticks of mohair at 4 d per stick	00. 02. 4	
To	1 wafer box and 2 shill's in cash	00. 02. 6	
To	a sett of bills of Exchange	09. 15. 2	
To	1 Cyphering Slate	00. 02. 6	

Total valuation L 694. 15. 2
        Signed James Boughan
           John Gatewood his mark
           Rich'd Dudley

10 June 1714.
Presented by Sarah ffullerton and James Griffin Exors.

page 259. Inventory of Est. of John Garnett deceased, taken by order of Court 11 March 1713/14. Total valuation L 39. 04. 10

                       signed James Rennolds Junr
                                  Cornelius Sale
                                  Thomas Streshley
                                     his mark

Presented by Thomas Garnet and William Taylor Admrs 10 June 1714.

page 259. Bond. 10 June 1714. L 1000. Sterl. "Leon'd Tarent has obtained a Commission for the office of Sheriff of Essex County"
Wit:
Ja Alderson   signed Leo Tarent
Wm Covington Junr   Richd Covington
                                          Richd Buckner
                Rec. 10 June 1714

page 259. Bond. 10 June 1714. L 100. Sterl. William Vickary (sic) Admr. Est. of John Sidey deceased.
Wit:
Ja Alderson   signed Will i Vickers (sic)
Robt Jones   John Anderson
                                         William x Mason
              Rec. 10 June 1714.

page 260. Appraisal of Est. of Robert Moss, deceased.
Includes:

1	old desk and a parcel of old books	00.	13. 0
2	Com'on prayer books 1 silver Clasps	00.	05. 0
1	old sword	00.	04. 0
1	taper bitt and tooth drawers	00.	01. 6
	a parcel of trifling things	00.	02. 0
1	pr Silver Shoe buckles	00.	03. 0
1	pr Silver Shirt buttons	00.	00. 6
1	Silver Seal	00.	02. 6
1	pr Spectacles and Case	00.	01. 0

Total valuation L 150. 07. 1

                             (continued)

Appraisal of the Estate of Robert Moss (continued)

        signed Salvator Muscoe
                 Robt Brooke Junr
                 John Mills

Presented by Martha Moss Extrx 9 July 1714.

page 261. We the Subscribers do by virtue of a former order of Court appraise one black horse branded R.B. about four years old five pounds Sterl as witness our hands the 16 of June 1714 It being the Estate of John Waters Dec'd.
Presented by Edward Price and Kath his wife and others Exor's of John Waters Dec'ed to Essex County Court the 8th day of July 1714 and is Recorded
        Test
          Richard Buckner Cl Cur

       signed Henry Woodnott
               his mark
             Vincent Godfrey Pile
             Fran: Moore

page 261. Appraisal of Est. of Class Caston, decd, 6 July 1714.
Includes:
To 1 Case of pistolls and holsters and sword
       and sadle at   03. 00. 0

Total valuation L 55. 02. 0
                signed Thomas Dicks
                         Wm Covington
                         John Crow

Presented 8 July 1714 by Cary Caston, Administrator.

page 262. Deed of Gift. 10 June 1713. Alex'r Doniphan of Richmond County gives, for love and affection, a young mare to Agatha Hay daughter of Mr John Hay deceased.
                signed Alex'r Doniphan
This deed ack in Court by Benj'a Robinson, Attorney of Alexander Doniphan
        Rec. 8 July 1714.

page 263. 8 July 1714. Bond. L 200 Sterling. Robert Ranson (or Rauson) Admr Est of William Montague, deceased.
Wit:
Benj'a Robinson   signed   Robert Ransone (Rausone ?)
Ja Alderson   Thomas Walker
                                          Rich'd Buckner

                      Rec 8 July 1714.

page 263. Appraisal of Est. of John Sidey, deceased. Taken by order of Court 10 June 1714.
Includes:
To 1 old Sword and parcel of head Lin'en 1 Gound
      and 1 pr of Bodies 1 knife and fork   00. 16. 0
To 3 pr of Stockins 2 combs 2 pr of old sicers
      to 1 piece of tape 2 aprons 1 old Towell   00. 05. 0

                            signed   Tho Ramsey
                                      Sam'll Ellitts
                                      James Noell

Presented by William Viccary Admr 8 July 1714

page 263. Appraisal of Est of Rachel Warren, deceased.

"To one Mair at   3. 10. 0
  To one horse at   1. 10. 0

Being part of Rachel Warrens Estate"

                           signed   Anthony Samuell
                                     Anthony Samuell Junr

Presented by William Warren Ex'r of Rachel Warren dec'd 8th July 1714.

page 264. Appraisal of Est of Mrs Rebecca Tomlin made by order of Court dated 10 June 1714. Total valuation approx L 310.
                            signed   Tho Winslow
                                    Tho Munday
                                    Thomas Davis
Presented by William Winston and Martha his wife exor'x 8th July 1714.

page 265. Will of John Williams of South Farnham Par. Essex Co.,
Dated 15 Mar. 1713/14. Probated 8 July 1714.
To son Thomas Williams land after the death of his Mother in Law.
Personal Est to be equally divided betw wife and children.
Wife, Elizabeth, exor. Children's names not shown excepting son
Thomas.
Wit: signed   John Williams
Henry Adcocke
John Twisdall his mark
Hugh Williams

page 265. Bond. 8 July 1714. L 400. Sterling. Martha Moss Exor
of Robert Moss, deceased.
Wit: signed   Martha Moss
Jno Picket   Salvator Muscoe
Richd Covington   Wm Winston
                                 John Hawkins

          Rec. 8 July 1714.

page 266. Appraisal of Est of William Harper, deceased, taken by
order of Court dated 8 Apl. 1714. Total valuation L 31. 04. 01
                    signed   Edward Rowzee
                             John Boughan
                             John Cooke
Presented 9 July 1714 by Henry Berry Admr.

page 266. Lease and Release. 11 and 12 August 1714. Richard Taylor
planter, of So Farnham Par. sells Henry Reeves of same par, planter,
plantation known as Richard Taylors quarter with 200 acres adj.,
on branches of Piscataway Creek, adj., land of William Ball and
John Price, 300 acres of a tract granted Mr. Henry Awbrey on the
19 March 1677 , and by John ffry purchased of sd Awbrey, Maj'r
George Morris and Benj Goodrich, and by Charles Walker and John
Southerland purchased of John ffry by deed dated 1 June 1696, and
by Jonathan ffisher purchased of sd Charles Walker and John
Southerland by deed dated 28 June 1690, and by Robert Taylor
purchased of Jonathan ffisher by deed dated 27 December 1692, and
by the will of sd Taylor dated 7 Sept 1699, 200 acres part thereof given to Benja Cook and by Cook conveyed to Richard Taylor by

deed dated 10 Nov. 1702, to whom of Right it doth now belong.
Wit:
Salvator Muscoe
Ro Brooke Junr
Nicho Smith Junr

signed The Marke of Richard Taylor

Susannah Taylor, wife to Richard, relinq her dower rights.

Rec. 12 Aug. 1714.

page 268. Deed. - August 1714. Thomas Bell of So. Farnham Par., exchanges Henry Gatewood 125 acres of land, being part of a tract of 1100 acres formerly granted John May of Essex Co., 20 Oct 1704, and by May sold to Tho. Tinsley of Essex Co., and by Tinsley sold to Thos Bell by deed dated 10 Apl. 1710.
The foregoing being in exchange for 50 acres in South Farnham Par., it being the remaining part of 75 acres given the said Henry Gatewood by his father John Gatewood's will dated 14 Nov. 1706, and adj. the land of Mr Henry Awbrey and Colo Thomas Gutteridge, and also adj the land of William Allen.
Wit:
Jos Baker
V. Godfrey Pile
Wm St John

signed Thomas Bell

Hannah Bell, wife to Thomas, relinq. her dower rights.
page 270. Deed in duplicate of above signed Henry Gatewood.
Dorothy Gatewood wife to Henry Gatewood relinq. her dower rights.

page 271. Bond. 12 Aug. 1714. L 2000. Sterling. Samuel Thompson of Surrey County, at a Court held for Essex County 10 May 1710, had Admr. granted of Est. of Benjamin Moseley deceased, and likewise the same day and year obtained a Probate of the will of Eliz'a Moseley deceased, wid'o and Relict of the aforesaid Benj'a Moseley, and did then enter into two bonds with Edward Moseley, William Thompson and John Williams now deceased, his Securities in the sum of L 500. each. He now agrees to keep harmless Joseph Lemon Exor of John Williams, etc.
Wit:
Samuel Stallord
Richard Booker

signed Samuel Thompson
John Hawkins
Wm Thompson

Recorded 12 August 1714.

page 271. Bond. 12 August 1714. L 200. Sterling. Joseph Lemon as Exor of John Williams deceased.

Wit: signed   Joseph x Lemon
Jno Bates   John x Cooke
R Buckner   Ja Alderson

                       Rec 12 Aug 1714.

page 272. Appraisal of Est of John Boulware, deceased, taken 4th August 1714. Total valuation L 70. 05. 07
Includes
To 26 geese   1. 06. 01
                    signed Edw Rowzey
                              P'r Godfroy
                              Ralph Rowzee
Presented by Samuel Stallord and George Berry Exors of John Boulware deceased 12 August 1714.

page 273. Deed of Gift. 12 Aug. 1714. Nicholas Smith of Petsworth Par., Gloucester Co., Virginia, gives "unto my welbeloved Son Nicholas Smith Junr of Essex County in Southfarnham Parish", a tract of land, acerage not shown, being part of a certain tract of land that he, Nicholas Smith Sr., bought of Mr Richard Cook, which was patented by Mr Thomas Bowlar, containing 500 acres, adj. to the plantation "that my said son now live on".

Wit:
Wm Upshaw   signed   Nicho Smith
Tho Munday
John Wills

                     Rec. 12 Aug. 1714

page 273. Lease and Release. 8 and 9 June 1714. Leonard Tarent, Gent., of St. A. Par., sells Francis Graves of So. Farn. Par., carpenter, 200 acres in St. A. Par., adj land of Charles Brown, land of John Coleman and part of a tract of 500 acres purchased by Tarent from Thomas Tinsley.

Wit:
Ja Alderson   signed   Leo Tarent
Robt Parker
Salvator Muscoe

Mary Tarent, wife of Leonard, relinq dower rights.

                     Rec 9 Sept 1714.

B-E   98

page 276. Lease and Release. 6 and 7 Sept. 1714. Augustine Smith, Gent., of St Mary's Par., Essex Co., sells Peter Byrom, "Gunn Smith", of So. Farn. Par., for L 10., 100 acres on So. side of Rappahonnock River, about 4 miles above the falls thereof in St. M. Par., adj. a branch of Hasle run (Hazel Run), the land of Henry Reeves, which 100 acres is a part of a tract formerly granted to John Bowsey (evidently phonetic spelling) and since granted to Augustine Smith by patent dated 22 October 1712, for 1708 acres.

Wit: signed   Aug't Smith
Ro Brooke Junr
Henry Bryom
Salvator Muscoe

page 280. Power of Atty., Aug't Smith to Salvator Muscoe to ack. above sale. Dated 7 Sept. 1714.

Wit: signed   Aug't Smith
Ro Brooke Junr
Henry Byrom

                        Rec. 9 Sept. 1714.

page 280. Lease and Release. 6 and 7 Sept. 1714. Augustine Smith, Gent., of St. M. Par., sells Henry Byrom "Gunn Smith", of South Farnham Par., for L 15., 150 acres on So. side of Rappahannock River, about 4 miles above the falls, etc., see foregoing entry.

Wit:
Ro Brooke junr   signed   Aug't Smith
Peter Byrom
Salvator Muscoe

Power of Atty., Smith to Muscoe, to ack sale.

                        Rec. 9 Sept. 1714.

page 284. Lease and Release. 7 and 8 Sept. 1714. Augustine Smith, Gent., of St. M. Par., sells to Henry Reeves, planter, of S. Farn. Par., for L 20., 200 acres, on So. side of Rappahannock River, about 4 miles above the falls, on a branch of Hasle run, etc., see above.

Wit: signed   Aug't Smith
Ro Brooke junr
Henry Byrom
Salvator Muscoe

Power of Atty. Smith to Muscoe to ack sale.

                        Rec. 9 Sept 1714.

page 288. Deed of Gift. 8 Sept 1714. Samuel Henshaw and Kazia his wife, for love, good will and affection "for our Loving Son in law Samuel Bezwell and our dear daughter Elizabeth his wife" give 40 acres, adj. Catletts nie tho main Road popoinas swamp being part of land where Saml. and Kazia now dwell.

Wit:
John Man his marke
John Adkinson his marke
John Boughan

signed Samuel Henshaw
Kazia Henshaw
her mark

Rec. 9 Sept 1714.

page 289. "To all to whom these presents shall come I William Cooke Esq'r her Ma'ties Secretary of State of Virginia send Greeting. KNOW YEE that I the said William Cooke Esq'r Secretary as afores'd by Virtue of her Ma'ties Letters Pattents bearing date the Twenty fifth day of January in the tenth year of her Ma'ties Reign have and by these presents do appoint place ordain Invest and confirm Richard Buckner Gent'l in the place and office of Clerk of the County of Essex x x". Dated 3rd December 1712. (seal)   signed Wm Cooke

page 291. Deed. 8 Sept 1714. Samuel Henshaw, planter, and Kazia his wife, of St. Anns Par., sell Arthur Onbee, planter, of the same Par., for L 20. Sterling, 30 acres in St. A. Par. adj land of John Catlett and Ralph Rowzee, the land of Thomas Hawkins now in possession of John Boughan and others, the land of John Cooke

Wit:
John Man his mark
Sam'll Bizwell
John Boughan

signed Samuel Henshaw
Kazia Henshaw
her mark

Rec. 9 Sept. 1714

Note: In the year 1737 an appraisal of an estate under the name of Arthur Oneby is entered.   B. F.

page 292. Deed. 8 Sept. 1714. Nicholas Copland of St Anns Par., sells Samuel Henshaw, in consideration of 30 acres sold by Henshaw and wife to Arthur Oneby (onbey), 30 acres in St. Anns Par., on

8-E

West side of Popoman Swamp, etc.,
Wit:
John Man his mark   signed Nicholas Copland
Sam'll Biswell   his N mark
John Boughan

Ann Copland, wife to Nicholas, relinq. her dower rights.

    Recorded 9 September 1714.

page 294. Bond. 9 Sept 1714. L 300. Sterling. Eliz'a Williams as
Extx Est of John Williams, deceased.
Wit: signed Eliz'a Williams her mark
Ja Alderson   Robt Webb his mark
Salvator Muscoe   Henry Adcocke
    Rec. 9 Sept 1714.

page 294. Deed of Gift. 9 Sept 1714. John Spiller of Richmond Co.
and Sarah his wife, only sister and only heir at Law of William
Harper late of St. Anns Par., Essex Co., give George Pley Berry
son of the said Sarah, for natural love and affection,"but more
especially in consideration of three thousand pounds of good
Tobacco", the plantation where William Harper dwelt at the time
of his death, upon Occupation Creek, adj the land of Richard
Mathews deceased, etc.
Wit: signed John Spiller his mark
Ja Alderson   Sarah Spiller her mark
Thomas ffenwick
A Somervell   Rec. 9 Sept 1714.

page 296. "Received this 9th day of 7'ber of George Berry (sic)
the three thousand pounds of Tobacco within mentioned by us"

    signed John Spiller his mark
      Sarah Spiller her mark

    Recorded 14 September 1714.

8—E

page 296.

" Mr Jos Groughere dr

London
1707
Aug 24   To Goods shipt on board the Corbin
          Cap't Walt'er Cooke   16. 12. 1
1709
June 21   To cash paid his bill to Cap't
          Isual   9. 0

          To postage of Letters &c   9. 2
                                                 ----
                                                 17. 10. 3
          Ballance   21. 02. 1
                                                 ----
                                                 38. 12. 4

Per Contra or
1706
9'ber 27 By Mr John Gilsons bill on
          Messrs Berry & Co   9.   6. —

Mar 12   By the Proceeds of 2 hhd Tob'o
          per Capt Graves   11.   1. 3
1709
9'ber 24 By ditto 4 per Isual   15. 14. 2

          By ditto 1 per Forrester   2. 10. 11
                                                 ----
                                                 38. 12. 4
          By ballance of Contra   21.   2. 1

Errors Excepted. Jan'ry 31 1711
per Henry Offley

At a Court held for Essex County the 9th day of September 1714
At the mo'con of Joseph Growhere this Account was ordered to be
Recorded and is Recorded
                         Test
                              Richard Buckner Cl Cur "

Index.

Abbott, Eliz. 87
    Fra: 87
Adcocke, Edw. 26. 33. 39.
    Fra: 33.
    Henry 59. 95. 100
Alderson Ann 25. 78
Alderson, James (as a witness)
    2. 4. 6. 7. 9. 12. 13.
    14. 17. 20. 21. 25. 31
    34. 37. 43. 45. 46. 48
    54. 55. 56. 58. 61. 72
    74. 76. 77. 78. 80. 81
    82. 84. 85. 88. 91. 92
    94. 97. 100
Alderson, James (other entries)
    12. 25. 55. 61. 77. 97
Allen, Erasmus 48. 34. 49. 85.
    Vallentine 30. 63
    William 22. 96
Allerton, Willoughby 56
Allieson, Jas 22
Allin, Jas. 85. 86. 89
Ambrose, Jno. 75. 76
Anderson, John 68. 92
    Jos. 62
    Richd. 33
    Richd, Jr. 38
Andrews, John 6. 14. 19. 44. 68
Arnold, Wm. 25
Atkins, Anne, 29
    Jane 29
Atkinson, Jno. 99
    Tim. 9. 10. 41
Avery, Mary 77
Awbrey, Francis 12
    Mrs Frances 12
    Henry 12. 95. 96
    John 12
Ayres, Tho. 14
Ayrnold see Arnold

Baker, Folin 1
    Joseph 32. 48. 62. 70.
        87. 88. 96
    Thos. 12
Bacon, Hon. Nath'l. 86
Bald Eagle Neck 1

Ball, John 44. 47
    William 95
Barker, John 2
    Penelope 2
Bartlett, Patience 25. 28
    Thomas 25. 27. 28
Bates - 33
    John 81. 89. 97
    Phebe 81
    Thos. 57
Battaile, Jno. 53. 64. 65
    Lawrence 53
Beasley, William 80
Beckham, Simon 60
Bell, Hannah 96
    Robt. 9. 12
    Robert, Jr. 9
    Tho. 88. 96
Bentley, Nath'l. 25. 28. 36
Berkeley, Sir William 90
Berry, Geo. 86. 97
    George Pley 100
    Henry 80. 81. 95
    Margt. 14. 41
    Nicho: 44
    Wm. 14. 41. 83
Berry & Co. 101
Bessill see Biswoll
Beverley, Chr. 28. 87
    Harry 32. 73
    Robt. 11. 12. 28. 51. 61
Bickloy, Jno. 77
Bidlecom, Eliz. 58
    James 58
Billups, Dorothy 76. 77
    John 76. 77
Bizwoll, Eliz. 99
    Jeremiah 6. 52. 53. 83. 89
    Mary 53
    Robt 69. 87
    Robt. Sr. 89
    Sam'l. 32. 83. 99. 100
Blackburn, - 53
    Elias 5. 69
    Martha 5. 69
Blackstone, Argill 63
Blatt, Thos. 56
Blundell, Jane 90

Booker, Edmund 52
       Edward 52
       Richd 52. 96
Booton, Joshua 26
Bondall, Jno. 28
Bonnitt, Wm. 9. 12
Boughan, Alex. 62
       Henry 17. 22. 28. 29. 62
       James 25. 26. 28. 29
              35. 37. 38. 42
              43. 61. 63. 70
              76. 77. 87. 89
              91
       James, Junr. 70
       James, Senr. 37. 62
       John, 14. 17. 26. 27
              28. 29. 32. 35
              36. 37. 38. 40
              41. 52. 62. 63
              64. 68. 69. 76
              77. 88. 95. 99
              100
       John, Senr. 37. 42
Boughton, Joshua (see Booton)
Boughan, Sarah 38. 85
Boulin, Simon 4
Boulware, - 90
       Eliz. 85. 86. 89
       Jas. 14
       Jno. 85. 86. 89. 97
       John, Jr. 85. 86. 89
       Mary 85. 86. 89
       Susanna 85. 86. 89
       Thos. 97 (Bowlar)
       Wm. 85
Bourne, Jno. 39. 54
       Peter 54
       Robt. 39. 54
       Wm. 34
Bowcocke, H. 51
Bowers, Arthur 10. 31. 61. 77
Bowrne see Bourne.
Bowsey, Jno. 98
Boyd, Robt. 50
Brazer or Brazier.
       Elizabeth 43. 48
       John 43. 48
       John, Jr. 43
       Richd 43

Brechin, Rev. Jas. 55. 57
Briant, Will 44
Brice, Henry 4
Broadley, John 54
Brockenbrough, New 84
              Wm. 84
Broocke, Richd 12
       Wm 12. 33
Brooke, Mary 55. 78
       Richd. 9
       Robt. 55. 56. 81
       Robt. Jr. 5. 38. 49. 55.
              71. 80. 81. 93
              96. 98
       Tho. 9
Brooking, Robt. 25. 46
Brooks, Eliz. 39
       Frances 39
       Joseph 57
       Richd 54
       Thos 54
Browne Bucken 6
       Charles 5. 10. 52. 53. 58
              90. 97
       Dan'll 38. 42. 81. 88
       Edw. 90
       Francis 42
       Henry 85
       James 90
       Sarah 31
       Susanna 90
       Tho. 22
       Wm. 30. 31. 58. 68. 79. 80. 90
Brown's Mill 64
Browning, Fra. 14
Bryan, Thos. 42
Buckner, Richd. (as Clerk of Court)
       1. 3. 8. 13. 15. 16.
       17. 21. 26. 29. 40. 48.
       49. 59. 60. 61. 62. 87
       91. 93. 99. 101
Buckner, Richd. (other entries)
       1. 4. 12. 17. 19. 45
       46. 48. 49. 50. 51. 57
       58. 75. 77. 85. 92. 94
       97
Burgess, Jos. 35
Burnett, Jno. 40
Burnett's Rolling House 40

Burton's Range 57
Burwell, Lewis 75
          Nath'l 75. 76
Butler, Agnes 69
        Amory 9
        Jno. 68. 69
Button, Robt. 1
        Thos. 1
Button's Range 1
Byrom, Henry 5. 60. 63. 74. 86
        98
        Peter 5. 91. 98

Callay, Jos. 14
Cambwell, Alex 57
Cammock, Warwick 9
Campbell, Patrick 12
Carter, Richd. 57
        Hon. Robt. 87
Caston, Cary 82. 93
        Class 82. 93
Catlett, - 99
         John, 5. 47. 53. 99
         Col. John 18
         John Jr. 65. 72
Chamberlain, Jno. 29. 63
             Leonard 86
Chance, Wm. 50
Chenault, Stephen 86. 89
Cheney, Jno. 54
Cheney, Wm. 54
Chew, Mrs Hannah 50
      Larkin, 3. 47. 50. 51. 52
             59. 63
Cheyney, Jno. 31
Cleveland, Jno. 11
Clowder, Jeremiah 50. 51. 52.
                  63

Coates, Saml 16
Cook, Richd. 97
Cooke, Capt Walter 101
       Hon. Wm. 99
Cooker, James 69
Coffee, Edw. 77
Cofflin, Fra. 12
Coghill, Jas. 10. 30. 58
Cole, Wm. 11. 86
Coleman, Ann 7. 81
         Edwd. 7. 14. 81
         John 88. 97

Coleman, Richd. 69
         Robt. 7. 19. 23. 28.
               29. 81. 88
         Spilsbee 42
Collins, Jas 57
         Mary 30
         Mathew 30. 45. 58
Combes, Mary 10
        John 9. 10
        Wm. 10
Comton, Wm. 85
Connally, Thos. 47
Connarnell, Mary 55
Connelly, Ann 45. 47
          Tho. 45
Conner, Timothy 57
Connoly, Thos. 82
Cook, Benj. 95
      Susanna 89
Cooke, Jno. 83. 95. 97. 99
       Robt. 30. 90
       Thos. 32
Copeland, Jno. 3
Copland, Ann 100
         Nicholas 99. 100
Coplin, Nicho. 57
Corbin, Gawin 1. 51
Cornwell, Peter 69
Covington, Ann 88
           Richd. 18. 20. 21. 24
                  41. 56. 70. 71. 77
                  78. 92. 95.
           William 3. 13. 21. 27
                   35. 61. 88. 93
           William, Junr. 5. 13
                   20. 21. 34. 36. 41
                   46. 92
Covington's Mill 32
Cox, Mrs Eliz'a 86
     John 86
Creighton, -. 39
Crokett, Robt. 75
Crompills, -. 22
Crow, John 41. 93
      Tho. 50
Crowdas, Sarah 40
         William 40

Daingerfield, Wm. 10. 13. 18. 24
              36. 45. 48. 78
              John 8.

Daniel, Wm. 43. 60
Davenport, Jos. 51
Davies, Evan 41
Davis, Robt. 43
      Thos. 11.34.72.94
      Wm. 27. 42
Day, Thos. 41
Dayle, Timmotha 7
de Graffenried, the Baron 51
Dickason, Tho. 23
Dicke, Susanna 56
Dickinson, Ealse 82
      Jno. 40.41.55.77
      Thos. 82
Dicks, Thos. 93
Dier, Jno. 74
     Wm. 74. 86. 91
Dike, Jno. 54. 56
     Susanna 54
Dinker, Jos. 10
Diskin, Danl 2. 61
     Jno. 2. 61
     Mary 61
Divilliard, Jacob 89
Dobyns, Cath. 40. 55
     Chas. 39.40.55
     Danl.37.39.50.54.55.
         59.64.
     Danl. Jr. 39. 55
     Drury 40
     Edmund 39
     Eliz. 40.54.55.59.65
     Griffin 40
     Isaac 40
     Richd. 39. 55. 59
     Wm. 39. 55
Doniphan, Alex. 93
Douchberry, Jas. 74
Dougherte, Dennis 9
Doughty, Enoch 14.41.44.82
     Jno. 12. 46
Driscoll, Timothy 16
Dudding, Andrew 54.55.68
Dudley, Richd. 47. 91
Dunn, Wm. 82
Dyer see Dier
     John 86
     Wm. 85

Edmondson, James 42. 43. 56. 61.
              62. 63. 64. 67.
              68. 77. 78.
     Joseph 46
     Thos. 86. 87
Edwards, Mary 14. 19
     Richd 14. 19. 63
Elliott, Saml. 19. 46
Ellit, Jno. 24
Ellits, Saml. 11.44.57.68.94
Evans, Edw. 49.53.54. 65. 72
     Eliz. 53. 54. 72
     John 5. 53. 59
     Mary 53. 74
     Rees 53. 54. 72
     Thos. 86
Evis, Alice 74
Evitts, Tho 22

Falconer, David 76
     Nicholas 77
Farmer, Thos. 61
Farrell, Charles 53. 89
Fenwick, Tho. 52. 53. 68. 100
Fisher, Benj. 19. 27. 29. 31. 32.
         35. 37. 38. 48. 50. 54.
         55. 70. 76. 78. 79. 84.
         87.
     Eliz. 28. 37
     Jonathan 27. 31. 32. 37.
         38. 95.
     Rebecca 37
Fisher's Mill 32
Fitzhugh, Hon. Wm. 50
Fitsjefres, Thos 40
Fletcher, William 73
Fogg, Nath'l. 11. 17. 33. 52. 75.
         77. 80. 81. 82. 89.
Forrester, Capt. 101
Foster, Jno. 7. 46. 68. 84
     Robt. 68. 69
Fox, John 47
Foxhill's Mill 41
Franklin, Nicho. 11
Fry, John 75. 95
Fullerton, Jas. 35.44.85.91.

Fullerton, James Jr. 85
    Sarah 85. 91

Gaines, Danl. 69
    Jno. 63
    Robt. 14
    Thos. 38. 42
Garnet, Ann 42. 77
    Anthony 77
    James 77
    John 42. 77. 92
    John, Jr. 77
    Thos. 77
    Richd. 57
Gatewood, Dorothy, 96
    Henry 96
    Jno. 31.47.91.96
    Rachel 87
    Richd. 48.81.87.88
Geffereys see Jeffries
Gibbons see Gibins
    Ann 43
Gibins, Ann 37
Gibson see Gipson
    John, 11. 50. 101
Gillett, Jno. 15
Gills, Jno. 22
Gilson, Mrs Beth 37
Gipson, Fran: 69
Glary, Jno. 56
Godfrey, Dr. Peter 1. 2. 13.
                  20. 48. 97.
Gold, Pierce 35
Golding, Wm. 2
Goode, Richd. 10. 47
Goodrich, Benj. 95
Gorbill, Mary 55
    Thos. 55
Gordin, William 68
Goudye, Geo. 90
Goulding, Casandra 15
    Dan'l. 15
Gouggee, Richd. 6
Gouldman, Edw. 1. 57. 70
        Francis 1. 2. 12.
            48. 54. 57. 58.
            90.
        Francis, Jr. 90
        Martha, 1. 57. 90. 91
        Thos. 12. 70. 90

Grafford, Philip 82
    Pollatia 82
Graves, Capt. 101
    Alex. 50
    Francis 61. 97
    Jno. 8. 34. 42
    Thos. 42. 55.
Gray, Abner 68
    Warwick 78
    William 78
Green, Paul 35. 54
    Thomas 86
Gregory, John 34
    Sarah 34
Grennell, Wm. (Various Spelling)
    11. 13. 34. 48. 86
Gregson, Anne 25
    Capt. Thos. 25
Gresham, Charles 31
Griffin, James 85. 91
    John 87
    Thos. 20. 21. 34. 88
    Wm. 41
Groughere, Jos. 101
Guggey, Richd. 89
Gutteridge, Tho. 96
Guttrey, Joan 87

Hackley, James 44
    John 85
Haile, Jno. 22. 44. 85
Hakes, William 31
Hall (or Nall), Mary 87
Hall, William 76
Halsey, Robt. 87
Hardee, Robt. 38
Harding, Wm 16
Harper, Sarah 100
    John 35. 42
    Tho. 44. 62
    William 25. 81. 95. 100
Harrison, -, 46
    Andrew, Jr. 49. 65
    Andrew Senr. 19
    Elizabeth 65
    James 20. 23
Harrood, Mary 16
    Peter 16
Hart, John 21. 81

Hart, William 21. 81.
Harvey, Thos. 10.
Harwar, Eliz. 56. 72.
   Thos. 12. 20. 26. 56. 72.
Haslewood, Jno. 23
Hawes, Saml. 88
Hawkins, Jno. 23. 64. 68. 69. 80. 95. 96
   Thomas 99.
Hay, Agatha 93
  Mrs. Anne 18. 24
  John 93
  Timothy 11. 12. 21. 57
Hayes, Danl. 14. 21. 25. 56. 81
Henley, Saml. 7
Henman, Thos. 81
Henshaw, Eliz. 99
   Kazia 99
   Saml. 99
Hewlett, Wm. 1
Hide, Jonathan 75
Hill, Charles 53
  Edwd. 12
  John 11
  Leonard 39. 56. 67
  Richd. 61
Hilliard, Thos. 3. 24. 65
Hines, John 13
Hobbs Hole 48
Hollow, Peter 81
Holloway, Jas. 11. 33. 45
   Richd. 89
Holt, - , 29
  Plunkett 42
  Richd. 37. 38. 42
  William 38
Hopson, Margaret 44
Hoskins, John 40
Housing, Isabella 66
How, Alex 47
Howlett see Hewlett
   William 78
Hudson, Edwd. 22. 39. 40
  Eliza 43
  Henry 59
  Isaac 22
  John 22
  Rebecca 22
  William 22. 43. 62
Hudson's Plantation 32

Hughes, Arthur 28
Hunter, John 25
Hutchens, Cath. 31. 33
   Jane 31. 33. 36
   John 33
   Richd 31. 32. 33

Indian Field Island 1
Ingram, Martha 80. 83
   Thos. 38. 53. 80. 83
   Thos. Jr. 80
   Tobias 38. 80
Isual, Capt. 101

Jackson, Thos. 44
Jamison, David, 4. 6. 14
   Mary 4. 19
Jeffries, William 50
Jenkins, Thos. 88
Jinkinson, Eliz. 27
   Jane 27
   John 27
Johnson, Christian 54
  Henry 36
  Richd. 47. 54. 74
  Saml. 90
  Thos. 35. 36
  Wm. 48. 62. 63. 85
Jones, Eliz. 33. 74
  Hugh 18. 24
  James 42
  Richd. 35. 36. 42. 78. 85
  Robert (as a witness)
   4. 6. 11. 17. 19. 21.
   31. 36. 44. 45. 53. 54.
   55. 58. 61. 65. 72. 74.
   76. 77. 80. 81. 82. 90.
   91. 92.
  Robert (other entries) 38.
   69. 71. 85.
  Susanna 28. 29
  William 6
Jordan, William 89
Juge, Jas. 84

Kay, Robert 5. 23. 24. 72.

Kay, Robert, Jr. 5. 60
    Robert, Senr. 60
Kelly, Danl. 90
Kemp, Ann 87
    Elinor 87
    Martin 5
    Rachel 87
    Richd. 5. 23. 36. 87. 88
    Richd. Jr. 87. 88
Kilman, Geo. 55
Kilpin, Wm. 43
Kirbey, Henry 28
Kirk, Thos. 10. 58

Lacey, John 55
Lambert, Tho. 74
Lampart, Geo. 30
    Jno. 30
Landrum, Jas. 2. 79
    Saml. 79
Latane, Rev. Lewis 58
Lawless, Michael 64. 65
Leaso, Jno. 55
Leitch, David 15. 16
Lomon, Jno. 89
    Joseph 88. 89. 96. 97
    Joseph, Jr. 89
    Margaret 88
Lewis, Zach. 19. 36. 58. 70. 78
Ley, Tho. 38. 69
Linch, Capt Israel 69
Lomax, Jno. 1. 4. 18. 24
Long, Christian 63. 64
    Gabriel 59
    Henry, 4. 63. 64. 83
    John 3. 19. 22. 46
    Kath. 19.
    Richd 4. 6. 11. 15
        19. 20. 21. 45
        46. 49. 64. 65
Lough, Tho. 20. 26
Loyd, Ann 61
    Eliz 4. 61
    Geo. 3. 11. 17. 19
        25. 34. 61. 71
        83.
    Johanna 61. 71. 78
    Martha 61.
    Saml. 61
    Stephen, 4

Lucas, - , 80
    Henrick 64
Lumpkin, Robt. 40

Machen, Henry 53
Mackdonel, Arthur 25
Mackey, Tho. 50
Mackie, Hen. 54
Mackdaniell, Arthur 90
Makenny, Jno. 68. 88
    Wm. 63
Man, Jno. 99. 100
Marchant, Wm. 74
Marshall, Florandin 36
Martin, Benj. 36
    Henry, 36
    John 26. 36
    William 12
Mason, Flower 77
    Geo. of Virginia 50
    Geo. of Bristol 50
    Peter 77
    Wm. 92
Mathews, Eliz 86
    Frances 86
    Richd. 85. 86. 100
May, John 35. 88. 96
Mayfield, Robert 14
McCall, Andrew 76
    George 56
McCay, Charles 16
    John 15
    Wm. 15
McGilchriss, John 15
McMerkins, John 15
Meadar, Thos. 83
Meades, Thos. 30. 36. 41
Meadows, Jno. 9
Meders, Jno. 30
Merchant, Abraham 37
Meriwether, Francis 3. 12. 18. 24
        45. 61. 66. 67
        87.
    Mary, 45. 67
Merrit, Edw. 82
    Eleanor 56
    John 8
    Thos. 4. 61. 81
Micall see McCall

Micou, Margaret 30
      Paul 1. 4. 8. 18. 24. 30. 78,
Midleton, Kath. 60
      Priscilla 60
Mills, Jno. 13. 75. 93
      John, Junr. 5. 6
      Robt. 60
Minor, Eliza. 87
Moncaster, Jas. 63
Montague, Jno, Webb als 62
      William 94
Moody, Jno. 67
      Robt. 40
Moore, Fran: 8. 16. 35. 61. 72. 93.
      George 73
      Richard 56
Morand, Nicho. 53
Morgan, Jno. 5
Morraine, Jno. 38. 42
Morris, Geo. 19. 95
      John 13
Moseley, Benj. 96
      Edward 6. 38. 47. 81. 83. 84. 90. 96.
      Elizabeth 96
      Robert 43
      William 38
Moss, Ann, 84
      Frances 84
      John 84
      Martha 84. 93. 95
      Rebecca 14
      Richard 84
      Robert 14. 25. 81. 84. 92. 95
      Robert, Junr 84
      Thomas 84
      William 84
Munday, John 45
      Thomas 6. 7. 8. 61. 63. 94. 97
Murdock, Peter, 16
Murrell, Geo. 77

Muscoe, Salvator 1. 5. 11. 15. 19. 32. 33. 37. 38. 41. 49. 61. 77. 80. 93. 95. 96. 97. 98. 100.

Nalle, Martin 70. 85
Nall (or Hall) Mary 87
Neale, Ralph 63
      William 62. 63
Newell, Danl. 44
Newman, Thomas 2. 14. 52
Newton, Benj. 83
      Elizabeth 72. 75. 76
      Henry 72. 75. 76
      Martha 76
      Pollatia 82
      Thomas 76
Nichols, Jno. 35
Noell, Jas. 94
North, Anthony 6. 48
Nott, Sir Edward 39
Nowell, Mess 68
Nowland, Jno. 90

Owen, Mary 16
Owens, Owen 9. 16. 43. 79
Offley, Henry 101
Onbeo (Oneby) Arthur, 99
Orkney, George Earl of 50
Orpen, John 76

Page, - , 69
      Thomas 14. 19. 64
Paget, Ephriam 14. 17. 77. 80. 82
      Francis 10
      Mary 82
Pain, - , 69
Pannell, - , 53
      Thos. 70
      William 70

Parker, Elinor 2
    John 22. 31. 33
    Margt. 2
    Martha 31. 34. 56
    Robert 1. 2. 4. 7
        20. 23. 31. 37. 44
        45. 54. 60. 65. 68
        73. 81. 83. 97.
    Thomas 14
Parsons, Robt. 31. 33
Payne, Jno. 23
Peach, Tho. 12
Pearce, Elizabeth 27
    Francis 27
Peatross, Thos. 27. 30
Peck, Robt. 80
Peirson, Richd. 36
Perry, Saml. 32
Peters, Henry 9. 30
Petrus, Henry 83
Petties, Thos. 86
Pettit, Thos. 19
Phillips, Ann 69
Picket, Henry 63
    John 22. 29. 31. 63.
        81. 84. 85. 95.
    William, 85
Pigg, John 27
Pile, Vincent Godfrey 79. 93. 96
Pitts, John 79
Pleas, John 19
    Robt. 19
Potier, Isaac 35. 36. 84
Powell, Honour 41
    Jane 64
    John 19. 64
    Tho. 19. 64
Priccet, Andrew 74
Price (also Prise) Edward 13
    88. 93
    John 44. 47. 95
    Kath: 13. 93
    William 27. 35. 64. 84
Pritchett see Priccet
Procter, Richd. 49
Prosser, - , 39
    John 60. 65
    Kath: 3.
    Roger 3. 5.
    Saml. 5. 15. 59. 90

Purkins, Henry 50. 82
    Tabitha 50

Rackley, John 11. 15. 48. 49
Ragon, John 39
Raines, William 78
Ramsey, Thos. 87. 94
Ransone, Francis 57
    Robert 57. 94
Rauson (prob. Ranson) Robt. 94
Read, Eleanor 61
    William 61
Reeves, Ann 7
    Eliz. 6. 7. 13
    Henry 6. 95. 98
    Joseph 6
    Martha 6
    Mary 6
    Rebecca 6
Rennolds, Eliz. 45
    James 45. 46
    James, Jr., 92
    John 82
    Sarah 45
    Thos. 45. 46
    William 82
Retterford (also Rotterford prob.
    meaning Rutherford)
    John 30
Rice, Mary 60
Richards, Mary 55. 68
Richardson, - , 35
    Robt. 22
    Wm. 35
Ridgdale, Eliz. 44
    Jno. 44. 68. 69
Riding see Wriding
Righcraft, Joshua 2
Ripley, Eliz. 2
    Richd. 2
Robards see Roberts
    John 68
Roberts, Jno. 55
Robertson, Wm. 50. 51. 77
Robins, Tho. 52
Robinson, Major 68
    Benj. 93. 94
    Henry 18. 24. 32. 72.

Robinson, Richd 37
Rodan, Homer 41
Rose, Dr. Henry
Rotterford, Jno. (this name is prob. Rutherford - being familiar with the name I've heard many varied pronunciations and seen it spelled in curious ways. B.F)
30. 64
Rouse, John 79. 80
Rowlson, Jos. 79. 80
Rowzee, Captain Edward, 2. 6. 53. 89. 95. 97
    John 2
    Ludowick 2
    Ralph, 57. 91. 97. 99
    Rebecca 86. 90
Roy, John 52. 60. 63. 65
    William 52
Rushell Thos. 37
Russell, Christian, 41
    Nehemiah 40. 41
    Thos. 43
Rutherford, Robert 4
Rycraft, Joshua 70

St. John, William 96
Sale, Cornelius 14. 15. 47. 75. 84. 92
Sallavand, Timo. 78
Samuell, Anthony 94
    Anthony, Jr. 94
    James, 78
    Sarah, 78
Sanders, Thos. 61
Sarle see Searle
Scott, William 1. 30
Seager, Jno. 19
    Oliver 38. 42
Searle, Jno. 13
Shackelford, Henry 22
Shepard, Robt. 52
Ship, Josias 43
Short, Abigail, 52. 53
    Samuel 14. 20

Short, Thomas 25. 26. 28. 36. 43. 52. 53.
    Thomas, Jr. 52. 53
Sidey, John 92. 94
Siles, Jno. 22
Skey, Jno. 9. 10
Slaughter, Jane 66
Slater, Robt. 47
Slaughter, Robt. 23. 47
Smart, Edw. 77
Smith, Ann 90. 91
    Augustine, 1. 2. 17. 20. 28. 29. 37. 49. 53. 54. 64. 69. 73. 74. 98.
    Daniel, 83
    Edward, 77
    Francis 83
    John 77. 80. 82. 87
    Joseph, 13. 18. 24. 32. 37. 40. 48. 58. 63.
    Capt. Lawrence 69
    Mary 90
    Nicholas, Junr., 12. 50. 64. 68. 72. 96. 97.
    Nicholas, Senr. 97
    William, 37. 63. 73. 90
Smither, William 46
Sneed, Thos. 88
Sollomans Garden 39
Somerville, Alexander 9. 19. 21 28. 100
Sorrell, Jno. 80
Sorsbe, Thos. 25
Southerland, Jno. 95
Spann, John 59
Spearman, Job. 69
Spicer, John 89. 90
Spillor, Jno. 100
    Sarah, 100
Spiers, John 89. 90
Spires, Jno. 6. 53
Spiers, Thos. 83
Spotswood, Hon. Alexander, 18 24. 51
Stallord, Saml. 4. 6. 31. 53. 68 69. 79. 80. 86. 96. 97

Stanard, Wm. 23. 60
Stapp see Stepp.
Stapp, Abraham 81. 84
    Abraham, Jr. 81
    Dorothy 81. 84
    Jacob, 81
    James 81
    Joseph 81
    Joshua 81
    Martha 81
    Rebecca 81
    Ruth 81
    William 81
Strang, John 4. 41. 72. 81
Stark, - , 53
    Frances 28
    James, 90
    John 28
    Thomas 28
Steevens, Edward Junr 73
Stevens, John 73
    Henry 73
    Rebecca, 73
Stemson, Wm. 60. 64
Stepp see Stapp
Stoaks (or Stokes) William, 11 25. 75. 76
Stone, Fran: 70
    Mary, 70
Streshley (also appears in these records as Strechley and as Thrashley - this last being the pronunciation of the name)
    Thomas, 46. 73. 92
    Thomas, Jr. 25
Sullivan see Sallavand
Surkings, Madam 1
Sutton, John 59
Swyney, Ann 50
    Morgan 50

Talburt, Catherine 87
Taliaferro, Ann 87
Taliaferro, Charles, 23. 39.47. 53. 54. 73. 74. 83 87. 88.
    Elizabeth 36. 47
    John 64
    Lawrence, 72. 73. 82. 88
Tapley, Jonathan 15.
Tarent, Leonard 2. 8. 18. 20. 24. 46. 48. 71. 77. 78. 83. 88. 92. 97.
    Mary, 77. 78. 97
Tayloe, John 52
Taylor, James 87
    John 83
    Mary, 83
    Richd 35. 95. 96
    Robert, 95
    Susanna 96
    William 42. 77. 92
Thacker, Mary, 56
    Samuel, 1. 7. 18. 24. 55. 56. 77
    Silvester 30. 78
Tharp, William 82
Thelwell, Jas. 36
Thewall, James 47
Thomas, Cath. 21. 24
    Elizabeth 34
    John 21. 24
    Marg'ry 23
    Robert, 21. 34. 39. 73
    Robert, Junr., 21. 39. 73.
    Sarah 73
Thomson, George 36. 55
    Saml. 96
    William 1. 3. 29. 96
Thornton, Francis 23
Thrashley, Thos. 73
Tinsley, John 44
    Sarah 44
    Thomas, 43. 44. 88. 96. 97
Todd, Thomas 75
    William 70
Tomlin, Lancelot, 90
    Rebecca, 90. 91. 94

Trawhere, Joseph 5
Trible, George 88
Tucker, Daniel 14. 15
    Eliza. 15
    Lacmedon 14
Turner, Thomas 52
Tutt, Richard, 9. 10
Twisdell, John 31. 95
    Sarah 36

Underwood, Wm 9
Upshaw, William 73. 97

Vash see Vass
Vass, Ann 27
    John 22. 56. 58
    Vincent 27. 58
Vaughan, Cornelius 88
Vawter, John 68. 79
Vickary, William 92. 94
Vickers (also Vickary)
    Nath'l. 49. 65
Virgett, Elizabeth 43. 45. 57
    Job 42. 43. 45. 57
    Mary 27. 42

Waggoner, John 16
Waite, Robert 65
Waklin, Wm. 82
    Richard 82
Walker, Charles 95
    Thomas 94
Waller, Charles 45. 55. 68. 73
    Edward, 12. 73
    Susanna, 45. 73
Walter, Isaac, 37
Ware, Nicholas, Junr. 46
Warren, Rachel, 94
    William 94
Waters, Cath: 13
    Isaac 28
    John 13. 86. 93
    Winifred 13

Wayde, William 56
Waye, William 58
Webb, Eliz. 62. 76. 79
    Isaac, 12. 13. 26. 39. 64
    James 33. 68. 72
    John 62. 76. 79
    Richard 76
    Robert 62. 100
    Winifred 19
Webster, William 53
Welsh, Mary 68
    Reub'n 12. 32. 35. 36. 51. 55. 57. 67. 83.
West, William 84
Wheeler, Elizabeth 60
    Thomas 48
White, Henry 86
    J. 74
Whiteside, John of the Kingdome of Great Britain. 10.
Willard, John 30. 31. 69. 79.
    Martin 79. 80
    Sarah 30. 31. 79
Williams, Eliza. 89. 95. 100
    Hugh 36. 37. 39. 95
    Jaell, 20. 23
    John, 33. 36. 37. 39. 59. 79. 80. 88. 89. 95. 96. 97
    John, Junr. 31
    Joseph 59
    Margaret 88
    Thomas, 36. 95
    William, 1. 20. 23. 70. 78.
Williamson, Thomas 2
Willis (Willis) Mary 10
Willis, William 10
Wills, Jno. 97
Willson, David 4. 27
Wilton, Richard 4. 8. 9. 49. 76.
Winnam, Peter 89
Winslow, Thos. 63. 71. 77. 80. 82. 94.
Winston, Martha 90. 91. 94.

Winston, William, 74. 76. 90. 91.
　　　　　　　94. 95.
Wood, Henry, 10
Woodford, William 4. 18. 24. 51.
Woodnot, Eliz. 32
　　　　Henry, 3. 9. 22. 32. 79.
　　　　　　93.
Wriding, John 31. 64. 68.
Wright, John 11.
　　　Mottrom (Makum) 1. 78.
Wyatt, Mrs. Katherine 19
　　　Richard. 19

Yard, Robert 86. 87
Young, Catherine 13
　　　Henry 13
　　　Robert 32. 62.
　　　William, 13. 18. 19. 21.
　　　　24. 39. 45. 57. 68.
　　　　79.

PREFACE

This volume is a continuation of Volume VIII.

It seems the more I see the less I know. Here are Harwar, Guggey and Hueklecot. What they are or how to pronounce them baffles me. I can only hope the reader knows. Even the clerks who wrote the second did'ent know.

There are items in Volumes VIII and IX that have already been included in the King and Queen County collections. They are repeated here to keep these Essex records in due order.

Beverley Fleet.

Nov. 25th 1940.

VIRGINIA COLONIAL ABSTRACTS

Vol. IX
Essex County - Wills and Deeds
1714 - 1717

*This book is a consolidation of
two volumes into one
with two separate indexes*

Compiled By:
Bevereley Fleet

Southern Historical Press, Inc.
Greenville, South Carolina

Ex 9.   1

                    Essex Co., Virginia. Wills & Deeds.
                         Number 14. 1714-16.

page 296. Bond. 9 Sept 1714. L 300. Sterl. Sam'll Stallord as Exor. of
Estate of John Boulware, dec'd.
Wit: signed   Sam'll Stallord
Salvator Muscoe   John Hawkins
Wm Thompson   John Boughan
                         Rec. 9 Sept. 1714.

page 297. "An account of things unknown at the praisement May 1st of
William Harpers Estate".
        to 1 sow and seven pigs
        to 3 old sider caskes
        to 1 old bed cord
Henry Berry Adm'r of the Estate of Wm Harper dec'ed presented this
further acc'ot of the sd de'ceds Estate to Essex county court the 9th
day of 7'ber 1714 which is Recorded.
                    Test Richard Buckner Cl Cur

page 297. Appraisal of Est. of John Williams, dec'd. taken by order of
Court 12 Aug. 1714.
Long inventory, including a number of textile items, totals L. 85.17.6
Also includes:
"to one servant man named William Kelly 20 months to serve 5. 00. 0
"Susanna Williams Apparell"
                              signed   John Boughan
                                        Edward Rowzee
                                        Ralph Rowzee

page 299. "At a Court held for Essex County the 9th day of September
1714 Joseph Lemon Surviving Ex'or of John Williams dec'ed presented
this Inventory to the Court which is ordered to be Recorded and is
Recorded".

page 299. An account of the Estate of Robt. Moseley dec'd.
Includes: to pd Mr Benj'a Moseley   10. 11. 5
Totals L. 101. 9. 1.
                         signed Martha Moss Adm'r.

page 299-A. Deed. 10 Sept. 1714. Godfry Stanton and Dorothy Stanton his
wife of "the County of Essex and Parish of farnham" for love and affection and also for L 50. sell "Thomas Wyatt our nephew and godson, son of

Ex. 9

Richard Wyatt and Catherine his wife of King and Queen County and parish of St Stephens", 280 acres on Hoskins Creek in F. par. in Essex Co., which land Thomas Pettit by his will dated 20 September 1663 devised to his daughter Dorothy now the wife of the above sd Godfry Stanton. If said Thomas d.s.p. then the land to his father Richard Wyatt.

Wit:
John Haymon
George Brook his mark
Richard Owens his mark

signed Godfry Stanton
Dorothy Stanton
her mark

Rec. 9 Sept. 1714.

page 300-A. Appraisal of Est. of Mr. Richard Kemp, dec'd., taken by order of Court dated May the 13th 1714.
Includes:

To a parcell of old Books	5. 4. 0
To one clock not fixed	2. 0. 0
To one p'r of Pistolls and holsters and sword	1. 5. 0
To 4 Silver Spoons at 7 s.	1. 8. 0
To one pr Money Scales and weights	0. 5. 0
To one punch Bowl	0. 5. 0
To one large Sun dyall	0. 7. 0
To Mrs Kemps wareing apparell	5. 19. 0
To one Razar and hone a flask & wafer Box	0. 5. 0

Totals L. 480. 0. 0 . Appraisal made 9 June 1714 and presented by:
Sam'll Stallord
Buckner Brown
Jno Vawter 1714

(Richard Kemp)
(Cha Taliaferro) Exors.
(Richard Gatewood)

Rec. 9 Sept. 1714.

page 303. Power of Atty. Reuben Welsh, merchant of Essex Co., to William Dangerfield, Gent., of Essex Co., to collect accounts and transact other business. Dated 11 Nov. 1714.

Wit:
Robert Beverley
Robert Jones

signed Reuben Welsh

Ack. by Welsh to Daingerfield and recorded 11th Nov. 1714.

page 304. Deed. 27 Sept. 1714. Henry Woodnot, planter, of Essex Co., "for affection that I do bare", lends to William Hudson and Rebecca his wife and to John their son of the same Co., a negro girl slave and her increase.

Wit:
Benjamin Morris
John Coutance

signed Henry x Woodnot

Rec. 11 Nov. 1714.

page 304. Deed. 14 Oct. 1714. John Bagge of the Parish of St. Anns, in the County of Essex, Clerk, and Mary his wife, late widdow of Samuel Thacker of the said county, Gent'l., deceased, sell to Thomas Streshley, Junr., of Southfarnham Parish, planter, for L 300., that tract of land whereon the said John Bagge now liveth, 276 acres in St. A. par. adj. land of John Walker deceased, the land of William Axam (this name also spelled William Amax in this same deed), a creek called Ralfs Creeke, also the Mill crook, which 276 acres were granted to Ralph Warrener, deceased, by Patent dated 18 Nov. 1663, and by Samuel Thacker and Mary his wife the only daughter and heir apparent of the said Ralf Warrener, were sold to Thomas Winslow, Taylor, of St. A's Par., 7 May 1698, and by sd Winslow sold to sd Samuel Thacker 8 Aug. 1698, and by sd. Thacker bequeathed to Mary his wife, Executrix of his will.

Wit:
John Walker
Jane Cornew
John x Halloway

signed John Bagge
Mary Bagge

Rec 11 Sept. 1714.

page 307. Lease and Release. 11th and 12th Oct. 1714. Robert Parker and Margaret his wife of St. A. Par., sell Samuel Stallord of same Par., 25 acres, for 1500 lb. tobo., this land bequeathed by Mr. Robt. Pley, deceased, to George King, and being in St. A's Par., on S. side of Occupation Creek.

Wit:
Buck'en Brown
Thomas ffenwick
George Gorden

signed Robert Parker
Margaret Parker
her mark

Rec. 11 Nov. 1714.

page 311. Lease and Release. 10 and 11 Nov. 1714. Edward Coffey of St. A. par., planter, sells John Barbee of the same par., for 5000 lbs. of "Lawful sweet scented Tobacco", 118 acres, which land Coffee bought of Augustine Smith, and is on branches of Occupation Creek, adj. land of Thomas Warren, on E. side of Chickahomony Path, the land of Coll. Francis Gouldman "to a corner red oake and white oake corner to Mr Beverley his Great Tract", etc.

Wit: Tho. Ramsey
     Saml. Stallord
     Robert Parker

signed Edward x Coffey

Ann Coffey, wife to Edward, relinq her dower rights.

Rec. 11 Nov. 1714.

9-Ex

Lease and Release. 8 and 9 September 1714. ffrancis Gouldman and Thomas Ramsey, Church Wardens of St. Ann's Parish, in the County of Essex, sell to Paul Micou of Par and Co. aforesaid, gentleman, for 8000 lb. tobo., for the benefit of the said Parish, and "by the order and consent of the Vestrymen thereof", the Plantation formerly purchased by the Church Wardens of the Parish aforesd, for the time being, of Richard West for a Globe for the use and benefit of the said Parish, this land being upon Blackbournes Creeke in the Par. and Co. aforesd. adj. the land of George Green, etc.

Wit:
Richard Gatewood
Robt. Parker

signed ffrancis Gouldman
Tho. Ramsey

Rec. 11 Nov. 1714.

page 318. Lease and Release. 8 and 9 Sept. 1714. Leonard Tarent of St. A. par., gentleman, sells ffrancis Gouldman and Thomas Ramsey, Church Wardens of Parish of St. Ann's, for 50,000 lbs. tobo., the plantation where Leonard Tarent now dwells, with the order, advice and direction of the Vestry, which he lately purchased from Garet Neale and Jane his wife, 140 acres, less the burying ground 50 ft. square, lying in St. A. par., adj. the old road leading from the plantation to Tandy's mill at the head of a valley proceeding out of a branch of Occupation Creek called Wasanauson, the land of Mr. Brooke, the land of James Alderson and the land of the late Thomas Gregson deceased.

Wit:
Richard Gatewood
Robt Parker

signed Leo: Tarent

Mary Tarent, wife of Leonard, relinq. dower rights, by letter of atty. to Robert Parker.

Recorded 11 Nov. 1714.

page 322. Appraisal of the Est. of John Williams, deceased.
Includes:

To one suit horse Arms	1.	00.	0
To a parcell of old books one pr horse fleems and Tob'c box	0.	03.	0
To three old Piggins	0.	04.	0

Totals approx. L 50.

Sworn before Capt William Young one of her Ma'ties Justices 11th 9ber 1714.

signed Jno Vass
William Broock
Joshua x Booten

Presented by Eliz'a Williams, Extr'x.

page 323. Bond. 11 Nov. 1714. 10000 lb. tobo. "Thomey Ley hath obtained a License to keep an ordinary at his house in this County of Essex"
Wit: Signed Tho's Ley
Ja Alderson John Boughan
John Hawkins

Rec. 11 Nov. 1714.

page 324. Bond. 11 Nov. 1714. L 20. Sterl. "Thomas Ley is by the Court of Essex County Lycenced to keep the ferry over the Rapp'a River from his Land to William Pannells Now if the said Thomas shall constantly keep sufficient boats for the Passage of foot and horse with able hands to attend the same and also give Passage without Delay to all Publick Messages and Expresses (according to an Act of Assembly x x) men'coned to be ferry free x x " etc.
Wit: Signed Thos Ley
John Hawkins John Boughan

Rec. 11 9'ber 1714.

page 324. Deed. 20 Nov. 1714. Thomas Strashley, Junr., of So. Farnham Par., planter, sells John Bagge, Clerk of St. Ann's Par., for L 300., the tract of land, 276 acres, where John Bagge now dwelleth, in St. A. Par., adj. land of John Walker deceased, the land of Wm Axam down by a Creek side called Ralfs creek, etc. This land originally patented by Ralph Warrener 18 Nov. 1663, etc. See p. 304.
Wit: Signed Thomas Streshley Junr
Thomas Munday
Nathll ffogg
Ro Brooke Jun'r Rec. 12 Nov. 1714.

page 326. Bond. 12 Nov. 1714. L 200. Sterl. Samuell Stallord as Admr of Est. of Elizabeth King, deceased.
Wit: Signed Sam'll Stallard
Ro Brooke Junr. Tho Ramsey
Ja Alderson Jo'ph x Leeman

Rec. 12 Nov. 1714

page 327. Bond. 12 Nov. 1714. 10000 lb. tobo. Rich'd Taylor to keep an ordinary at his dwelling house in So. Farnham Par.
Wit: Signed Rich'd x Taylor
Ja Alderson Benj'a ffisher
Wm Winston John Boughan

Rec. 12 Nov. 1714.

page 328. Bond. 12 Nov. 1714. L. 2000. "Joseph Smith by the Hon'ble Governors comission appointed Agent for Boulwares Storehouse on Rappahannock River in the County of Essex".
Wit:
Tho Henman
Richd Covington

Signed Joseph Smith
ffrancis Gouldman
Jno Lomax

Rec. 12 Nov. 1714.

page 328. Bond. 12 Nov. 1714. L 50. Sterl. Robert Jones as Guardian of William Moss, an orphan.
Wit:
Tho Henman
Ja Alderson

Signed Robert Jones
Jno Pickett
Sam'll Stallord

Rec. 12 Nov. 1714.
Test
    Richard Buckner Cl Cur

page 328.
" By the Lords Justices

A Proclamation requireing all persons being in office of Authority or Government at the decease of the late Queen to proceed in the Execution of their Respective offices x x x Given at the Court of St James the fifth day of August 1714 in the first year of his Majesties Reign
    God Save the King "

"Whereas it hath pleased almighty God to call to his Mercy our late Soverign Lady Queen Ann of Blessed memory by whose decease the Imperial Crown of Great Brittain France and Ireland and all the other dominions thereunto belonging are solely and rightfully come to the High and Mighty Prince George Elector of Brunswick Lunenburg: We therefore the High Sherif Justices of the Peace and Principal Inhabitants of the County of Essex do hereby with one full Voice and consent of tongue and heart Publish and Proclaim that the High and Mighty Prince George Elector of Brunswick Lunenburg: is now by the death of our late Soverign of happy memory become our only Lawfull and Rightfull Leigh Lord George by the Grace of God King of Great Brittain France and Ireland defender of the faith ote. to whome we do acknowledge all faith and constant obedience with all hearty and humble affection Beseeching God by whom King and Queen do reign to Bless the Royall King George with long and happy years to reign over us

    GOD SAVE THE KING

    Truly Recorded
    Test
        Richard Buckner Cl Cur

page 330. Bond. 13 Jan. 1714/15. L 20. "x x whereas the Court of Essex County have this day ordered that a Petition of the said Francis Thornton be Granted wherein he prays to have one Acre of the said Taliaferros Land appraised and delivered to him to build a mill as the Law directs x x from which order the said John Taliaferro prays an appeale to the 8th day of the next Generall Court x "
Wit: Signed Jno Taliaferro Jun'r
Robt Jones Aug't Smith

page 330. Deed. 13 Jany 1714/15. James Edmondson of Essex Co. sells to Samuel Edmondson of same Co., for L 45. Sterl., 150 acres bought from Mr. Leo Tarent, being part of Buttons Rainge Pattent formerly belonging to William Williams and sold by him to Edward Gouldman and by his Ex'or, Mr ffrancis Gouldman sold to Mr Samuel Thacker late dec'd, and by his will given to Mary Brooks now the wife of Mr. Leo Tarent. Adjs. land of William Howlet, the land of Makum Wright.
Wit: Signed James Edmondson
Will Edmondson
Robt Elliott
Bryant Edmondson

Power of Atty. Judith Edmondson wife to James Edmondson to Mr. James Boughan to relinq. Right of Dower. Dated 8 Jan. 1714/15.
Wit: Signed Judith Edmondson
William Edmondson
Bryant Edmondson
 Rec. 13 Jan. 1714/15

page 332. Lease and Release. 10 and 11 Nov. 1714. Augustine Smith of St. Marys Par., Essex Co., Gentleman, sells Cornelius Saile of St. Anns par., Essex Co., planter, 200 acres in St. M. par., about 3 miles above the falls of the Rappahannock River, adj. land sold by sd Smith to Peter Byrom, and the land of Henry Reeves.
Wit:
Salvator Muscoe Signed Aug't Smith
Ro Brooke junr
 Rec. 13 January 1714/15

page 335. Lease and Release. 8 and 9 December 1714. John Spicer, Junr of Sittenbourne Parish in Richmond Co., Gent., ~~sells~~ Rowland Thornton
 buys from
(continued)

Ex 9

of Hanover Par. Richmond Co., planter, all that part of 2750 acres "w'ch in Right belongeth to him" in Essex Co., adj. land formerly granted to Alexander ffleming 17 April 1667.
Wit: Signed   Rowland Thornton
Nicho Smith
James Phillips
                          Rec. 13 January 1714/15

page 337. Will of Robert Thomas of St Maries Parish, Essex Co. D. 1st Jan. 1714/15. P. 13 Jan. 1714/15.
To two grandsons Robert and John Thomas 600 acres of land lying on the branch of Ware Swamp to be equally divided. The residue of that patent, 370 acres, to daughter Ann Griffin.
To wife Susannah all the full Estate both real and personal that she brought with her.
Balance of estate to son Robert Thomas and daughter Ann Griffin.
Son in Law Thomas Griffin to be Exor.
Wit: Signed   Robert Thomas
Jno Taliaferro   his mark
ffran: Thornton
Mary x Mackor

Bond. 13 Jany 1714/15. L 200. Sterl. Thomas Griffin as Exor. of Robert Thomas, deceased.
Wit: Signed   Thomas x Griffin
Robt Jones   William Pickett
                                                 Robt Thomas

                          Rec. 13 Jany 1714/15

page 339. Deed of Lease. Dated 11 November 1710. (sic). Place Powell, of St. Anns Par., planter, leases, for 99 years, to Augustine Smith, Gentleman, 300 acres in the Parish of St. Maries in the County of Richmond, whereon George and William Prockters now liveth. This land in the freshes of Rappa. River, in the fork of Lambs Creek, and was formerly granted to ffrancis Place by patent "dated the 7:br 1654".
Wit:
John Golding   Signed   Place Powell
  his mark   his marke
Casandrey Golding
  her mark
John Wood
  his mark

Proved by oaths of the three witnesses on 13 Jan. 1714/15 and Recorded.

page 340. Bond. 13 Jan. 1714/15. L 100. Sterl. James Booth "de bonis non Administrates"·(Adm. of remaining part of an estate not settled by exors) of Humphrey Booth, deceased.

Wit: Signed   James Booth
James Alderson   Salvator Muscoe
A Somervell   Robert Brooke Jr

                      Rec. 13 Jan 1714/15

page 340. "Know all men by these presents that I James Griffin of South farnham Parish x x Exor x x of Mr James ffullerton decd x x have in my hands all the Goods x x of the sd James ffullertons Estate x x and that neither x x James Webb nor Sarah his wife by virtue of her right to Executorship in her widdowhood have taken or converted any part of the said Testators Estate x x I do hereby acquitt and discharge the said James Webb x x forever x x ". Dated 13 Jany 1714/15.

Wit:
P Godfrey   Signed   James Griffing
Nicholas Smith Junr
                      Rec. 13 Jany. 1714/15

page 340. Appraisal of the Estate of Elizabeth King, taken by order of Court dated 12th day of 9ber 1714. Presented by Samuell Stallord, Admr. Includes:
   To 1 Taylors Goose and Iron Sitt   0. 02. 0
Total valuation L 05. 12. 05
                                Signed
                                Edward Rowzee
                                Ralph Rowzee
                                Joseph Leamon

                    Rec. 13 Jan. 1714/15

page 341. TO ALL TO WHOM these presents shall come I William Cocke Esq'r his maj'ts Secretary of State of Virginia send greeting KNOW YE that I the said Wm Cocke Esq, Secretary as afore'sd by Virtue of her late maj'ts Letters Patents x x do appoint x x Thomas Henman Gent'l in the place and office of Clerke of the County of Essex x x Given under

Ex 9

my hand and seal this seventh day of ffebruary 1714 In the first year of his Maj'ts Reign"

         Signed Wm Cooke

"At a Court held for Essex County on Thursday the 10th day of February 1714
  Thomas Henman Presented the above Commission for Clerk of this County and being by Virtue thereof Sworn Clerk the said Commission is admitted to Record"

page 341. Bond. 10 Feb 1714/15. L 40. Sterling. Thomas Ayres as Guardian of Robert Moss, orphan.
Wit: Signed Thomas x Ayres
Wm Covington Junr   Robt Jones
                Robert Thomas

       Rec. 10 Feb. 1714/15.

page 342. "Memorandum of words spoken by Robert Thomas of the County of Essex on the first day of Jan'ry to Mr ffrancis Thornton when he was on his death bed vizt he being asked by the said Thornton whether he had any more Land than what he had Given away by his will or whether he did design to give any more to his two Grandsons then the six hundred acres he had men'coned in his will his answer was that that six hundred acres was all the Land he could give them or did design to give them x x"
              Signed ffran Thornton

"on mo'oon of Robert Thomas the above named ffrancis Thornton made oath to what is above written x x "
         Rec. 10 Feb. 1714/15

page 342. Lease and Release. Both dated 20 January 1714/15. William Stoks of St. Anns Par., planter, sells Aron Porry of So. Farnham Par., planter, 30 acres in St. A. Par., adj. William Jones Bridge, land of Thomas Davis, etc.
Wit: Signed William x Stoks
Ro Brooke jr
Salvator Muscoe
Mary Muscoe
        Rec. 10 Feb. 1714/15

Ex 9   11

page 345. Deed. 9 Feb. 1714/15. Robt Richison, planter of So. Farn. Par. sells Wm. Richisone, planter, of same par., 150 acres in So. F. par., adj. land of Daniel Brown, Senior, land of John Sills and land of Henry Shackelford.
Wit: Signed   Robt x Richisone
Alexand'r Younger
Henry Shackelford   Rec. 15 March 1714/15

page 347. Lease and Release. Both dated 6 March 1714/15. John Chick of So. Farn. par. sells Erasmus Allen of same par., 100 acres in So. F. par., being part of 1563 acres formerly granted the said Chick by Mr. Edwin Thacker and to the said Thacker by Patent dated 20 of April 1687. Adj. land of Thomas Hucklecot, land of James Taylor, land of James Boughan, land of Andrew Dyer and land of John Gatewood.
Wit: Lease signed   John x Cheeke
John Allen   Sinor x Cheeke
Herbert Wagoner
Jane x Richason

page 348. "At a Court held for Essex County on Tuesday the 15th day of March 1714 John Cheeke acknowledged this his deed of Lease to Erasmus Allen which is ordered to be recorded and is recorded
                                    Test
                                         Tho Henman Cl Cur

                        Truely Recorded
                            Test
                                  W Beverley Cl. Cur   "

Note: It would appear from the records that Thomas Henman was not a particularly efficient or accurate clerk. It may be assumed that Wm. Beverley, clerk of a later period, went back through the records and verified certain entries. Hence his name as clerk on the records of this date.   B.F.

page 351. Will of John Henderkin of Richmond County. Dated 30 Dec. 1712. Prob. 15 March 1714/15.
To loving sister Katherine Handerkin, tobo.debts, horse, bridle and
     saddle.
To Loving Brother Tho Handerkin all wearing clothes.
Friend John Griggs Exor.
Wit: Signed   John x Henderkin
Abr'm Velden
Thomas Barnett
John Griggs

Ex 9

page 351. Power of Atty. "William Boulter late of Eggbury in the County of South'ton in Great Britain and now of Steake within the parish of S. Mary Bourne in the same County Taylor Eldest son of John Boulter late of Eggbury aforesd yeoman and of Margarett his wife sister of Thomas Robey late of the County of Middlesex in Virginia all since Dec'ed and Nephew and heir of the sd Thomas Robey sendeth greeting"

"Know yee that the said William Boulter x doth x x appoint x x Richard Martin and Thomas Martin both of the County of King William in Virginia aforesd his true and Lawfull Attorneys x x to enter into all and Every Messauges Mills, plantations, Lands x x given or devised by the Last Will x x of x Thomas Robey bearing Date the 15th day of April wch was In the Year of our Lord God one thousand six hundred ninety and five x x x."   Dated 8th Sept. 1714.

Wit:
George Martin   Signed   Will'm Boulter
James Hardwicke
George Hardwicke
ffrancis fisher

   At a Court held for Essex County on Tuesday the 16th Day of March 1714
   This power of attorney was present' by Thomas Martin and proved by oath of ffrancis ffisher one of the witnesses thereto and is recorded "

Note: This name may be Robey or Roboy. The Parish Register of Christ Church, Middlesex County, Va. page 35, shows:
"Thomas Robey and Ann Wallis both of this pish was marryed 27th of June 1687"

page 353. Power of Atty. John Goare of South Farnham Par., Essex Co., to "my Trusty and well beloved kinsman Timothy Driscoll" of same par. and Co., to collect debts. Dated 9 Feb. 1714/15.
Wit: Signed   John Goare
Benjamin Morris
John x Hubbard
                          Rec. 15 March 1714/15

page 354. A further Inventory of the Est. of Robt Moss, deceased, taken 9 Feb. 1714/15. Totals L 4. 13. 6
                          Signed   Salvator Muscoe
                                    Ro Brooke Junr
                                    John x Mills

                          Rec. 15 March 1714/15

Ex 9

page 354. "Jorimah Biswell Recomeds Three pounds of ffeathers Lately Com to hand of the Estate of David Ginkins forgot to be appraised
At a Court held for Essex County on Tuesday the 15 March 1714
The ffarther Inventory of David Jenkins's Estate was presented by Jeremiah Beoswell and is recerded"

page 354. "Essex County St Marys Parrish January 19th day 1714/15"
By order of Essex Court dated 13 Jan 1714/15, an appraisal of the Est. of Robert Thomas, decd., sworn before Mr John Lomax, one of his Maj'ts Justices.
Includes:

One orphan boy bound by the Vestry att	12. 00. 00
One paire of Spatter lashes of Deers Leather att	00. 03. 00
One Grafting Instrument att	00. 00. 06
One Spoon mould anvill and hamer att	01. 10. 00
a Small old bible and an old family book att	00. 03. 00

Total approx. L 50.

At the end of the list appears:
"Here Ends the Inventory of the sd Thomas own proper Estate"

"Here begins the Inventory and appraisement of the Estate of the Widow and Legatee of the said Thomas dec'd which shee brought wth her to the Estate of the sd Thomas dec'd as followeth"

"ffirst the fethers in a bed ticking weighing fifty Eigh pounds att	02. 10. 00
one old rug att	00. 05. 00
one Chest att	00. 10. 00
one Chest att	00. 04. 00
one Court Cubbord att	00. 10. 00
x x x	
twenty Six pounds of old pewter att	00. 15. 02
x x	
two young Virginia born negroes a man and a woman att	60. 00. 00
Seventy three pounds of Cotton in the Store att	00. 12. 12
x x x "	

Total approx. L 75.

"This is all the Estate that she brought that is in being product to uss to Inventory and appraise
and here follows that part of the sd Widows Estate which she brought to the Estate of the sd Robt Thomas decd which is not in being

(continued)

Ex 9

nor to be found which we do Inventory and appraise as followeth"
This list includes:

first one Cow killed for beef att	01. 10. 00
Eight barrows of about two year old one of them lost att	01. 00. 00
Seven flitches and a halfe of Bacon and five Joles of bacon att	01. 10. 00
five bushells or thereabouts of Indian pease att	00. 10. 00
one horse sold for five hundred pounds of Tobacco by the sd Thomas	01. 15. 00
Two bushells of beans att	00. 06. 00
forty five pounds of fatt	00. 15. 00
Eleven hundred pounds of bad Tobacco and the Cask att	04. 00. 00
(which sd Tobacco was sent down among the shiping to be put of by John James In his Shallop)	
Two Cows and two yearlings and a two year old heifer which dyed of themselves att which wee think they Might have gotten by the hides or otherwise to have bin of no vallue"	

Total approx. L 10.

"All which goods have bin Inventoryed and appraised by uss as witness our hands and seales"

                               Signed   Robert Key
                                                 Henry x Brice (or Price)
                                                 John Ellitts

"At a Court continued and held for Essex County on Wednesday the 16th 1714 (sic)
     Thomas Griffin presented this Inventory of Robt Thomas's Estate dec'ed which is recorded"

page 357. Bond. L 100. Sterl. 15 March 1714/15. Richard Covington as guardian for Daniel Diskin an orphan.
Wit: Signed   Rich'd Covington
Tho Honman   Will Young

                               Rec. 15 March 1714/15

Ex 9

page 356. Agreement. 5th April 1715. John Hunter and Ann Coleman of the County of Essex of one part and Thomas Coleman, son of the said Ann Coleman of the County of King and Queen of the other part. "Whereas there is a marriage (by Gods Grace) intended Suddainly x x between the sd John Hunter and her the sd Ann. It is agreed x x between x x John and Ann x to and with Thomas Coleman x x that the whole personall Estate x x now in the possession of her the sd Ann which she holds and Enjoys by vertue of the Last Will and Testam't of Robert Coleman dec'ed her late Husband shall and may when required by him the sd Thomas either before the said marriage be solemnized or after, be divided into two Equal parts x x "one part thereof being retained and kept by her the sd Ann as her own proper Estate the other half to be divided between the sd Thomas and the rest of the children of the sd Robert Coleman x x x"

Further that John Hunter shall not dispose of timber, negroes etc. on the land. "Notwithstanding the sd Intermarriage as also that she may not Dispose Give or bequeath of all and Every the plate as Tankards and other things weighing Seventy four ounces and a half without the License or consent of the sd John x x ". John Hunter and Ann Coleman bound to John Coleman in the sum of L 500. Sterl. to keep this agreement.
Wit:
Ja Alderson   Signed   John Hunter
Miles x Short   Ann Coleman
Catherine x Short   Tho Coleman

Presented by Thomas Coleman and by his attorney Mr Zachary Lewis.

Rec. 21st June 1715.

page 359. Deed. 18 April 1715. "Leonard Hill gent of Southfarnham parish in the County of Essex within the colony of Virginia Attorney General for George Cappell Merch't in the City of London and Richard Jones planter of the same", sell Alexander Younger, planter, of the same par., for 3250 lb. tobo., 100 acres of land, adj. that of ffrancess Browne, Senr., the land of Thomas Wood, the land of Major Aylotts, land formerly belonging to George Kephill, land of Nicholas Newton, etc.
Wit:
James Boughan   Signed   Richard Jones
Henry x Browne   Leo Hill 1715

Rec. 17 May 1715

Note on curious nomenclature: There are times, and this is one of them, when I feel just like the above witness, Miles Short. But imagine going through life, from one end to the other, like that.   B.F.

Ex 9. 16

page 361. Power of Atty. "John Collier of the City of Bristol merchant (one of the Creditors of Lem Coxe late of Virginia Plantor decd)" to "my loving friend Nicholas Smith Liveing on Rappahannock River in Virginia Merchant", to receive settlements from Benjamin Deverell, merchant, and George Downing, planter, Exors of Lem Coxe. Dated 3rd Jan. 1712/13.
Wit: Signed   Jno Collier
Walter King
John Paine

Presented by Smith and proved by oaths of King and Paine 17 May 1715.

page 362. Bond. 17 May 1715. 10000 lb. tobo. Arthur Bowers to keep an ordinary at the Courthouse.
Wit: Signed   Arthur Bowers
Thomas Munday   Wm Winston
H Brooke   Thomas Streshly Junr

Rec. 17 May 1715.

page 362. Bond. 17 May 1715. 10000 lb. tobo. Robert Ellitt (sic) to keep an ordinary at the Courthouse.
Wit: Signed   Robert Elliott   (sic)
Tho's Ley   John Hawkins
H Brooke   Robt Jones

Res. 17 May 1715.

page 363.

"Capells Letter
   to Hill
                                     London the 27th of Ap'll 1705
Mr Leonard Hill
              Your last Letter I rec'd, and S'r, I hope as I being such a Distance from my Effects you will in Choice See that there is Justice done me between Mr Richard Jones and my Selfe for I Desire nothing but the fair thing and in Case Mr Jones refuses to give his affidavit to the bargaine betweene us I will Leave it to his owne Conscience and S'r according to the power you have I would desire you to turne my Land into

(continued)

money or Tobacco or if Mr Jones will take it up on accompt I will leave
it to y'r Judicious management as to vallue of it and S'r, Mr Jones
hath more of mine as follows besides w't I gave you an accompt og w'n
I sent you my power (Vizt) 1 Mare Coalt and fold as he writ me word of
1 pr of stiliards w't 900 lb. 1 large buckskin and 1 fawne skin and
perhaps some other odd things wch I cannot now remember

 I pray S'r bring all to a faire accompt and take and give releases
on both sides and S'r bring all your Charges to an accompt if there is
any Effects over plus besides satisfying Mr Jones Consign them pray this
shipping to whome you see fitt and S'r In case there be a Deficiency
send an accompt and I will allow it is all

 Desireing y'r rememberance in the business above is from yr
ffriend to Comand
        Geo Capell

Sr Direct y'r Answer to be left at the Virginia Coffee house in St
Michaels Alley Cornehill London
To
Mr Leonard Hill
Merchant on the South Side
of Rappahannock River
 Virginia

At a Court held for Essex County on Tuesday the 17th day of May 1715
 This Letter was presented by Alexand'r Younger and at his mo'oon
is ordered to be recorded and is recorded
        Test
         Tho Henman Cl Cur

page 364. Bond. 21 June 1715. 10000 lb tobo. Robt. Elliott as
guardian of John Diskin, an orphan.
Wit: Signed Robart Elliott
Robert Jones   James Webb
Wm Covington Jr   Thomas Munday

      Date of record omitted.

page 364. Bond. 21 June 1715. L 1000. Sterl. Leonard Tarent having
"obtained a Comission for the office of Sheriff of Essex County" x x x
"according to the Commands thereof and shall Diligently Enquire and
find out the true quanity of Land held in the abovesaid County of Essex

      (continued)

Ex 9

by any and Every person and persons whatsoever and return a perfect List or rent roll of the same x x "
       Signed Leo Tarent
            Richd Covington
            Paul Micou
   Rec. 21 June 1715.

page 365. Bond. 21 June, year omitted from record. L 50. Sterl. John Golding as admr. of Est., of Place Powell dec'd.
Wit: Signed John x Golding
Robert Jones   Will: Tayler
Hum Brooke   Wm Winston
   Rec. 21 June 1715.

page 365. Add'l Inventory of the Est. of James ffullerton, dec'd., Cattle, etc. Total L 8. 14. 0 . Appraised by Mr James Boughan, Mr John Gatewood.
       Signed James Griffing

   No date of record shown.

page 366.
"March the 4th 1714/15 Surveyed for Mr James Scott in Richmond County one hundred and seventy three acres of Land scituate in the parish of St Ann in the County of Essex binding on Little Portobacco Swamp December the 2d 1714. Surveyed for Coll Richd Covington two hundred and Thirty Six acres of Land scituate in the parish of St Ann in the County of Essex binding on the Land of John Smith and Tho Winslow
January the 2d 1714/15 Begun to Survey for James Griffin a Tract of Lan near Tapahanock Town the chain to be - up by Mrs Ann Coleman
Aprill the 8th 1715 Surveyed for Mr James Alverson and Robert Brooke Junr one hundred and Eighty acres of land found to be Escheat from John Walker scituate in the parish of St Ann in the County of Essex in the mouth of Lawson Neck
May the 30th 1715 Surveyed for Majr William Aylett of King William County five hundred acres of Land scituate in the parish of South farnham in the County of Essex Lying on the branches of Pascataway Creek "
       Signed Ro Brooke Junr
           D.S.El

page 366. Deed. 10 July 1715. Francis Browning of St. Mary's Parish, gives for "natural affection which I have for my well beloved Daughter Anne Browning", 100 acres, "where I now live", which land was purchased out of a tract formerly granted to Enoch Doughty. This land adjs. 100 acres sold to Joseph Calloway and land recently taken up by Jno. Sanders. Wife to retain right of dower.
Wit: Signed   ffrancis Browning
Jno Ellitts
John Morgan
                      Rec. 20 July 1715.

page 367. Lease. 20 Sept. 1714. ffrancis Smith of St Anns par., planter, leases Leonard Tarent, Gent., of same par., 5 acres, being part of a plantation on which Francis Smith now lives, adj., land of Wm. Tompson, formerly called Thicket point, "to have and to hold the sd five acres of land unto him the said Leonard Tarent his heirs and Ex'rs and assignes for and during the Lives of him the sd Leonard Tarent and of Mary his wife and of Mary Boughan and for and during the Life of the Longest Liver of them x x ". Yearly rent of 3 bbl. Indian corn. Also to build a dwelling house and leave it in good condition at expiration of lease.
Wit:
Wm Tompson   Signed   ffran Smith
John Boughan   Leonard Tarent
                      Rec. 20 July 1715.

page 369
            "Essex County   The Deposition of Elizabeth Pley
    Your deponent says that Thomas Jewell and his Mother before him has been twenty years about getting the land that was in Diferance between him and John Parker, and your Deponent went to Mr Gillson who sold the sd land to one Thomas Rowson w'ch the sd Thomas Jewell Claims from, and the sd Gillson told your deponent that the sd Jewell had right to but fifty acres and your Deponent says that the Land the said Thomas Jewell has taken away by a Survey from John Parker was the land that was In difference between Geo Jones and Robert Tomlin and that your Deponents Husband took possession of the said land in the behalf of Robt Tomlin the said Tomlin being sick at that time and that Thomas ffreshwater then Subsheriffe at that time who Delivered possession to yo'r Deponents Husband by the consent of the sd Tomlin and your Deponents Husband bought the said land of the sd Tomlin for sixty acres more or less and your Deponent further saith not"

Ex 9

page 369. Power of Atty. 13 Nov. 1714. " x Samuell Randall the younger of the City of Corke merchant and Mary his wife the Daughter of Thomas Pope late of Bristol merchant deceased send Greeting Whereas an Estate In Virginia called Nettle patch plantation at the mouth of Popes Creek in the County of Westmorland containing five hundred acres of land or thereabouts with a parcell of negroes and buildings thereon is descended to the said Mary Randall als Pope and for a Certain Consideration in hand paid the Land Negroes and Buildings were let to Lewis Merchant late of Virginia dec'ed untill the said Mary should come to age or be marryed Now know ye (that) we the said Samuel Randell and Mary Randall als Pope (his wife) reposeing Speciall Trust and Confidence in our Loving kinsman Thomas Wiles of Bristoll merchant have made ordained Constituted and appointed and by these presents do make ordain Constituted and in our place and steed put and authorise the said Thomas Wiles our true and lawfull attorney for us in our name and to our use, by himself or such other person or persons as he shall think fit to substitute and appoint to Enter into and upon the said lands buildings and Improvements thereof or otherwise and to take possession thereof and of the said negroes and being thereof so possessed for us in our names and to our use to sell and Dispose of the said land negroes and Improvements x x x "

Wit: Signed   Samuel Randall Jun'r
Thomas Thomas   Mary Randall
ffrancis Hart
John Clark
Stephen x Richardson   Date of record not shown.

page 370. Power of Atty. 30 Nov. 1714. "Jacob Nicholson of St Bees in the County of Cumberland and Kingdom of Great Britain yeoman and Richard Sanderson of Morresby in the County and Kingdome aforesaid yeoman, Exors of the last will and testam't of ffrancis Whiteside late of Whitehaven In the sd County and Kingdome marriner dec'd x x appoint x x x Paul Mackew and John Lomack both of Rappahannack In Virginia our Lawfull attorneys x x to x x receive of and from the Heirs Exor's or Admr of George Lloyd late of the County of Essex in Virginia aforesd, the sume of six thousand pounds of Tobacco wch was due us from the said George Lloyd by a note under his hand being (sic) date the twenty third day of August anno Dm One thousand seven hundred and tenn x x "

Wit:
Antho Nicholson   Signed   Jacob Nicholson
William Whiteside   Rich'd Sanderson

At a Court held for Essex County on Tuesday the 16th day of August 1715
   The within power of attorney was proved by the oath of William Whiteside one of the Evidences thereto and is truly Recorded
                            Test
                               Tho Harman C. Cur

Note: The above names are Paul Micou and John Lomax, both of Essex Co.

Ex 9

page 371. Deed. 16 August 1715. **William Berry and Marget his wife**, of the par. of Hanover in the Co. of Richmond, planter, sell Wm. Daniell of the par. of St. Mary in the Co. of Essex, planter, for 2500 lb. tobo. 114 acres, part of a patent granted Enoch Doutey in St. M. Par., adj. land of ffrancis Browning, etc.

Wit:
Richard x Edwards
Richard Goode Junr
Robert Parker
Thomas Shortt Junior   Rec. 16 Aug. 1715.

Signed   William Berry
         Marget Berry

page 373. Deed. 24 July 1715. John Hodgson of St. A. par., and Elizabeth his wife, for love and affection for "our Loving Son in Law Josias Ship and our dear Daughter Elizabeth his wife of the sd Co. and Parish", gives all land whereon Ship now lives, in fork of a swamp called Long Bridge Swamp, adj. land sold by Hodgson to Thomas Peatross, and being 30 acres.

Wit:
John x Hodgson
Samuel Biswoll
Thomas Peatross

Signed   John x Hodgson
         Eliza x Hodgson

"John Hodgson and Elizabeth his wife presented and acknowledged their within Deed for Land to their Daughter Elizabeth x x "

Rec. 16 August 1715.

page 374. Deed. 18 July 1715. John Hudson, planter of St. A. par., sells Thomas Peatross, planter, of same par., for 6800 lb. tobo., 62 acres, part of a tract Hudson now lives on in St. A. par., adj. Long Bridge Swamp, land of William Pitte, boundry line according to Hudson's deed from Valentine Allen.

Wit:
Saml Biswoll
Richd Ship
Charles x Brown   Rec. 16 Aug. 1715.

Signed   John x Hudson

Bond for foregoing witnessed by Samuel Biswoll, John x Harrison, Josias Ship.

page 377. Lease and Release. 18 - 19 July 1715. Samuel Prosser, planter, of St. M. par., sells Joseph Throwhero, Taylor, of same par., 214 acres

(continued)

Ex 9

in St. M. par., on Pewmansend Swamp and on a branch of Golden Vale Swamp. Name also appears as Trowhere.
Wit: Signed   Sam'll Prosser
Gabriel Long
Richard Buckner
Eliz: Buckner

This entry signed "Test Tho Henman Cl Cur"
And further "Truly Recorded Test W. Beverley Cl Cur"

page 381. Lease and Release. 15 Aug. 1715. Capt. James Boughan of So. F. par., sells John Cheeke of same par., 117 acres, in So. F. par., part of a tract of 550 acres granted Mr. William Johnson of So. F. par., 26 April 1704, and by him sold to sd James Boughan's father.
Wit:
Jos: Baker   Signed   James Boughan
A Somervell
                          Rec. 16 August 1715.

page 385. Will of Robert Mayfield, Senior. Dated 3 Dec. 1714. Probated 16 Aug. 1715.
To wife Sarah Mayfield all Land and Movable Est. during life.
One shilling each to sons : Robert Mayfield, Abraham Mayfield, John
     Mayfield and Isaac Mayfield.
To son Jacob Mayfield all land at decease of wife.
One shilling each to daughters : Catherine Gregory, Jane Graves, Anne
     Connoley.
Ext'x and Exor wife Sarah and son Robert.
Wit:
Daniel Hayes   Signed   Robert x Mayfield
Cornelius Sale

Proved by oath of Sarah Mayfield, widow, Executrix, etc., 16 Aug. 1715.

Note: Robert Mayfield refers to each of his children as "wel beloved". Therefore they are by no means out off with a shilling. He simply leaves his estate to be settled by his wife.

page 386. Bond. 16 Aug. 1715. L 50. Sterl. Sarah Mayfield, Extrx of will of Robt. Mayfield, dec'd.
Wit: Signed   Sarah x Mayfield
(names omitted)   John x Mayfield
                                                           John x Loyde

                          Rec. 16 Aug. 1715.

page 387. Bond. 16 Aug. 1715. L 2000. "The Condition of the above written obligation is such that if the above bounden Joseph Smith gent: shall and faithfully performe the office and Trust of an Agent according to the Directions of an Act of Assembly begun the twenty second day of October one thousand seven hundred and Twelve entitled an act for preventing ffrauds in Tobacco payments and for the better Improveing the Staple of Tobacco, Then this obligation to be void or else to be and remaine in full force and Virtue".

                      Signed   Joseph Smith (seal)
                                  Leo Hill 1715   "
                                  John Bagge   "

Rec. 16 Aug. 1715.

page 387. Bond. 16 Aug. 1715. L 200. Sterl. "Ann Kemp widdow of Richard Kemp Dec'ed adm'r x x "
Wit: Signed   Ann Kemp
Robt Jones   Rich'd Covington
                                    Rob't Elliott

Rec. 16 Aug. 1715.

page 388. Bond. 16 Aug. 1715. L 200. Sterl. Salvator Muscoe as Guardian of James, Phoebe, William and Margaret Booth, orphans.
Wit:
John Boughan   Signed   Salvator Muscoe
                                  Nicholas Smith Junr
                                  Robt Jones

Rec. 16 Aug. 1715.

page 389. Bond. 16 Aug. 1715. L. 200. Sterl. John Boughan and Thomas Leftwich admrs of Est. of Thomas Ley deceased.
Wit:
Nicholas Smith Junr   Signed   John Boughan
Salvator Muscoe   Thomas Leftwich
                                  John Chamberlain
                                  Richard Gatewood

Rec. 16 Aug. 1715.

Ex 9

page 390. Bond. 16 Aug. 1715. L 60. Sterl. William Berry of Richmond Co., Admr. Est. of Thomas Landrum, Dec'd.
Wit:
Robt Jones   Signed William Berry
                                          Richard x Long
                                          William x Dan'll
                    Rec. 16 Aug. 1715.

page 391. Bond. 16 Aug. 1715. 10000 lb. tobo. Richard Taylor to keep an ordinary at his home in Essex Co.
Wit: Signed Richard x Taylor
Wm Covington Ju'r   Benja ffisher
                                          Henry x Boughan
                    Rec. 16 Aug. 1715

page 392. Will of Thomas Todd the younger of the County of Baltemore in the province of Maryland.
Dated 11 Jan. 1714/15. Probated at Annapolis 3 June 1715.
To son Thomas Todd all lands "where I now live" below the head of Bare Creek and at the head of Back River. He failing in heirs to the heirs of son Robert. Son Robert failing in heirs then to heirs of brother William. If he fail in heirs then to the heirs of Philip Todd. If he fail in heirs then to the heirs of brother Christopher Todd.
To son Robert Todd land called Shewan Hunting Ground lying on Draughts of Gunpowder River. 1500 acres.
Land in Virginia to be equally divided betw. wife and children.
Tract lived on in Virginia to him my father shall give his dwelling on condition my father gives his personal est. in Maryland of equal value to my heirs.
To son Thomas Todd "all my Rings Sword and plate Books and Surveying Instruments".
To Richard Colegate and James Phillips each L 10. Sterl. on condition they act as Exors.
To Jonathan Hide L 10. on same condition.
To brother William and Martha his wife each a ring of 25 shillings.
Refers to business transactions betw. Mr Loury Offley and himself.
Bal. of estate betw. wife and children.
Father to take the two sons Thomas and Robert.
Wit:
Richard R —   Signed Tho's Todd Junr
Paul Phillpotts
Jacob Bull

Bond. 20th September 1715. L 500. Sterling. William Todd of King and

Ex 9.

Queen County, Jonathan Hide of Gloucester County and Elizabeth Todd admr Thomas Todd deceased.

                Signed   Elizabeth Todd
                              Will Todd
                              Jona'th Hide

page 395   Jan'r 6th 1712

INVENTORY of the Estate of Mr Step'h Loyde deceas'd

In the Hall			
8 black fram'd Chairs at 3 s	1.	4.	00
6 high fram'd Leather Chears 3.6	1.	1.	00
1 Kane Couch pillow and Quilt	0.	15.	00
1 oak ovel Table and Covering	1.	0.	00
1 small square Do and Covering	0.	10.	-
1 Esintor	1.	5.	-
1 pr back Gammon Tables and appurten'd	0.	7.	06
a parcell Earthen ware on the Shelfe	0.	3.	08
2 Glasses 2 Cruits 1 Incerperator	0.	3.	06
2 mapps	0.	5.	-
	6:	14:	8

In the Little Chamber			
1 feather bed bolster 2 pillows 3 blankotts 1 rugg Curtins Vallens bedsted etc	8.	0.	-
1 Small oval Table	0.	8.	-
	8.	8.	-

In the Hall Chamber			
1 Standing bed bolster 5 pillows 2 pillow Cases 2 blankitts 1 rugg Quilt 1 pr sheets	10.	00.	-
1 Em'l Chist	00.	10.	-
1 Spining Wheele	00.	5.	-
	10.	15.	-

(continued)

Ex 9

Inventory of the Estate of Mr. Stephen Lloyd (continued)

In Mist'rs roome
1 Standing bed bolster 2 pillows 1 pr blankett 1 rugg quilt Curtains Vallens shets 2 pillow oases	10. 0. -
1 Looking Glass Table covering and Window Curtains	2. 0. -
3 Low Leather Chairs	0. 9. -
5 Chen cupps and dishes	0. 10. -
2 Drinking Glasses 1 broken	0. 2. -
1 Tea pot 1 Do Chony shug'er Do and Tea Table	0. 10. -
1 Glass Globe	0. 0. -
1 Silver watch and Chain	4. 0. -
3 Silver Castors 1 Large pottle Tankard	20. 0. -
76 ounces of old Silver and Grath (?)	20. 19. -
Scales bras weitts 3 old Candlesticks and snuffers	0. 15. -
1 pr Tongs and Iron ffire shovell	0. 3. -
1 flock bed 1 feather bolster and pillow rugg 2 blankett and sheets old	1. 15. 0
1 box Iron 2 heaters and 2 pad Irons (sic)	0. 7. -
	61. 12. 00

Looking Glass Table and Covering and Curt	- 15. -
3 Glass Cupps and Sawcers, warming pan	- 12. -
	1. 7. -
	88. 16. 8

Lennin vist
1 old Cheq'er Table Cloath 2 w'th Lin Do	0. 11. 6
5 huggaback Table Cloaths	1. 5
1 fine Diaper Do	0. 7. 6
1 Doz'n Linin Napkins	0. 10. -
20 old Huggabak Napkins	0. 10. -
11 Diaper Napkins	0. 11. -
3 p'r Cource worn sheets	1. 4. -
1 pr of cotton Do	0. 10. -
1 Do	0. 8. -
2 pr holland sheets	2. 10. -
7 huggaback Table etc	0. 5. 3
1 pr of old Table Cloath and 2 Lin' Towels	- 2. -
	8. 14. 3

1 Trunk 2 Chest 1 box 1 Danriek Cse	1. 10. -
1 Doz'n Maple hafted 1 do forks	0. 15. -
a par'll old Glass Eathen ware and saddle baggs	0. 1. 6

(continued)

Ex 9

Inventory of the Estate of Mr. Stephen Lloyd (continued)

1 ould umbrella	0. 2. -
4 old knives and 6 old fforks	0. 2. 6
2 old brushes	0. 0. 6
15 doz'n of bottles and 2 pottle Do	1. 10. 6
1 4 gals wickerd bottles	0. 2. 6
1 brass pestill and mortor	0. 5. -
a par'll Tin patty panns	0. 2. -
2 pr sheep shares bill hook	0. 2. -
5 Grubin hows	0. 6. 3
1 Deale box in the buttery	0. 2. 6
	- - - - - - -
	5. 2. 3

In the new room	
Bed bolster blankets quilt Curtains and sheets	10. 00. 00
Chest of Drawers	1. 10. 00
4 Cushion Chairs	1. 8. 00
a parcell of Cheny ware	1. 00. 00
Looking glas Table Wind'w Curtains	00. 10. 00
	- - - - - - -
	14. 8. 00

New room Closet	
Books by Invoyce	6. 9. 4
Trunks bottles and Galipots	7. 6
	- - - - - - -
	6. 16. 10

1 sett of wrought Curtains and Val	10. 00. 00
2 old brushes	2. 6
2 pr pistoles	2. 10. -
	- - - - - - -
	12. 12. 6

Dairy vizt	
Earthenware	00. 3. 00
6 brown milk pans	0. 2. -
3 butter pots	0. 1. 6
12 patty pans wooden tray	0. 4. 6
2 Coffee potts pepper box drudgin box Skimmer and Earthen Mugg	0. 4. -
3 dozen plates	1. 10. -
	- - - - - - -
	2. 8. -
	138. 15. 6

Ex 9

Inventory of the Estate of Mr. Stephen Lloyd (continued)

Wareing apparell vizt
4 pr Ticking britches 2'6	00. 10. -
1 pr Leather Do 1 old pr Druggett	00. 12. -
2 Ticken 1 flannin vest	00. 10. -
1 Drugget 1 Cloth Do	00. 12. -
1 Drugget Coat	1. 10. -
1 ffrize 1 old Do	1. - -
2 old Silver hilted swords	3. - -
1 pr old boots and Spurrs	00. 5. 0
1 old wigg	00. 15. 0
	8. 14. -

1 Elm Chest 7 s. 2 Truss and Cradle 10 s.	17.

Wareing linin in the Chest of Drawers
8 New holland Shirts at 12 s.	4. 16. -
3 halfe worn Do 6 s.	00. 18. -
12 Muslin neckcloths 4,6	2. 14. -
10 Kenting hankerchiefs	00. 10. -
5 old night Capps	- 5. -
1 silk Do 2.6 6 pr thread Stockings 6.	- 8. 6
5 pr good worsted stockings 3/6	00. 17. 6
5 pr worn Do 2/6	00. 12. 6
2 pr yarn Do. 2.6 3 pr gloves 8.	00. 5. 6
	11. 7. -

One Truss of Linnin imported in the Eliza shipt by John Earle of Liverpoole on account of Mr Loyde amount'g as by Invoyce	17. 9. -
25 - - - advance (illegible)	4. 7. 3

Kitchin ffurniture
2 Large spits at 5 s.	00. 10. -
1 brass kettle 48 lb at 14 d per lb	0. 6. -
1 bell mettle skillot	0. 6. -
5 old brass kettles wt 63 lb at 9 d	2. 7. 3
150 lb of Iron pots at 3 d	1. 17. 6
Sawse pan ffrying pan Ladle, Ladle flesh fork	0. 10. -
2 old Sifters 1 Seive and riddle	0. 3. 6
80 lb of pewter at 9 d	3. - -
Table form pales, piggins treas chest troa and Stilliards	2. - -

(continued)

Ex 9

Inventory of the Estate of Mr. Stephen Lloyd (continued)

	£	s	d
3 ordinary beds and bed Cloaths	3.	-	-
	16.	10.	3
	198.	-.	-

In the Store
	£	s	d
7 pr thread ordinary Stokins	0.	10.	6
5 1/2 Thread	0.	8.	3
a parcell Trompery	0.	5.	-
a fflock bed &c	1.	10.	-
a par'll wash Gloves	0.	3.	-
2 deale and 1 oak Chest	0.	16.	-
1 man Saddle and furniture	2.	0.	-
1 Sin'll old Saddle	0.	5.	-
1 Cart and wheels	2.	0.	-
	7.	19.	9

Cattle
	£	s	d
41 sheep at 6 s	12.	6.	-
19 Cows at 40 s	38.	0.	-
2 steares at 50	5.	-	-
8: 2 year old 20 s	8.	-	-
4: 3 year olds 30 s	6.	0.	-
1 Bull	1.	10.	-
9 Yearlings at 8	3.	12.	-
	74.	8.	-

Horses
	£	s	d
1 White Cart horse	3.	0.	0
1 Do mare	3.	0.	0
2 saddle Horses	10.	0.	0
1 yearling Colt	2.	0.	-
Cart Harnes	00.	10.	-
	18.	10.	-

Hoggs
	£	s	d
5 Large Barrows	5.	-	-
6 Sows and Barrows 8 s	2.	8.	-
18 Small Hoggs at 4 s	3.	12.	-
8 sucking piggs 12d	0.	8.	-
	11.	8.	0

(continued)

Ex 9   30

Inventory of the Estate of Mr. Stephen Lloyd (continued)

Prize house
2 new Collars and harnes
1 new haler down
4 Blocks 2 Single and 2 Double Lignumvite Sheeves &c   2. 10. -
4 Single 4 Double Do worn   2. 10. -
   1/2 belongs to Mr Ja Loyde   7. 18. 0
                                                           ----
                                                          13. 19. -

9 M 4d nailes   0. 18. -
2 S of 10 d Do 4/3   - 10. 7 1/2
3 750 8d Do 3/5   - 12 10 1/2
                                                           ----
                                                           1. 1. 2

   1/2 whereof belong to Mr Ja Loyde

1 old Gunn   - 10. -
3 how 3 axes   1/2 Ja Loyde   - 3. -
Made up of by Mrs Loyde since Mr Loyds decease
57 bar'll of Indian Corn at 6   17. 2. 0
6 steers at 50 s   15. 0. 0
15 hoggs at 8 s   6. - -
4 sheets at 6 s   (sheep ?)   1. 4. -
                                                           ----
                                                          39. 6. 0
                                                         354. 9. 11

Brought Over
2 pr Scales and Weights 1 pr fflegins 1 gaging rod
    razes   0. 8. -
Plow Irons and file   0. 6. -
1/2 of a fflat an old Canow   3. - -
1 sm'll oald boat   3. 5. -
                                                           ----
                                                           6. 19. -

Negroes
Sambo   30. - -
Dick   30. - -
Primas   30. - -
Rachel   27. - -
Betty   27. - -

                        (continued)

Ex 9   31

Inventory of the Estate of Mr. Stephen Lloyd (continued)

Moll	27. - -
Sarah	27. - -
Nero aged 10 years	22. 0. -
Will Molotto 4 years	15. 0. -
Arthur 2 years	10. 0. -
Nany 1 1/2 rickets	3. 0. -
Roger	30. 00. 00
	278. 00. 00
1 old chest 3 pottle bottles 2 old Cask	0. 8. -
Pewter Chamber pott	0. 3. -
	11.
1 Gold watch	15. - -
Side Saddle	00. 5. -
2 Tin panes	00. 3. -
L	655: 7: 11

Essex County
    Pursuant to an order of the Court date the 12th of Decemb'r Last we have valued and Inventoryed the Estate of Mr Step'n Loyde dec'ed amounting as above to six hundred fifty five pound seven shilling and Eleven pence.
    Given under our hands this 7th of Jan'ry 1712

                        Joseph Smith
                        Wm Daingerfield
                        James ffullerton

At a Court held for Essex County on Tuesday the 20th day of 7'br 1715
    The within Inventory was presented by John Tailoe and on his mo'con is ordered to be recorded and is recorded
                        Test
                            Thos Henman
                                        Cl Cur

Stafford
    Wee the Subscrib'rs at the request of Lyonel Loyd attorney of James Loyd and Isaac Elton of Bristol merch't and John Tayloe who Intermarryed w'th the relict of Stephen Loyd dec'd did meet on the

(continued)

Ex 9

Inventory of the Estate of Mr. Stephen Lloyd (continued)

plantation called Chatterton in the aforesd County on the 7th day of June 1714 and value the Estate that was in partnership betwixt the sd James Loyd Isaac Elton and Stephen Loyd as by the Inventory underwritten

To 4 Cowes and Calves each at 1: 15: 0	7. - -
To 3 barren Cows each 1: 10: 0	4. 10. 0
To 4: 2 year old each 0: 12: 0	2. 8. 0
To 1 yearling	0. 6. 0
To 1 4 yr old steer	1. 04. 0
To 2 8 yr old Do, 0: 18: 0	1. 16. 0
To a parcel old bed Covering	1. 03. 0
To 2 potts and 2 ffrying panns	1. 17. 6
To 2 Wedges a pestle and broad axe	0. 9. 0
To 1 Mare	2. 10. 0
To 1 Cart and wheels	1. 15. 0
To 2 old pales	0. 1. 0
To 1 Sett of Horse harness	0. 15. 0
To 2 double and 2 Single blocks	0. 10. 0
To a handsaw drawing knife and twelve lb Rope	0. 06. 6
	----------
	26. 11. 0
	290. - -
	----------
	316. 11. 0
one third is	105. 10. 4

Negro man Ned	35. - -
Negro man Robin	35. - -
Negro man James	35. - -
Negro man Peter	32. - -
Negro man Charles	33. - -
Negro man Thom	20. - -
Negro wom'n Nanny and her Child Nell	30. - -
Negro wom'n Jenny and her child Sarah	30. - -
Negro wom'n Judy	25. - -
Negro wom'n Rachell distempered	05. - -
Negro boy Tom	10. - -
	----------
	290. - -

             Henry Fitzhugh
             Jno Fitz-hugh
             John x Grigsby

At a Court held for Essex County the 20th day of 7'br 1715 The above Inventory was presented by John Tailoe and on his mo'con is recorded   Test
           Thos Henman Cl Cur

(continued)

Ex 9   33

Inventory of the Estate of Mr. Stephen Lloyd (continued)

Stafford
These are to Certify that the apprassors were this day Sworne before
me James Jameson one of her Maj'ts Justices of the peace for the sd
County. Given under my hand the Day and year above sd
                                                    Ja Jameson

An accot from   1714 The Estate of Mr Stephen Loyde dec'ed Dr
J Loyd concerning   To Sundry Bills drawn Eliza Loyde on acc't of the
Ste: Loyds Esta.   Estate vizt:

            in fav'r of Larkin Chew   L   30. 0. 0
                        Wm Allen   34. 13. 6
                        Cha: Chiswell   15. 10. 6
                        John Naylor   5. 12. 6
                        Jos Smith   20. -   -
                        John Parker   6. 11. 8

                                    L   112. 8. 2

To the Moiety of Sundry bills drawn on the Joint acc'ot of Mr James
Lloyde and the Estate of Mr Ste Loyde in fav'r of
                        Sam'll Thacker   7: 9: 11
                        Jno Picket   13: 18: 8

                                             21: 18: 7
            1/2 is   10: 19: 8 1/2

                                            123: 7: 5 1/2
                                            287: 15: 0 1/2

                                            411: 2: 6

P'r Contra   Cr
By the Bills of Mr James Loydes ac'ot   )
date Dec'r 1st 1713   )   324: 18: 1

By the Moiety of a bill drawn in ffav'er   )
of Jno Pickett being on the Joynt acc't   )
of James and Ste Loyde   )   4: -: -

By Sundry remittances since Step'n Loydes   )
Death to Ja: Loyd   )   59: 6: 7

Pay one Years Interest for 324: 18: 1   19: 10: -

                                                  407: 4: 8
By the Moiety of one hhd from Potomack   3: 7: 10

                                                  411: 2: 6

                        (continued)

Ex 9   34

Inventory of the Estate of Mr. Stephen Lloyd (continued)

Virga. July 23d 1714 Errors Excepted per me
Lyonell Loyde attorney of Mr James Loyde
of Bristol merch't.

At a Court held for Essex County on Tuesday the 20th day of 7br 1715
The above account was presented by John Tayloe Gent and at his mo'oon
is ordered to be recorded and is recorded
                                          Test
                                            Tho Honman   Cl Cur

- - - - - - - - - - - -

page 403. By order of Essex Court 16 August 1715 the subscribers, first
sworn before Mr Paul Micou one of his Maj'ties Justices of the peace,
the Inventory and appraisal of Thomas Landrum late of this county dec'd
was presented by William Berry Admr.
Includes:
To one Earthen punch Bowle and Ten powter spoons   0: 1: 6
          Total valuation 14: 1: 6

Given under our hands the 17th day of Septem'br 1715
                                  John Boughan
                                  Sam'll Stallord
                                  Richd x Edwards
               Rec 20 Sept 1715.

page 404. By order of Court 16 Aug. 1715. Inventory of Est. of Robert
Mayfield.
Includes:
To 4 Trayes 1 bole 1 piggin 1 old noggin   00. 05. 0
To 1 parcel of Earthen Ware 12 Tranchers   00. 03. 0
          Total valuation 13. 00. 0 1/4

                                  Signed   John Merritt
                                           Cornelius Sale
                                           William x Jones

             Rec. 20 Sept. 1715.

Note: LYDE * Loyde

There never was any question in my mind until I came upon this record. Lyde not Loyde.

"Mt. Airy" the colonial estate of the Tayloe family is across the Rappahannock River from Tappahannock. Over the entrance door in the dining room there hangs a portrait of a lady. The Tayloes, and everyone else who knows this stately room, have always understood that this picture is that of Mrs. Elizabeth Lyde, widow of Stephen Lyde, who married secondly John Tayloe. Between the long windows overlooking the numerous terraces, gardens and fields to the Rappahannock River and beyond, in this same room, hangs a remarkably quaint portrait of a child, her son David Lyde. Here also portraits of Henry Corbin in his official robes, that of Katherine Griffin wearing a high lace headdress, a Governor of Maryland, Hon. John Tayloe of horse racing fame and other members of the family.

The Tayloe family bible and various original records at "Mt. Airy", all carefully examined the day of my last visit, November 3rd 1940, show this name as Lyde. Not Loyde. And Lyde it shall be so far as I am concerned. I might remark, that even if Miss Estelle Tayloe had not actually shown me the records, I still would believe anything she had to say about the family regardless of any written record.

The Essex County records have the name as Loyde. There is no doubt about that, for I examined them again this day, November 6th 1940. There is no loop in the small 'o'.

Now there was a young gentleman who had a country place at Lloyd's in Maryland. Friends would ask him where it was and he would say at 'Lieds'. They would laugh and say he has 'lied' again. So the old joke went threadbare. Evidently that explains it. The early pronunciation of Lloyd was 'Lyde'. Phonetics again, to the confusion of us moderns.

                                            Beverley Fleet.

page 405   The Estate of George Loyd Dec'ed 1715

To the Estate of Dan'll Diskin after my thirds deducted	7828
To Mr Robt Beverley as per his Receipt	
2 Judgmts L 36: 12: 18	
To Martin Palmer as per Judg't L 20: 18: - 1/2	
To Costs thereon	227
To Mrs Thacker L -: 16: 6	
To Do	476
To John Graves	497
To ffrancis Paget	408
To Ruben Welch	732
To Do	754
To Do	172
To Mr Orlando Jones	180
To Jeremiah Parker for bringing a)	
bed and furniture from New Kent)	200
To my Expenses and fforrige over 2 ferrys)	
to New Kent concerning a Debt due)	
from Wm Wms to the dec'd)	400
To Mr Muscoe	1117
To Capt Clowder L 2: 14: -	
To Clks ffees	543
To Mrs Churchill L 60: 17: 1 1/4	
To Mr Robert Beverley	1200
To Mr Bewers L 3: -: -	
To Do	100
To Coll Gouldman	414
To John Worden	1000
To Do	1080
To Capt Walker	1260
To John Loyd	173
To Thomas Winslow	764
To Capt Hawkins	250
To John Hill	1910
To Joseph Smith	3000
To Erasmuss Allen	200
To Leonard Tarents w'th Interest	2280
To Coll James Taylor	200
To Martha Parker	1076
To Nath ffogg for making up acco'tt	606
To Capt William Young	3260
To Thomas Lilliard	1908
To Coll Gouldman	140
To Mr Muscoe	172
To John Cooke	1200
To Mr John Bagg	566
To Do for a ffunerall Sermon	500
To Thomas Jewell	145
To the funerall Charges	200

(continued)

Ex 9

The Estate of George Loyd (continued)

To Patrick Courtney	200
To pd Robt Parker sub sheriff	1265
To Joseph Trohare	120
To James Renolds Junr	551
To X'pher Boverley	118
To Wm Price	500
To John Vawters	400
To Mr X'pher Boverleys bond	3358
To Mr Richard Buckner	1933
To 10 p'ct of 19008 lb of Tobo for receiving and paying	1900
To Mr X'pher Boverley	700
L 124: 18: 3 3/4	
	48137
Deducted per article to Ruben Welch	732
and for the funerall sermon	500
	1232
because it is supposed there is not sufficient to pay the debts	
	46905

Per Contra	Creditt	
By the Inventory and apprais'l	L 254: 6: 9	
By Mr Upshaw		300
By Isaac Mercer		200
By Mr Muscoe		993
By Martha Moss		400
By Cornelius Sale		53
By James Ronolds Senr		126
By Bernard Gaines		830
By John Vawters		2995
By Tobo ret'ed		560
By Ross Allin		600
By Sev'erll parcells ret'd		500
By Benja ffisher		1353
By James Williamson		630
By David Leach		625
By Ross Allin		483
By Ruben Welch		559
By the Estate of Jno Parker		1191
By Thomas Davis		71
By John Hunter		500
By Capt Rousey		400

(continued)

Ex 9

The Estate of George Loyd (continued)

By Godfroy Pile	121
By Thomas Threshley Junr	658
By Mr Bowers	1040
By Thomas Merritt	298
By Robt Parker	270
By ffrancis Pagett	406
By Thomas Lilliard	2673
By Rich'd Gatewood L 1: -: -	
By Wm Taylor	226
By Henry Kirby	226
By James Garnett	21

```
                        L 255: 6: 9      Tobo  19008
                    Signed   Robert Elliott
                             Johannah x Elliott
```

At a Court for Essex County on Tuesday the 20th day of September 1715
 Robert Elliott and Joanna his wife formerly Joanna Loyde wid'o presented the above acco't of their administration of George Loyde dece'd his Estate and delivered in the vouchers of the articles above men'coned which was allowed by the Court they the sd Robert and Joanna his wife makeing oath thereto which they did.
 And is ordered to be recorded and is recorded
```
                              Test
                                    Tho Honman   C. Cur
```

- - - - - - -

page 407. Deed. Charles Brown of St. A. par. Essex Co., "in Consideration of the Love good will and affection which I have and do bear Towards my Loving ffriend and son in Law William Tiller Junr of the said County and parish and Towards Catherine my Dear Daughter, wife of the said Tiller x x give x x the sd William Tiller and Catherine his wife and to their son Thomas Tiller x x", 63 acres part of a tract called Kirks Land, adj. land of Bernard Gaines, etc. Dated 19 Sept. 1715.
Wit:
Josias Ship   Signed   Charles Brown
Wm Davis
         Rec. 20 Sept. 1715

page 408. Bond. 19 Sept. 1715. 5000 lb. tobo. William Tiller to allow Charles Brown, referred to as Charles Brown Senior, to get timber and operate his mill on the foregoing 63 acres of land.
Wit: Signed   W x Tiller
Tho Barttlot
Josias Ship
Wm Davis   Rec. 26 Sept 1715.

Ex 9

page 409. Lease and Release. 19 - 20 Sept. 1715. Capt. James Boughan of So. F. Par., sells James Walls of same Par., 102 acres in So. F. Par., being part of 500 acres granted Mr. William Johnson by pat. dated 26th April 1704, and by him sold to James Boughan's father. Adj. land of Wm. Wilson, land of Mr. Robt. Beverley, etc.
Wit: Signed   James Boughan
J Baker
Wm Johnson   Rec. 20 Sept 1715

page 413. Lease and Release. 19 - 20 Sept. 1715. Jas. Boughan, Gent., of So. F. Par., sells William Willson, planter, of St. A. Par., 101 acres in St. A. Par., at the head of Gilsons run, adj. land of John London.
Wit: Signed   James Boughan
J Baker
Nicholas ffaulconer
Will Taylor   Rec. 20 Sept. 1715.

page 416. Bond. 20 Sept. 1715. L 200. "Martha Moss, widow shall x x pay fifty nine pounds Eleven Shillings and Eight pence (which she now hath in her hands and possession) unto Edward Moseley and Benjamin Moseley two Orphans of Robert Moseley dec'ed or to their order being their proportionable parts of their sd late fathers Estate x x as soon as they or Either of them shall be of Lawfull ages x x "
Wit:
Salvator Muscoe   Signed   Martha Moss
Ro Brooke Junr   Henry x Reeves
                 Rec. 20 Sept. 1715.

page 417.
                  The Estate of John Parker dec'ed   Dr
Acco't Parkers
    Estate

To paid Mary fforbush for Servants wages	L	-. 4.	-
To paid Mr John Bagg for a funerall sermon		-. -.	-
To paid for rum and sugar at the ffunerall		1. 10.	-
To paid Elizabeth Waters servants wages		-. 5.	-
To paid Ann Smith		-. 4.	-
To paid Peter Byrom	190		

(continued)

Ex 9

Estate of John Parker (continued)

To paid Coll Covington his Sheriffs fees at	827		
To paid Samuel Kill Patrick		1. 10. -	
To paid for ffinishing the Courthouse stable		- 16. 2	
To 500 nailes to the sd Stable		- 4. 6	
To paid Mr Joseph Smith		- 5. 4	
To paid Wm Hakes per Judgm't & C'sts	1021		
To paid Mr Tho Honman	1000		
To paid John Worden per Judgmt & Costs	2154		
To paid Mr Robert Beverley per Judgmt & Costs	49		
To paid ffogg & Pagett per Judgmt & Costs	1574		
To paid Geo Loyde the Levys	138		
To Robt Elliott	1191		
To Wm Hamor Judgmt & Costs	1326		
To Robt Parker	636		
To Thomas Ingram	70		
To Xpher Man	25		
To Benjamine Deveroll		- 15. -	
To the appraizers for 2 days	120		
To Mr Winstone	580		
To Coll Gouldman		- 19. -	
To Mr Rob't Beverley	1200		
To Simon Bookham	160		
To Capt Pew on acc't of a bill of four pds sterling		1. 10. 0	
To Mr Ruben Welch		- 7. 6	
To Mr Rich'd Buckner Clks ffees	256		
To Jonathan ffisher per order and Costs	125		
To Matthew Davis	102		
To my Trouble in receiving and paying	1269		
	----	-------	
	14013	12. 1. -	
for the sermon deducted		2. 10. 0	
		-------	
		9. 11. 0	
To 12513 at 12/6		78. 4. 4	1/2
		-------	
		87. 15. 4	1/2

Per Contra   Cr

By the Inventory and appraisement		75. 5. -
By James Touchberry	300	
By Joseph Reeves	125	
By Thomas Bene	125	
By Rich'd Cane	145	

(continued)

Ex 9

Estate of John Parker (continued)

By Martha Gouldman	250		
By Robt Jones	60		
By Robt Hardee	60		
By James Graves	50		
By Benj'a Deverell		7. 5. 4	
By James Alderson	120		
By John Munday	100		
By John Evans	125		
By Mr Robt Brooks Junr	40		
By John Danbly		- 2. 16 1/2	
	1500 Tobo	82. 12. 2 1/2	
Dr as per the other side		87. 15. 4 1/2	
Ballance due from the Estate		5. 3. 2	

A Somervell
Martha Somervell

- - - - - - -

page 419

A proc'l concer'g
Courts of Claims

    VIRGINIA Sc.
        BY His Maj'ts Lt Governor and Commander in Chief of this Dominion
        A Proclamation for enforcing the Laws for the better regulateing the manner of signing and Certifying Propositions and Grievances to the General Assembly.

    Whereas the act made at a General Assembly held at James City the 8th day of June 1680 Entitled an act for the presentation and Delivery of Grievances: Tho still unrepealed hath been so neglected and disused that notwithstanding the plain directions therein given for preventing ill disposed persons from transmitting to the Generall Assembly Scandalous and Seditious papers under the General name of Grievances of the County wherein they dwell although the same be unknown to the greater part of his Maj'ts good subjects of the County whose title they bear. I have received Information that such has been the Licentious practices of divers evill disposed persons of late that Scandalous and Seditious

(continued)

Proclamation Concerning Grievances (continued)

papers have been framed and the names of divers persons put thereto, and others have been handed about through the Countys and the meaner sort of people called together in a riotous manner to sign the same and the said papers called by the Generall name of the Grievances of the freeholders or Inhabitants of such Countys not signed at the Courts appointed for Certifying such Grievances as the sd act directs nor presented by the persons signing the same but only by one or two of the sd subscribers have been certifyed by the Justices of such Courts altho it could not appear to them whether the names affixed thereto were really the writeings of the persons said to be subscribers neither doth it appear by the Certificates annexed thereto whether the same be the General Grievances of the Countys or only of the persons subscribing nor which of the subscribers did present the same By which evil practices the minds of his Maj'ts good Subjects have been seduced by private insinuations of Crafty and ill designing men, the good intention of the sd Act evaded and the time of the General Assembly to the great burthen of the Country spent in reading trifling propositions or such papers as require rather the punishm't of the authors than to be considered as Grievances for prevention whereof, for the future and to the end the propositions and Just Grievances of the people may be presented in a Decent manner and regularly certifyed I have thought fit by and with the advice and consent of His Maj'ts Councill to Issue this proclamation Hereby strictly chargeing and requireing all Justices of the peace within this Colony that they diligently observe the directions of the aforerecited act and that they Certify no Grievances but such as shall be signed at the time and place therein appointed and duely presented by the persons signing the same and the sd Grievances being so signed and presented they shall cause to be attested as the Grievances of the person or persons signing and presenting the same as by the aforementioned act and a clause in the act for regulating the Election of Burgesses &c, passed in the year 1705, is injoyned and directed AND WHEREAS the power of redressing the Just Grievances of the people is Lodged in the General Assembly consisting of the Governor Councill and Burgesses and not in Either of the Houses of Assembly Seperately I doe further with the advice aforesaid direct and appoint that all such propositions and Grievances as shall be legally signed and presented in the manner aforesaid be certified to the Generall Assembly as law they ought to be and to the End all riotous and tumultous meetings for frameing and signing such propositions and Grievances may be prevented I Doe hereby strictly charge and require all magistrat within this Colony that they use their utmost Diligence to discover and punish all such persons their aiders and abetters as shall be found to assemble in a riotous manner for drawing up or signing papers under the name of Grieveances otherwise than the Laws in that case direct and I do appoint this proclamation to be read and published by the Sheriffs at the Courthouse of every County at the first Court held in the County after the receipt thereof and to be entred upon the records of the

(continued)

Ex 9

Proclamation Concerning Grievances (continued)

respective County Courts and that this present proclamation be also published in the Severall Countys together with the writts for the Election of the Burgesses and at the Courts of Claimes
    Given at the Councill Chamber in Williamsburgh the 24th day of August 1715 in the second Year of His Maj'ts Reign
                                            A Spotswood
God Save the King

Note: If anyone will examine these old petitions it is evident that many of the signatures were written by the same person. Whether or not with the consent of the owner of the name we will never know. Most of them could not write anyway.
    Also see Journals of the House of Burgesses, Vol.5, Assembly of 1715, first page concerning the arrest of local Justices in this matter.
    Governor Spotswood's efforts to bring the easy going Virginians to the letter of the law did not increase his popularity. Col. Gawin Corbin of King and Queen County did not like it for one. That sort of thing is all right in the modern business world - but just try it in the mountain backwoods of Virginia even now. But if you must, don't fail to start the experiment with an iron frying pan in the seat of your pants.   B.F.

- - - - - -

page 420. Bond. 20 Dec. 1715. L 40. Storl. Margaret ffarmer, Admr of Est. of Thomas ffarmer, dec'd.
                        Signed   Marg't x ffarmer
Names of witnesses omitted   Richard Goode
from record   Tho x Ayres
                Rec. 20 Dec. 1715.

page 421. Will of Thomas Edmondson of Essex Co. Date omitted. Prob. 20 Dec. 1715.
To son William Edmondson plantation "whereon I now live w'th all the Land on the West side of the maine Swamp known by the name of Samuell Porry Swamp".
To son Bryan Edmondson land on east side of sd swamp. Wife Mary Edmondson to have 1/3 int. in all land during life.
To two sons James Edmondson and Joseph Edmondson all money now in the hands of Mr. Micajah Perry and Compa and Mr Richard Lee Merchants in London

(continued)

Ex 9

Will of Thomas Edmondson (continued)

To son James Edmondson, feather bed, "my new riding Coate my best hat my wigs and my Silver headed Cane"

To son Thomas Edmondson a negro slave to be delivered to him when he is 21. Also a horse, saddle and bridle, 2000 lb of tobo being 1/2 of 4000 lb tobo now due by bill from his son Saml Edmondson.

To son John Edmondson a slave when 21. Also 4000 eight penny nails to build a dwelling house when he demands them. Also 2000 lb. tobo., the other half of 4000 lb. due by bill from son Samuel to be paid when John is 21.

To daughter Sarah Boughan 10 s. for a ring. To daughter Ann Hayman the same.

Exors to give L 5. for the relief of three of the most ancient and poorest people in this parish to be paid as soon as possible.

Balance of Est. to wife Mary "during the time she remains a widdow and no longer". If she marry again estate to be divided betw. "my six sons James Edmondson, Joseph Edmondson, William Edmondson, Bryan Edmondson, Thomas Edmondson and John Edmondson".

Exors wife and son James.

Witness names   Signed   Tho. Edmondson
omitted from record.

Presented and proved by Mary Edmondson and James Edmondson, Exors., and recorded 20 Dec. 1715.

page 423. Deed. 3 Dec. 1715. Martin Willard of Essex Co., sells to Silvester Patty of same Co., for 1200 lb. tobo., land, acreage not shown, on S. side of Rappa River and on the branches of Lucas his Creek adj. land of John Martin, William Beesly and John Williams.

Wit:
John Pitts   Robt Parker   Signed   Martin x Willard
Thomas Short Junr

Sarah Willard wife to Martin relinq right of dower.

Rec. 20 Dec. 1715.

page 426. Will of Mary Marten of St. Anns Par., Essex Co.

To "my Youngest Daughter Elizabeth" feather bed, etc. and "do also ord that my sd Daughter Elizabeth shall be sett at age and be Left att her own disposing from the day of the date hereof".

(continued)

Ex 9

Will of Mrs. Mary Marten (continued)

Balance of estate to be equally divided betw. "my two said Daughters Mary and Elizabeth", they to be exors. Dated 19 Sept. 1715.
Wit:
Sam'll Bizwell   Signed   Mary x Marten
Elizabeth x Pitts
Silvester x Patty

20 December 1715. "The above will of Mary Martin (sic) dec'd was presented by Mary Short late Mary Martin and Elizabeth Martin Executrixes therein named as also by Thos Short Junr husband to the said Mary x x and is recorded"

Note: Mrs. Marten may not have been the wealthiest woman in Essex Co., nor yet the most aristocratic of her day, but I truly believe she was the wisest. She certainly knew a thing or two about human nature. B.F.

page 427. Bond. L 400. 20 Dec. 1715. Tho Short and Mary his wife and Elizabeth Marten, Exrx of will of Mary Marten Decd.
Witnesses names, if any,
omitted from record.   Signed   Thomas Short Junr
                                                           Mary x Short
                                                           Elizabeth x Martin
                                                           Thomas Short
                                                           Richard Booker
                                 Rec. 20 Dec. 1715

page 428. Will of Mary Duckbary of St. Anns Par., Essex Co.
Dated 21 April 1715. Probated 20 Dec. 1715.
To Susanah Cogghill and Thomas Coggill and Mary Cogghill a cow calf each.
To "my well beloved Dafter Mary Willis all my waring Close and a ring of
     Twenty Shilling Price".
Bal. of Est. to be equally divided betw: "my sone ffreadurick Cogghill my Dafter Mary Willis and my Sone George Ducbary and I Leave my Son ffreadrick and my son in Law John Willis and Gorge Duckbary hole and sole Exsecutators of this my last will and Testament"
Wit: Signed   Mary x Duckba   (sic)
Thomas x Smyth
Jesper x Pite (or Pile or Jasper Pellow ?)
Mary x Smith
                         Rec. 20 Dec. 1715

page 429. Bond. 20 Dec. 1715. L 50. Sterl. ffred: Cogghill and John Willis exors of Mary Ducksbury deceased.
Witnesses names if any
not shown on record   Signed   ffrederick x Coghill
                                               John Willis
                                               Thomas Moakes
                                               William Pickett
                    Rec. 20 Dec. 1715.

page 430. Will of George Duksbery of St Marys Par., Essex Co. Dated 5 Nov. 1715. Probated 20 Dec. 1715.
To "my Brother ffrederick Coghills Eldest Daughter Susannah my plantation with all the land", she failing in heirs to Richard Booker.
To John Mellit 140 lb. tobo.
"I give my boy Henry Lea the mill unto hes (sic) mother Mary Smith untill he come to the age of Eighteen years".
To Jospor Pellow 550 lb tobo.
To John Kendall 200 lb tobo.
To Mary Munday 200 lb Tobo besides her wages.
If Hugh Crutcher deliver obligation to Exors. they to deliver man Tony to him.
To Hugh Crutcher 240 lb tobo.
Bal. of Est. to be equally divided betw. ffredrick Coghill, Richard Booker, John Willis and John Pillow.
Exors ffredrick Coghill and Richard Booker.
Wit:
Mary x Munday   Signed   George x Duksbery
Geo Robinson
                    Rec. 20 Dec. 1715.

page 431. Bond. 20 Dec. 1715. L 100. Sterl. ffrederick Coghill and Rich Booker Exors of Geo. Ducksbery, decd.
Witnesses names if any
omitted from record.   Signed   ffrederick x Coghill
                                               Richard Booker
                                               William Pickett
                                               Thomas Short

                    Rec. 20 Dec. 1715.

page 432. Deed. 11 Oct. 1715. Thomas Ayres of St. A. Par., sells to Matthew Collins of St. M. Par., for 4720 lb. tobo., 157 acres in St. M. Par. on S. side of Rappa. River, on S. side of the So. branch of Powmanzend Swamp, adj. land of sd Collins, etc.
Wit:
Jno Vawter   Signed   Mathew x Collins
Wm White
Timothy Monglothly

Matthew Collins' bond for above witnessed by John Boughan, George Robinson and Edmund Booker.
         Rec. 20 Dec. 1715.

page 435. Deed. 7 Dec. 1715. William Brown of Essex Co., sells James Masters of same Co., for 3200 lb. tobo., 100 acres in Essex Co., on S. side of Rappa. River, being part of a tract formerly granted Mr. Thos. Page, adj. land of John Willard, a path near John Pittes old field, the land of Richard Covington, Popeman branch, the land of Mark Boulware, James Landrum, etc.
Wit: Signed   William Browne
Sam'll Stallard
James Boulware Junr
Samuel Landrum

Margaret Brown wife to William relinq. right of dower.

         Rec. 20 Dec. 1715.

page 438. Bond. 20th day of 10br 1715 (20 Dec. 1715). L 40. Sterl. William Tiller Admr of Est of Saml Johnson decd.
Wit: names, if any
omitted from record.   Signed   Wm x Tiller
              Thomas Meadows
              ffreadrick x Coghill

         Rec. 20 Dec. 1715.

Ex 9

page 439. Inventory of Estate of Thomas Ley late of this County deceased. Taken by order of Court dated 16 August 1715.
Includes:

To nineteen Carpenters Chisells at	0.	6.	0
To 2 broad axes at 2/6 and three old box rules at 2/6	0.	2.	6
To a Small Iron Square and ffour Joyners hold fasts at	1.	10.	0
To a Small Joynter and Twenty two plaines at	1.	10.	6
To 4 old Augors adds three old hammers a parcell of old Locks and a Gimlet	0.	5.	0
To 2 hand saws a Joyners Saw a Compass Saw and a small file	0.	6.	0
To three old Chests and two old boxes and one new Ditto	1.	4.	0
To one old Grindstone and one new Ditto at	0.	3.	0
To one Druget Sute of Cloathes and a fine hatt	1.	15.	0
To the remainder of (Mr Ley) his wearing Cloathes at	1.	15.	0
To one pair of womans Shoes 2 razors 2 Inkhorns and a pair of spurrs	0.	5.	0
To some Inkpowder a brush a parcell of absom salt and some paper and a pair of horse fflegms an old Common prayer book	0.	5.	0
To Sixty four pounds of Nailes at 3 p	0.	16.	0

Total Valuation of Inventory L 52. 12. 10

John Boughan   Signed   Sam'll Stallord
Thomas Leftwich   Ralph Rowzee
                                   Nicho x Copeland

Wednesday 21 Dec. 1715. Presented by John Boughan and Thomas Leftwich Admrs and recorded.

page 441. Appraisal of Est of Mr. Thomas Todd, deceased.
Includes:
"one Scotchman named Will Young having two years and five months to serve"   8. 0. 0
Inventory consists of slaves, stock and farm implements. No household goods. Total valuation L 197. 3. 5

                         Signed   Tho Waring
                                  Chr. Beverley
                                  James Rennolds Junr

September 21st 1715. Presented by Thomas Wareing and recorded.

Ex 9

page 442. Lease and Release. 10-11 Nov. 1715. John Mills, planter, of Couth Farnham Par., sells William Johnson, planter, of same parish, 100 acres lying in Essex Co., "formerly known by the name of Lancaster County", on N.E. side of Piscatocan Creek, adj. land formerly belonging to Armstrong and Richard King, land formerly belonging to Wm. Johnson, the Grandfather of the aforesaid Wm. Johnson. "The sd Land being formerly sold x x by a certain deed x from the aforenamed Grandfather and Constance his wife unto John Mills the Grandfather of the aforesaid John Mills" on June 10th 1656, "and since descended to his Grandson John Mills above named as the Eldest Son of Robt Mills who was the Eldest Son and heir apparent to the Grandfather John Mills aforenamed". The lease refers twice to the purchaser as "William Johnson the younger". The lease also refers to John Mills as "John Mills the younger".
Wit:
James Boughan   Signed   John Mills
Wm Covington Junr
Thos Wheeler   Rec. 21 Dec. 1715.

page 445. Lease and Release. 17-18 Oct. 1715. James Boughan of Essex Co., sells John London of King and Queen Co., 100 acres in Essex Co., adj. land of John Chick, part of a tract of 550 acres granted to William Johnson, 26 April 1704, and by him sold to James Boughan.
Wit:
Jos Baker   Signed   James Boughan
John Pickett   Rec. 21 Dec. 1715.

page 449. Lease and Release. 1 Nov. - 1 Dec. 1715. Thomas Jewell, planter, of St. Anns Par., sells John Bagge of same Par., 149 acres in St. Anns Par., "being bounded as followeth, vizt. Beginning at a marked white oake by the side of Gilsons Creek, near the place where the old Corner red Oak stood, thence along a line of marked trees West Northwest three hundred and twenty poles crossing several branches of Gilsons creek to a white oak and red oak standing on the west side of a branch thence south by west half west one hundred and seven poles to a white oak by the side of Gilsons swamp thence down the sd swamp and Creek the several Courses thereof to the place it began", being part of a tract first granted 22 Nov. 1653 to Andrew Gilson and sold by him, 6th May 1657, to Thomas Reson, and by him sold to Stubble Stubbleson 29 June 1668, "wch sd Tract of Land upon the death of the sd Stubble Stubbleson an alien by an Inquisition taken in the County of Rappahannock the first day of May one thousand Six hundred and Sixty nine, being found Escheat was granted by patent bearing date the thirteenth day of November Anno Domini one thousand Seven hundred and thirteen to Thomas Jewell

(continued)

Ex 9

Land Transfer. Jewell to Bagge (continued)

aforesaid party to these presents, saving reserving and Excepting a parcell of the land containing twelve foot Square, where his Grave y'd is now".

Wit: Signed   Thomas Jewell
Thomas Streshly Junr
Wm Bagge

On page 450 the price paid by the Rev. Mr. Bagge for this 149 acres is shown: "That the said Thomas Jewell for and in Consideration of the sum of thirty five pounds Sterl, four Gallons of rum and four pound of Sugar to him in hand or Secured to be paid by the sd John Bagge"

Francis Jewell wife to Thomas relinq. dower rights.

                            Recorded 21 Dec. 1715.

Note: Stubble Stubbleson is ancestor of many American families, his daughter Anne having married John Ferguson. This means Pendleton, Willis Washington, Ryland, etc. He is also my ancestor, which permits me to remark that the name had always been to me the most country-punkin clodhopper name I'd ever seen, until this entry came to light. He was an 'alien'. Doubtless another of the Dutchmen who settled in this section.

One cannot but wonder. The Rev. John Bagge appears to have cancelled the fees for several funeral sermons. Any respectably bereaved family would certainly press a generous supply of the funeral rum upon the good minister in such cases. Little did they expect he would buy real estate with it. Beating the Devil around the bushes of St. Ann's Parish, as it were.   B.F.

page 458. Bond. L 300. Sterl. 21st 10'ber 1715. "Job Speerman Guardian of Elizabeth Martin during her minority". Refers to Elizabeth Martin as an orphan.

Wit: Signed   Job x Speerman
Names, if any,   Thomas Short
omitted from   Anto Samuell Junr
record

                        Rec. 21 Dec. 1715

Ex 9

page 458. Deed. 21 June 1715. "John Massey eldest son and heir of John Massey late of Essex County dec'd" sells to Wm and Katherine Young, Robert and ffrancis Ransone, 150 acres in So. Farn. Par., "it being formerly Exchanged by my dec'd father w'th Capt Edward Thomas" for another parcel of land 30 Sept. 1689.

Wit:
Wm Montague Sonr   Signed   John Massey
Benja ffisher
Jno Billups   Rec. 21st Feb. 1715/16.

page 458. Lease and Release. 20 - 21 Feb. 1715/16. "William Young of Southfarnham parish in the County of Essex Gent and Katherine his wife, and Robert Ransone of St Stephens parish in the County of King & Queen Gent and ffrancis his wife" sell Peter Richeson of Abington parish in the County of Gloucester Gent a plantation and appurtenances of 306 acres in South Farnham parish. The aforesd Wm Young and Katherine his wife and Robert Ransone and ffrances his wife in right of them the sd Katherine and Frances are seized in fee of this 306 acres, adj. the Dragon Swamp at the lower end of Essex Co which was formerly the land of Edward Thomas late of Essex Co., and known as Thomas's Quarter, which land the sd Edward Thomas by his will proved 10 Nov. 1699 was given to Elizabeth Merewether, and which at her death descended to them.

Wit:
John Evans   Signed   Will Young
Wm Smith   Katherine x Young
Wm x Hudson   Robert Ransone
     ffra: Ransone

Rec. 21 Feb. 1715/16

page 460. Lease and Release. 20 - 21 Feb. 1715/16. John Billups and Dorothy his wife of Essex sell Thomas Smith of Middlesex Co., 200 a in So. Farn. Par., being part of a tract granted Mr Henry Awberry, adj the main run of Hoskins Creek, etc.

Wit:
Tho Waring   Signed   Jno Billups
Fr Wyatt   Dorothy x Billups
Wm Clark
     Rec. 21 Feb. 1715/16.

page 465. Lease and Release. 12 - 13 Dec. 1715. John Dike and Judith his wife of So. F. Par., sell Thomas Bryant, 120 acres in So. F. Par., this land being given to the aforesd Judith by John Savage of So. F. Par. deceased, and adj. land of Richd Bush, the sd Tho Bryants old field, the Beaver Dam Swamp, etc.

Wit:
Jos Baker
Vt: Godfrey Pile

Signed John Dike
Judith x Dyke

Rec. 21 Feb. 1715/16

page 469. 4 January 1715/16. Inventory of Est. of Mary Ducksberry. Totals approx. L 35.

Signed Wm Pickett
Geo Robinson
Thomas Griffin

Rec. 21 Feb. 1715/16

page 470. Inventory of the Est. of George Duksbery deceased. Totals approx L 45.

Signed Wm Pickett
Geo Robinson
Thomas Grifin

Recorded 21 Feb. 1715/16

page 472. Bond. 22 Feb. 1715/16. L. 250. Sterl. Job Spearman admr. Est. of John Martin, decd.

Wit:
R. Hickman
Ralph Gough

Signed Job x Spearman
John X Willard
Joseph x Leemon

Rec. 21 Feb. 1715/16

page 473. Bond. 21 Feb. 1715/16. L 500. Sterl. Tho. Short Junr and Mary his wife and Job Spearman admrs of Est. of John Martin, decd, during the minority of Elizabeth Martin.

Wit:
Ralph Gough

Signed Thomas Shortt
Richard Booker
Tho Short

Rec. 21 Feb. 1715/16.

Ex 9. 52

page 474. Will of Ealse Shipley (Alice Shipley) of St. A. Par., Essex Co. Dated 8 Jan 1715/16. Prob. 21 Feb. 1715/16.
To "Sarah fflowers my Best Gound and petty Coate and a black hood and a Lased Henchefer"
To "martha fflowers my nex best gound and petty Coat"
To "my Son in Law John Shipley" all meat, corn, hogs, horses and mares.
To "my Daughter Elizabeth Virgett one shilling".
To "my Daughter Keziah Henshaw all my sheep".
To "my Daughter Susanna Cook the best Cow I have in my pen"
To "my Daughter Mary Cosston one Cow"
Balance of Est. to Son in Law John Shipley, he to be Exor.
Wit: her
         his   Signed   Ealse x Shipley
Arther x Onbee   marks
        mark
John Boughan

21 Feb. 1715/16. "The within written last will and Testament of Alice Shipley dec'ed was proved by the oath of John Shipley the Exor".

page 475. Bond. 21 Feb. 1715/16. L. 200. Sterl. John Shipley Exor. of Est. of Alice Shipley.
Wit: Signed   John x Shipley
Robert ffoster   Wm Thompson
Robert Jones   John x Cook

            Rec. 21 Feb. 1715/16

page 476. Bond. 21 Feb. 1715/16. L. 50. Sterl. Sam'll Henshaw ad'mr of est of Francis Gibson.
The Justices of Essex County listed in this bond are: Francis Gouldman, Joseph Smith, Wm. Daingerfield and Tho: Weren (this name also appears as Tho: Warren.
Wit:
Robert Payne   Signed: Sam' Henshaw
Ralph Gough   ffra: Smith
                                            Daniel x Smith

            Rec. 21 Feb. 1715/16

page 477. Bond. 21 Feb. 1715/16. L. 50. Sterl. ffrancis Smith, admr. of Est of Henry Smith, decd.
Wit:
Robert Payne
Ralph Gough

Signed ffra. Smith
        Sam' Henshaw
        Daniel x Smith

Rec. 21 Feb. 1715/16

page 478. Jan. 14th 1715/16. Inventory of Est. of Samuel Johnson as it was presented by Wm Tiller Admr.
Includes:
To 1 old chest and Wearing Close and a gold Ring at   2: 12: 00
Total valuation approx L. 15.

Signed Thomas Meades
        Thomas Ayres
        John Miller
        Richd Ship

Rec. 21 Feb. 1715/16

page 479. Bond. 22 Feb. 1715/16. L 30. Sterl. Richd Bush as Guardian of Sarah Mitchell, an orphan.
Wit: Signed Richard Bush
John Boughan   James Webb
R Hickman   John Michell

Rec. 21 Feb. 1715/16

page 480. Inventory of Est. of Tho ffarmer, Decd. Taken by order of Court dated 20 Dec. 1715. Total val. L 3: 16: 00

Signed Edwa Moseley
        Cornelius Sale
        John x Cooke

Rec. 21 Feb 1715/16

Ex 9   54

page 480. Will of Robert ffoster of St. Anns Par., Essex Co., Described
as "yea'men" which doubtless is intended for "yeoman".
Dated 6 Jan. 1715/16. Prob. 22 Feb. 1715/16.
To son Robert plantation where he lives.
To sons James and John "Land where I Dwelt", to be div. betw. them.
    James to have his choice.
To Barbary Loveing one shilling and to her son Richard Loveing "one
    heighfer with Calve named Rosbory". To her husband "all he is
    Indebted to me".
To "my three youngest children, Margret, Elizabeth and Anthony Each of
    them a Gold ring" etc.
To "my son Richard my pistols holsers and Sword and feather bed and
    bolster and a Cow and a heighfer".
To "my three sons George, Thomas and William" each a cow and heifer.
Exors: wife Elizabeth and sons Robert and James.
Wit:
John x ffoster   Signed   Robert x ffoster
Anto Samuell Junr
Thomas x Garnett   Rec. 22 Feb. 1715/16

page 481. Bond. 22 Feb. 1715/16. L 500. Sterl. Elizabeth ffoster,
Robert Ffoster and James ffoster, Exors of Est of Robert ffoster, decd.
Wit:
Robert Jones   Signed   Eliza x ffoster
                                                    Robert ffoster
                                                    James ffoster
                                                    William Smithee
                                                    Anto: Samuell Junr
                         Rec. 22 Feb. 1715/16

page 482. Inventory. "9ber 7th 1715. The severall things herein recited
vallued by ffran Gouldman, Wm Winston, John Boughan and Edw'd Moseley
as follows". List follows with a total valuation of 12340 lb tobo.
    "The severall goods above recited I the subscriber do acknowledge
to have rec'ed of John Bates as so much of the Est of James, Phebe,
Margaret and Wm Boeth and if it should over pay their pts or portions
of the above sd Childrens Estate then the sd John Bates do oblige himself to take so much of the Est above rec't as shall make a ballance"
Wit:
ffrancis Gouldman   Signed   John Bates
Edwa Moseley   Salvator Musoeo
Wm Winston
John Boughan
                    Rec. 22 Feb. 1715/16

Ex 9

page 483. Will of Thomas Tinsley of St. Anns Par., Essex Co.
Dated 25 Nov. 1715. Prob. 22 Feb. 1715/16.
To son Thomas a horse.
To son Phillipp a mare.
To each other of his sons, names not shown, a cow to be/delivered at the age of 20.
To each of daughters, names not shown, one Ewe.
Bal. of Est. to wife Sarah, she extrx. At her death land to son Thomas and to son Philipp 82 acres adj. land of Borry, he to have this when of age.

Wit: Signed Thomas x Tinsley
James Jameson
Sam'l Bizwell
Thomas x Jackson
James Coghill
Thomas Dickison

Proved by oath of Sarah Tinsley, widow, and rec. 22 Feb. 1715/16.

page 484. Bond. 22 Feb. 1715/16. L 100. Sterl. Sarah Tinsley, Extrx of Est. of Tho. Tinsley.
Wit: Signed Sarah x Tinsley
Robert Jones   James Coghill
     Thomas x Jackson

Rec. 22 Feb. 1715/16

page 485. Power of Atty. 14 Feb. 1715/16. William Hudson and Rebecca his wife and Edward Hudson son of sd William of So. Farn. Par., to Wm Young to ack. deed of Lease and Release and bond to John Evans for 160 acres of land.
Wit: Signed Willm x Hudson
Richd Ireland   Rebecca x Hudson
Paschal Greenhill   Edward Hudson
Wm Smith

Rec. 22 Feb. 1715/16

page 486. Will of Richard Guggey. Dated 3 Feb. 1715/16. Prob. 22 Feb. 1715/16. This entry mutilated.
To "my God Daughter Eliza Jones the daughter of William Jones one cow"
To "my Grandson Charles -owers (Bowers ?) one cow and my Carbine"
Bal. of Est. to wife Elizabeth, she extrx. and John Dunbar exor.
Wit:
Samuell Carter   Signed Richard x Guggey
Gabrill Smether (Smithee ?)
John Cardin

Proved by Elizabeth Guggey, widow, and rec. 22 Feb. 1715/16.

page 487. Bond. 22 Feb. 1715/16. L 50. Sterl. Eliz. Gougey Extrx. Est. of Richard Gougey, decd.
Wit: names omitted from record.
                          Signed   Eliza x Gougey
                                          Robert Jones
                                          Charles ffarrell
                    Rec. 22 Feb. 1715/16

page 488. Bond. 20 March 1715/16. L 50. Sterl. William Winston Admr. of Est. of Isaac Mercer decd.
     Justices of Essex shown in this bond are ffrancis Gouldman, Joseph Smith, Wm Daingerfield and Thomas Waring, Gentlemen.
Wit:
Ralph Gough   Signed   Wm Winston
                                                  Nathl ffogg
                                                  Jno x Marriott
                    Rec. 20 March 1715/16

Note: The pronunciation of Gough is "Goff" and of Marriott "Merit". B.F.

page 489. Will of Ann Whitehorn. Dated 9 Nov. 1715. Prob. 20 March 1715/16.
All Estate to "my son James Crosswell and his wife", he sole exor.
Wit:
Tho Crutcher   Signed   Ann x Whitehorn
Edmund x Camebridg

Proved by James Crosswell the Exor and rec. 20 March 1715/16.

page 490. Deed of Gift. 20 March 1715/16. Francis Gouldman, Gent. of Essex Co., gives 500 acres of Land to his neice Elizabeth Waring. "out of the Love and affection which I bear unto my Coz'n Elizabeth Waring Daughter and only heir of my Brother Thomas Gouldman deceased x x give unto my kinswoman Elizabeth one part or parcell of that my Tract x x lying and being a part of it in the County aforesaid the other part in King and Queen County, the same being granted to my father Thomas Gouldman deceased by patent x x the 23d of September 1674 which sd

(continued)

Ex 9

grant is for 2200 acres one moiety whereof is now in the possession of Mrs Mary Meriwether widdow".
Wit:
Salvator Muscoe
R Hickman
Daniel Hayes

Signed ffrancis Gouldman

"Tuesday the 20th day of March 1715/16
ffrancis Gouldman Gent acknowledged this his deed to Elizabeth Wareing wife to Thomas Waring gent: x x and is recorded".

page 490. Lease and Release. 20 - 21 Feb. 1715/16. Peter Godfrey, surgeon, of So. Farn. Par., sells Edward Rowzee, planter, of St. Anns Par., for 3300 lb. tobo., 55 acres on So. side of Rappa. River, on Occupation Creek, part of a tract of land bequeathed to Lodowick and John Rowzee by their father Edward Rowzee in his will. Adjs land of sd Edw. Rowzee, the bank of Occupation Creek. The burial place lying betw. the present dwelling house and the creek about 30 feet square excepted.

Also a tract of 40 acres adj. the first tract, Occupation Creek, etc. all of which land is now in possession of Peter Godfrey.

Both of the above tracts were in 1689 granted and sold to Thomas Parker, Senior.
Wit:
A Somervell
Ja Alderson
Ro Brooke Junr

Signed Pr (seal) Godfrey

Rec. 20 March 1715/16

page 496. Power of Atty. 17 Feb. 1715/16. Eliza Godfrey, wife of Peter Godfrey of So. Farn. Par., to Mr James Alderson of St. A. Par., to relinq. dower rights in land sold to Capt. Edward Rowzee, "being the Lands my Husband purchased some time since of one Rob't Parker".
Wit:
Jno Bates
Tho Wheeler

Signed Eliza x Godfrey

Rec. 20 March 1715/16

page 497. Lease and Release. 11 and 12 March 1715/16. "Thomas Cox and Ann his wife the only Surviving daughter and heiress of John Haile deceased of ffarnham parish in the County of Essex in Virginia planter" sell to "Samuell Clayton of St Stephens parish in the County of King and Queen in Virginia", for L 60., 100 acres in Farnham Par.
Wit:
Geo Moore
Thomas Williamson
Elizabeth x Williamson

Signed Thomas x Cox
Ann x Cox

Rec. 20 March 1715/16

Ex 9

Lease and Release. 16 - 17 Feb. 1715/16. Mathew Collins of St. Marys Par., Essex Co., sells to John Morgan of same Par. and Co., 53 acres formerly granted to Henry Peters, decd, on April 17th 1667, in St. M. Par., adj a corner of John Ellits land, the south fork of Pewmansend swamp called the Beverdam branch.
Wit:
William Bramlit   Signed   Matthew x Collins
Geo Robinson
John Smith   Rec. 20 March 1715/16

page 506. Power of Atty. 17 Sept 1715. "Henry Walter Esq'r (now Mayor of the Citty of Bristoll) John King Samuell Hartnell William Attwood Jeremia Junys John Lewis and John Templeton all of the Citty of Bristoll aforesd merchants and owners of the Good Shipp or Vessell called the Rappahannocke whereof Walter King is now Master x x authorize and appoint x x the sd Walter King our true and Lawfull attorney x x to x x receive x x from Nicholas Smith and William Thornton both of Rappahannocke in Virginia Merchants x x all x x money Debts Goods Wares and Merchandizes whatsoever now due x x"
Wit: Signed
Tho Hall
John x Williams   Jeremy Junys   Henry Walter
Jam Adams   Jno Lewis   John King
                             Jno Templeton   John King for
                                                      Sam'll Hartnell
                                                  Wm Attwood

Tuesday 20 March 1715/16.
Proved by oaths of Thomas Hall and John Williams and recorded at the motion of Walter King.

page 507. Inventory of Est of Richard Gougey decd., presented by Eliz: Gouggey Extrx.
Includes:
To one old Musquit and 1 Carbine   0: 11: 0
To 2 Swords at   0: 2: 0
To 1 Looking Glace 1 old hat and one old pestell   : 1:

Total valuation L 26: 19: 0
Appraisers names omitted.
                              Rec. 20 March 1715/16

page 508. Bond. 20 March 1715/16. L 50. Sterl. Elizabeth Sky admr. of Est. of John Sky, deceased.
Wit:
Robert Jones

Signed Eliza x Sky
John x Rodyford
Josias Ship

Note: Rodyford - Scottish, Rutherford. B.F.

page 509. Deed of Gift. 22 March 1715/16 (or perhaps 20 March) John Taliaferro of St. Marys Par., gent., gives "for the Natural Love and affection wch I beare unto my son Lawrence Taliaferro" of the same Par. and Co., a plantation of 300 acres formerly purchased by the sd John from Thomas Medos and Susannah his wife.
Wit:
J Thornton
Nicholas Smith Junr
Ro Brooke Junr

Signed Jn Taliaferro

Rec. 20 March 1715/16

page 510. Deed of Gift. 20 March 1715/16. John Taliaferro of St. M. Par Gent., gives "for the Natural Love and affection wch I bear unto my Loving Son Charles Taliaferro" of same Par., a plantation of 300 acres in St. M. Par., formerly purchased by sd John Taliaferro from John Smith Esq'r of Gloster and Elizabeth his wife.
Wit:
J Thornton
Nicholas Smith Junr
Ro Brooke Junr

Signed Jno Taliaferro

Rec. 20 March 1715/16

page 511. Inventory of Est. of Andrew Hardoe.

To Pd Saml Coates	175		
To 1 bar'll Corn per John Picket	120		
To Clks ffoe for admr	250		
To Sher ffees on the appraisal	230		
To pd the Ex'rs of Edwd Gouldman per Judgmt	276		
To pd Maj'r Boughan	150		
To pd Orlando Jones per ffees at	850		
To ffunerall Charges		3: 0: 0	
To per his bond to Leon'd Hill		11: 19: 0	
To Clks ffees	24		

(continued)

Ex 9

Inventory of the Estate of Andrew Hardee (continued)

```
To pd Robt Hardee per Judgmt              304
To Salary and Trouble                       -
To the 2 Negros wch ought to be Inventoried )
   being real Estate and desending to the  )
   Co heirs after dower Ended              )         54:  0:  0
To one bar'll Corn per Capt Coleman                   0:  7:  0
To Mr Buckners Clks ffees                  58
To Costs of Rich'd Perres acc'on          100
To pd Mr Beverley                                     3: 15:  -
                                         -----      ------------
                                         2537        73:  1:  -

To mony pd                                           73:  1:  -
To the ball in Tobo at 12 s 6                         6: 19
Due to ball                                          54: 19: 04
                                                    ------------
                                                    134: 19: 04
```

per Contra   Cr

```
By the appraism't                                   103:  9:  8
By Ball'l acco'ts in Mr Porrys hands                  1: 10:  4
By Ball'l in Mr Offleys hands not yet rec'd 42. s
Bene steer sold ffogg and Paget           615
By money recd of Jno Smith - bills        )
   from Mr Step'n Loyd                    )          24: 11:  4
By Stocke and Hoggs vizt:
   6 barrows 2 year old or thereabouts                2:  8:  0
   5 Do abt 1 1/4 year old                            1: 15:  0
   3 old Sows                                         0: 15:  0
   22 shotes and piggs                                1:  -:  -
By one hhd of tobo                        810
The rest of his Crop my wife pd to
   some of Hardees Crod'ers               ---       ------------
                                         1425       134: 19:  4
```

(continued)

Note: I, my father, my two grandfathers, at least one grandmother and several cousins named Ryland, all being nevertheless to the contrary in having deceived ourselves into thinking colored people were human beings, are set just right by this record. Negroes were real estate. They were as of and a part of the land. Still I rebel against the written record. That colored William who insists on my wearing clean shirts, who loads me in the car when I'm unable to enter alone, who hands me my stick when I emerge, is a Christian Gentleman. God knows more so than I ever hope to be.   Beverley Fleet.

Note: An apology for this waste space. There was a note introduced here concerning the activities and experiences of my own family in early attempts to educate the negroes. After this volume was made up I decided to omit this.
B. F.

page 512.

"March the 20th 1715
by me
Tho **Wheeler**
Ann **Wheeler**

At a Court held for Essex County on Tuesday the 20th day of March 1715 Thomas Wheeler presented and made oath to the within account w'ch on his mo'con is adm'd to record

Test
Tho Henman Cl Cur"

page 512. "Joseph Hardee in Christ Church parish and County of Middlesex x x do x x discharge Thomas Wheeler of the County of Essex and parish of Southfarnham x x from the full sum of Eighty Six pounds thirteene shillings x x being part of two orphanes Estates belonging to Andrew Hardee dec'd x x". Dated 2d day of July 1716.
Wit:
Page mutilated.   Signed   Jos Hardee
Names destroyed.

page 513. "x x John Picket and Alexander How of So. Farn. Par., Essex Co., discharge Thomas Whealler of same Par., "from all and every part of two orphanes Estates now in the hands of the sd Thomas Wheeler belonging to Andrew Hardee of this County dec'd". Dated 21 Jan. 1715/16
Wit:
Jno Billups   Signed   Jno Picket
John Griggs   Alix'a x How

Rec. 20 March 1715/16

page 513. An Inventory of the Orphans Estates belonging to Andrew Hardee, decd. Total valuation L 96: 13: 00

"We the subscribers did appriz the within mention Goods and Chattels for the orphans of Andrew Hardee des't witness our hands and seales this 23d of Jan'ry 1715"

       Signed Jon Gaines
           Martin Hall (or Nall)
           Tho Streshley
           Jno Chamberlain

Recorded on mo'con of Thomas Wheeler 20th March 1715.

page 514. Lease and Release. 13 - 14 Febry 1715/16. Wm. Hudson and Rebecca Hudson his wife and Edward Hudson his son sell John Evans, all of So. Farn. Par., 116 acres in So. F. Par., on S. side of Rappa. River, being part of a patent that Henry Woodnot "dwelt on last lately", which land was given by sd Woodnot to Wm. and Rebecca Hudson by deed dated 6 Aug. 1711, adj plantation of Wm Hudson, land of James St Aicson (? name illegible).

Wit: Signed Willm x Hudson
Richard Ireland   Rebecca x Hudson
Paschal Greenhill   Edward Hudson
William Smith

       Rec. 21 March 1715/16

19 March 1715/16. Delivery of above property to John Evans witnessed by :

        John Rodes
        Tho Emerson
        Charles x Baxter

page 519. Entry mutilated. Bond. 21 March 1715. L 100. Sterl. "in a suit in chancery brought by x John Picket plt agt Thomas Burnot Mary Merrewether and Mary Dyer deft and the plt x x had an appeal granted to the Eight day of the next General Court x x "

Witnesses names, if
any, not shown on   Signed John Picket
record.   Wm Winston

      Rec. 22 March 1715/16

Ex 9

page 520. Lease and Release. 9 - 10 Aug. 1715. Alexander Graves of Christ Church Par., Middlesex Co., sells George Stapleton, for L 50. Sterl., 200 acres in Essex Co., adj. lands of Thomas Crow, Wm Chanee, William Gefferys and Dan'll Dobbins, which 200 acres Graves bought of Morgin Swinney and his wife Ann and Henry Purkins and his wife Tabitha Purkins.
Wit:
Richins Brame   Signed   Alexander Graves
John Bristow
Nicholas Bristow

Mary Graves, wife to sd Alexander, relinq. her right of dower.

Rec. 15 May 1716.

page 523. Will of Timothy Driscoll of Essex Co.
Dated 14 Sept. 1715. Prob. 15 May 1716.
"I bequeve my sole to the Lord that gave it me"
To wife Katherine Driscoll "my whole Estate Reighall personall dureing her neightorall Life". At her death or if she remarry as follows:
To James Marsh a negro boy, if he d.s.p. to Wm Young Junior.
To "Timothy Driscoll Juner Godson to the sd Timothy Driscoll Sen'or" four negroes. If he d.s.p. a negro to Richard Carter and three negroes to James Coatleland.
To James Marsh 1/3 of Crop for 8 years, money, etc.
To Timothy Driscoll personal estate.
William Young sole exor.
Wit:
Richard Carter   Signed   Timothy Driscoll
Sarah x Harwar
James Marsh

15 May 1716 proved by oaths of Wm Young, Gent., Exor., and Richard Carter and James Marsh Evidences.
15 Jan. 1716/17 further proved by Sarah Harwar.

page 525. Bond. 15 May 1716. L 400. Sterl. Wm. Young as Exor of Timothy Driscoll, deceased.
Essex County Justices listed in this bond are: ffrancis Gouldman, Joseph Smith, Henry Robinson, Wm Daingerfield, Tho Waring, Augt. Smith and Tho Cattlet.
Wit: Signed   Will Young
Ralph Gough   Richd Covington
                                       Salvator Muscoe

Rec. 15 May 1716.

page 526. Will of Richard Meador of So. Farn. Par., Essex Co.
Dated 12 Dec. 1715. Prob. 15 May 1716.
To wife plantation "whereon I now live" during life and then to eldest
    son William.
To younger son Richard the land where William Borne now lives "that is
    to say after the sd William and hester his wife Decease the sd
    Land being fformerly In the possession of my Grandfather". If he
    d.s.p. then to "my youngest Daughter Addra". Following the word
    Grandfather is a word that may be either the surname White or the
    word white. It makes perfect sense either way.
To "my Brother John Meador my pistoles and houlsters".
Wife exor.
Wit: Signed   Richard Meador
Erasmus Allen
Thomas   x   Duden

Proved by oath of Ann Meader widow, Extrx therein named.

page 527. Bond. 15 May 1716. L 100. Sterl. Ann Medors, Extrx., of Est.
of Richard Medors, decd.
Wit: Signed   Anne x Meadors
Ralph Gough   Jno Pickett
                                                        Wm Pickett

Rec. 15 May 1716.

page 528. Inventory of Est. of Thomas Tinsley, Lately Deceased.
Total valuation L 46. 12. 0. Four feather beds and furniture listed,
otherwise nothing unusual.
                                          Signed   ffrederick x Coggill
                                                       Thomas Meades
                                                       Edmund Booker

Rec. 15 May 1716.

page 529. Inventory of Est. of Henry Smith, deceased, taken and
appraised 14 April 1716. Total valuation L 5: 10: 9
                                          Signed   Jasper Coston
                                                      Wm Thompson
                                                       Joseph x Leeman
                            Rec. 15 May 1716.

Ex 9

page 530. Inventory of Est. of John Martaine, taken by order of Court 20 March 1715/16 and presented by Tho. Shart, Junr., and Jebe Sperman, admrs. A lengthy inventory. Many items of woven fabrics indicating that he was a cloth merchant. Total valuation L 126: 04: 4

                            Signed   John Boughan
                                           Richard Booker
                                           Tho Ramsey
                Rec. 15 May 1716.

page 523. Will of John Waggner of Essex Co.
Dated 12 Feb. 1715/16. Prob. 15 May 1716.
To wife Rachell Waggner his plantation during life, then to son Benj.
    Waggner.
To wife 3 negroes, Doll, Martin and Jugg during life. Then Doll to "my
    Daughter Margarit Allen wife of William Allen". Negro Martin to
    son Benjamin. The negro girl Jugg to son Sam'l Wagoner.
To "my son harbert Waggoner one Cow being in full of his portion".
To sons Sam'll and Benjamin, beds and personal property.
To "my daughter Dinah Allen wife of Erasmus Allen one Cow".
Other bequests of personal property to children named above.
Bal. of Est. to wife, she exor.
Wit: Signed   John Waggoner
Wm Daingerfield
Peter Byrom

Bond. 15 May 1716. L 150. Sterl. Rachel Waggener Extrx Est. Jno. Waggener
Wit: Signed   Rachel x Waggener
Ralph Gough   Wm. Winston
                                                Erasmus Allen
                 Rec. 15 May 1716.

Note: In regard to the above will there are those indefinable indications that Herbert Waggener and Dinah Allen are not going to fare so well, and then to ease the sense of just distribution additional detail is left to them. As an experienced devisee I know the signs all too well. B.F.

page 535. Inventory of the Est. of John Skey late of Essex Co., decd., taken by order of Court dated 20 March 1715/16. Total val. L 18. 14. 6

                               Signed   Samll Stallord
                                           John Miller
                                           Thomas x Ayres

                Rec. 15 May 1716.

Ex 9.

page 536. Will of Charles Doores of St. Anns Par., Essex Co. This name may possibly be Deeres.
Dated 3 Jan. 1715/16. Prob. 15 May 1716.
"being very sick and weeak but of perfect mind and memory"
To eldest son James Doores a heifer 2 years old to be paid him when he is 16.
To son Charles Doores his gun to be delivered at the age of 16.
That James and Charles Doors "should have two years Schooling a peace at or after the age of Eight years and to be paid out of my Estate"
Bal. of Est. to "my Loveing ffriends Abner Gray and Richard Guggo for the bringing up of my Children", they to be exors.
Wit:
Jno Ridgdaile   Signed   Charles x Doores
Wm Gray

"The w'th in Last Will and Testam't of Charles Doores dec'd was presented by Abner Grey Surviving Exor therein named x x and is recorded" 15th May 1716.

page 537. Bond. 15 May 1716. L 50. Sterl. Abner Gray Exor of Est. of Charles Doors decd.
Wit: Signed   Abner x Gray
Andrew Harrison   John x Bell
Ralph Gough   Jer Biswell
                                  (Jeremiah Beeswell)
                     Rec. 15 May 1716.

page 538. Deed of Gift. 28 March 1716. Richard Booker of Essex Co. "do freely clearly and absolutly Give and Grant unto Susanah Coghill Daughter to ffrederick Coghill and Sarah his wife all that Tract or Dovidend of Land which was left to the sd Susanah Coghill by the Last will and Testament of George Duckberry Lately deceased x x ".
Wit:
Sam'll Bizwell   Signed   Richard Booker
John Miller
Thomas x Ayres   Rec. 18 May 1716.

page 539. Deed of Gift. 28 March 1716. Frederick Coghill of Essex Co., gives to Richard Booker of same Co., 340 acres, being all right, title and interest in a tract of land "in a patent granted by Governor Berkeley unto James Coghill" on 17 April 1667, of 1050 acres, that is all that is in St. Anns Par.
Wit: Signed   ffrederick x Coghill
James Bizwell
John Miller
Thomas x Ayres   Rec. 15 May 1716

page 539. Richard Booker makes over all right and title to the within

Ex 9

mentioned 340 acres. Dated 15 May 1716.
Wit:
John Boughan   Signed   Richard Booker
Wm x Price
                          Rec. 15 May 1716.

page 540. "Pursuant to an order of Essex County dated the 20th day of March 1715 we x x have Inventoryed and apraised all such of the Estate of Alce Shipley as was presented to our Vewy by John Shipley Ex'or of the sd Estate as followeth vizt: "
List includes:
To 1 ould ffeather beed Loe Beedsted Corde and hide Rugg
    and Blankett   2: 10: 0
To 5 puter plates 4 poringers and nine Spoones and 2 cups
    1 salt Siller 1 Scimer 1 Tankard   0: 07: 0
To 1 Gound and 2 petty Coates   1: 10: 0
To 1 Black hood a Lased Hanckercife and sum other Lining
    and 1 Earthen plate   0: 10: 0
Total valuation L 34. 17. 7

Given under our hands this 10th day of Aprill 1716
                                        John Boughan
                                        Tho Ramsey
                                        John andreces
                          Rec. 15 May 1716.

page 541. Bond. 15 May 1716. 10000 lb. tobo. Augustine Ley to keep an ordinary at his dwelling house in St. Anns Par.
Wit:
Andrew Harrison   Signed   Aug't Ley
Ralph Gough   Jer Beswell
                          Rec 15 May 1716.

page 452. Bond. 15 May 1716. L 20. Sterl. Aug't Ley to keep the ferry "usly Called Southings fferry".
Wit:
Andrew Harrison   Signed   Aug't Ley
Ralph Gough   Jeremiah Beswell
                          Rec. 15 May 1716.

Ex 9   68

page 543. Power of Atty. William Evered of Leverpoole in the County of Lancaster and Kingdom of Great Britain, Mariner, to Wm. Daingerfield on the freshes of Rappahannock River in the County of Essex in Virginia in america, planter, to transatt all business for her in Virginia. Dated 22 March 1715/16.
Wit: Signed   Wm Evered
Joseph Smith
Spilsbe Coleman

William Daingorfield Gent., presented tho above power of attorney x x which was proved by the oaths of Joseph Smith Gent and Spils-by Coleman

Rec. 15 May 1716

page 544. Bond. 15 May 1716. 10000 lb. tobo. Arthur Bower to keep an ordinary at his home in St. A. Par.
                              Signed   Arth Bowers
                                        Wm Winston
                                        James Rennolds Junr

Rec. 15 May 1716

page 545. Lease and Release. 14 - 15 May 1716. Richard Covington, Gent. of St. A. Par., sells William Saint-John of So. F. Par., 82 acres in So. F. Par., being part of a dividend "called by the name of bestlands". Adj. lands of Thos. Howerton and of Meriwether.
Wit:
Nicholas Smith Junr   Signed   Richd Covington
Wm Covington Ju'r
                  Rec. 15 May 1716.

page 549. Deed. 27 Sept. 1715. Henry Adcocke of So. Farn. Par., sells John Evans of same Par., 70 acres in Essex Co., on Rappa. River side, Adj. lands of Mr. Lewis Lattany and the land of Mr. Leonard Hill. This land in consideration for a third part "of a Grist water mill commonly call and known by the name of Evan's mill scituate and being in King and Queen County and parish of St Stephens".
Wit:
Wm Covington   Signed   Henry Adcocke
James Webb
Hugh Williams   Rec. 15 May 1716

Ex 9

page 551. Will of Sarah Bizewell of St. A. Par., Essex Co., "being very sick and Weake of body but of perfickt sense and memory". Dated 13 January 1715/16. Prob. 16 May 1716.
All land to be div. betw. "my two sons Erasmus Bizewell and Daniell Bizewell in Quanty and Quallety".
To daughter Ann Bizwell 1000 lb. tobo.
Bal. of Est. to be div. equally betw. "my three Children Erasmus, Daniell and Ann Bizewell"
Exors "my two brothers John Butler and Jeremiah Bizewell"
Wit:
Aug't Ley   Signed   Sarah x Bizwell
John x Bizwell
John Boughan

Presented by Jeremiah Beeswell one of the Exors., 16 May 1716.

page 552. Bond. 16 May 1716. L 200. Sterl. Jeremiah Beeswell admr of Est of Robt. Beeswell decd.
Wit:
Wm Covington junr   Signed   Jer Biswell
Ralph Gough   Aug't Ley
                                       John Mckenny

Rec. 16 May 1716.

page 553. Bond. 16 May 1716. L 20. "Whereas Judgm't being this day Given in Essex County Court unto Jane Peacock agt Leonard Hill upon a petition depending between the sd Jane and Leonard for the said Janes ffreedome", an appeal is granted Hill to the Gen'l. Court.
Wit:
Thomas x Griffin   Signed   Leo Hill 1716
Ralph Gough   Richd Covington

Rec. 16 May 1716.

page 554. Bond. 16 May 1716. L 10. Sterl. Jane Olive as Guardian of Elizabeth Brown an orphan.
Wit:
Zach Lewis   Signed   Jane x Olive
                                       Erass Allen
                                       (Erasmus Allen)

Rec. 16 May 1716.

Ex 9.

page 555. Bond. 17 May 1716. L 500. Sterl. Edward Coleman, John Chamberling and Danl. Brown. Administrators of the estate not settled of Robt. Coleman, decd.
Wit: Signed Dan'll Brown
Salvator Muscoe   Edward Coleman
Ralph Gough   John Chamberlaine
             James Boughan
             John Crow
      Rec. 17 May 1716.

page 556. Inventory of remainder of the Estate of Richard Kemp, decd. "and have set a part the Dower of Ellenar Kemp widow of the sd Richard"
Includes:
To his wareing apparell 3 wiggs gloves and hatt 03. 00. 00
Total valuation L 165. 19. 09 1/2

Anno Kemp   Signed John Hawkins
             John Boughan
             Salvator Muscoe
      Rec. 17 May 1716.

page 558. Lease and Release. 18 and 19 June 1716. Francis Smith of St. A. Par., planter, sells John Spicer Junr. of the Par. of Sittenburn in the Co., of Richmond, Gentleman, 100 acres in St. A. Par., formerly bought by John Smith of William Catlett, adj. Rappa River and the land of Robert Payne.
Wit: Signed ffran Smith
Nicho Smith
Joshua ffarguson Rec. 19 June 1716.

page 563. Mortgage, 7 April 1716. Francis Smith of St. A. Par. planter, sells Leonard Tarent of same Par., gent., for 4400 lb. tobo. "for the proper Debts of the sd ffrancis Smith (at the Instance and request of the sd ffrancis Smith) and in Consideration of the sd Tarents haveing ffreed and set at Liberty the sd ffrancis Smith out of the Goal of the sd County and in Consideration that no Interest is to be paid for the sd Tobacco x x all that his the sd ffrancis Smiths Plantation and Tract of Land whereon he now dwells", formerly purchased of one Catlett, in St. A. Par., on Rappa River, 95 acres. Smith agreeing to pay Tarent the

(continued)

Ex 9

4400 lb. tobo., on the 25th Dec. 1716. That if Smith decides to dispose of the land finally to Tarent, each will select an honest man to place proper valuation on the property.
Wit:
John Hunter
Richard Moss
Tho Henman

Signed   ffra Smith
         Leo Tarent

Rec. 19 June 1716.

page 567. Inventory of Est. of Robt. Bizwell decd., presented by Jeremiah Bizwell, admr., according to Court Order 16 May 1716.
Includes:
To a parcell of Sarah Bizwells old waring Close	1:	0:	0
To a pare of pistolls and houlsters Breast plate and Crupor	1:	0:	0
To a parcell of ould books	0:	04:	0

Total valuation L 60: 00: 8

Given under our hand this 15th day of June 1716
John Boughan
Ralph Rowzee
Augustin Ley

Note: Of these poor scattered words we must rebuild our history. What circumstances brought this armor to Virginia ? When ? What shot or blows had it turned aside from our ancestors' hearts ?   B.F.

page 569. Deed. 4 May 1716. Thomas Bartlett of St. Marys Par., Essex Co., planter, sells John Miller of St. A. Par., planter, for 3400 lb. tobo., 60 acres, granted to John Ayres 1662 (part of page missing here) bounded by the lines of Kirk, of Rotterford, of Thorp and of sd Miller.
Wit:
Sam'll Bizwell
John Millatt (Miller ?)
Robert Parker

Signed   Thomas x Bartlett

Patience Bartlett wife of Thomas relinq. her right of dower.

Rec. 19 June 1716.

Ex 9

page 572. Bond. 19 June 1716. L 1000. Sterling. Thomas Catlett, having obtained appointment, as sheriff of Essex Co.

        Signed   Thomas Catlett
                    ffran Thornton
                    Jno Taliaferro

Rec. 19 June 1716.

page 578. Lease and Release. 18-19 June 1716. Joanna Williamson, of St. A. Par., spinster, sells Elizabeth Pursell, of same Par., widow, her interest in half of a tract of land and dwelling house, 100 acres in St. A. Par., "nigh a certain place there com'only called Elliots ordinary, which land was devised to them (Joanna and Elizabeth) by their late father John Williamson decd".
Wit:
John Boughan   Signed   Joanna x Williamson
Ralph Gough
Tho Henman   Rec 19 June 1716.

Note: So here is a Williamson - Purcell connection early in the 18th century as well as later on.
    All of us make uncalled for remarks. Strictly in this class is the free information that the origin of the name Purcell is 'little pig'.
                                                                               B.F.

page 577. Inventory of Est. of Richd. Meador, decd.
Includes:
To a sett of Trupers arms	3:	-:	-
To 2 Saddles and 2 bridles	-:	15:	-
To a parcell of old bookes	-:	10:	-
To 1 pare of old Silver buckels	-:	3:	6
To 1 new felt hatt and 2 other felt hatts	-:	5:	-
To a parcell of Shewmakers tooles and Lasts	1:	1:	-
To a parcell of Shewmakers thred and flax	-:	3:	-

Total valuation L 63: 8: 8

Signed 12 June 1716.   Erasmus Allen
                                    John x Gatewood
                                    Jno Billups

                      Rec. 19 June 1716.

Ex 9.

page 579. Bond. 19 June 1716. L 20. Sterl. Peter Godfrey admr. of Est. of Richd. Owen, decd., he having died without a will.
Justices of Essex Co. listed in this bond are: Joseph Smith, William Daingerfield, Thom's Wairen and Ruben Welsh.

         Signed Pr Godfrey
               John Pickett
               Robert Jones

      Rec. 19 June 1716.

page 580. Will of Benja ffisher of So. Farnham Par., Essex Co. Dated 16 April 1716. Prob. 19 June 1716.
All land to be div. equally betw "my three sons Namely Benjamin ffisher James ffisher and John ffisher". Mill to be also div. betw. 3 sons, "it being in Lew of a bond w'ch James Boughan hath of mine for sixty pounds Sterl".
To wife Elizabeth ffisher a feather bed and her third of Est.
Bal. of Est. to be div. betw. "my children Jonathan ffisher, Elizabeth ffisher, Benjamin ffisher, James ffisher and John ffisher".
To wife Elizabeth a slave and she to be extrx. Other slaves to be div. betw. children.
"I give unto my father Jonathan ffisher all my wareing Cloaths Exeept that that is bound w'th Silver I give unto my son Benjamin ffisher to be given him at the Discretion of my Executrix"
Wit:
Benja Morris   Signed Benj'a ffisher
John Haile
Thomas Bryan
Richard Jones

page 582. Bond. 19 June 1716. L 400. Sterl. Elizabeth Fisher, widow, Extrx. of Est. of Benj. Fisher, decd.
          Signed Elizabeth x ffisher
               James Boughan
               John Boughan

      Rec. 19 June 1716.

page 583. Will of Thomas Peatrooss of St. A. Par., Essex Co. Dated 27th Dec. 1715. Prob. 20 March 1715/16.
Land bought of John Hudson to be sold to pay debts.
Land lying by William Biesle to be sold as follows: the first 50 acres, now seated by Henry Biesle to "my Cosen Thomas Petrese the son of John Petrose and Ann his wife". If he d.s.p. then to Elizabeth Petross. If she d.s.p. then to Metthew Petrose. If he d.s.p. then to John Petrose.

         (continued)

Ex 9.   74

The Will of Thomas Peatross (continued)

To Metthew Petrose 40 acres. Wording confused regarding this bequest.
    May be to Thomas Petross. This land now seated by Henry Biesle.
    We would assume, but do not know, that this name is intended to
    be Biswell or Beeswell.
To John Petrose 50 acres being the last part of 150 acres.
To Job Spearman 5 bbl. corn.
To "my Cosen Elizabeth Petross Daughter of John and Ann Petrose" bal of
    personal estate. If she should die this to be div. betw. her three
    children Thomas, Metthew and John Petross.
Exors. William Chaes (this name appears again as Wm Chace) and John
    Huson.
Wit: Signed   Thomas Peatross
Jno Skey
William x Hudson

Wm Chace relinq his exorship 20 March 1715/16.

page 585. Bond. 19 June 1716. L 250. Sterl. John Hodgson, also referred
to in body of will as John Huson and again in bond as John Hudson, as
Exor of Est. of Thomas Peatross, deceased.
Wit:
Daniel Hayes   Signed   John x Hodgson
Ralph Gough   Sam'l Stallord
                                                  Josias Ship

                        Rec. 19 June 1716.

Note: My apologies for the foregoing slovenly abstract. I can almost
hear some superior genealogist (and some are SO superior) exclaim
"It is perfectly clear and simple to me" - Well take notice and beware,
it is anything but clear to this block head. All I can do is to squirm
out and say I did not draw the original will.   B.F.

page 586. Lease and Release. 18 - 19 June 1716. Leonard Tarent, Gent.,
of St. A. Par., sells Thomas Hipkins and Cordela his wife, of same Par.,
202 acres, Tarent's part of 920 acres in Essex Co., on Occupation Creek
and run, and the branches of Cockelshell Creek, granted sd Tarent 28th
May 1716. See entry to follow.
Wit:
Ja Alderson   Signed   Leonard Tarent
Ephra Paget

                        Rec. 19 June 1716.

Ex 9

page 590. Lease and Release. 18 - 10 June 1716. Leonard Tarent of St. A. Par., Essex Co., Gent., sells to William Brooking and Susanna his wife of Petsoe Par., Gloucester Co., planter, 230 acres, being of Tarents part of 920 acres patented 28 May 1716.
Wit:
Ja Alderson   Signed   Leonard Tarent
Ephra Paget

page 595. Lease and Release. 18 - 19 June 1716. Leonard Tarent, Gent., sells James Rennolds Junr., planter, of So. F. Par., 460 acres as above.
Wit:
Ja Alderson   Signed   Leonard Tarent
Ephra Paget

page 598. Lease and Release. 18 - 19 June 1716. James Boughan of So. F. Par., Essex Co., sells Thos. Coleman of St. Stephens Par. in King and Queen Co., 542 acres, which land was granted to sd Jas. Boughan by Escheat patent dated 16 Dec. 1714. Adj. Gillsons Swamp, the land of Dan'll Swillivant, etc.
Wit:
Sam'l Clayton   Signed   James Boughan
Wm Covington Junr
Wm St John

Power of Atty. 19 June 1716. Sarrah Boughan, wife of Jas. Boughan, to John Boughan to relinq. dower rights.
Wit: Signed   Sarrah x Boughan
James Boughan Junr
John Harper
                        Rec. 19 June 1716.

page 605. Inventory of Est. of Charles Dowers. By order of Court dated 9 June 1716. Total valuation L. 22: 4: 6
Part of Est. of Charles Dowers delivered to Sarah Dowers L. 22: 4: 6

                         Signed   Edwn Moseley
                                     Tho Ramsey
                                     John Andrews

Date of record omitted - however 19 June 1716.

page 606. Inventory of Est. of Timothy Driscoll, by order of Court dated 15 May 1716.
Includes:
To a Case Pistoles and Trooping Saddle and sword	1: 5:	-
To a Buck anere Gun	1: -:	-
To a parsell books	0: 5:	-
To a Chafin Dish	0: 02:	-

Total valuation approx. L 190.

Signed   James Webb
         Isaac Webb
         Fran: Moore
         Nicholas Smith

Rec. 20 June 1716.

page 608. " June the 14th 1716 we the Subscribers being Summoned and this day Sworn to lay of and procession the Land of Richd Johnson persuant to an order of Essex County Court dated Wednesday the 16th day of May 1716 and we demand the sd Richard Johnson to shew us the bounds of his Land, and also to produce what writings he held his Land by, and he the sd Richard did answer us and said, that his Land was already bounded and that there was no occasion Either to show his writeings, or bounds of his Land for that Henry Hill and he had agreed on their bounds for which reason we could not further proceed to perform the said order.
      Given under our hands and seales the day and year above written"

Jno Ellitts foreman	Tho (T) Griffin	Rob't Kay Jun'er
Jno Long	Sam(ll Prosser	Wm Harrison
Geo Robinson	John Sanders	Nicholas Ware
Rob't Kay	Henry (H) Brice	Andrew Harrison J'r

page 609. Inventory of Est. of Jno. Waggner, decd. Long Inventory, Not appraised as to valuation. Presented by Rachel Waggener 20 June 1716.

page 611. By Court order 16 May 1716. The subscribers surveyed and processioned the land of John Hudson " x x beginning upon a point between Lucases Creek and a small branch thereof x x " etc., " and then we being stopt and the Surveyors Chaine then and there forcibly

(continued)

Ex 9

taken up by Wm Price of the sd County, for which reason we Could not proceed persuant to the sd order. Given under our hands and seales this 5th day of June 1716."

Tho Short foreman	Charles Brown	Thomas (T) Aires
ffra Smith	Charles Brown Jun'r	Wm (W) Daniel
James Cogghill	Thomas O'eson	Jno x Morgan
John Miller	Matt'w x Collins	Edwd X Scrimshaw

page 612. By order of Essex Court 14 June 1716. Being first sworn "in Company with Robt Brooke Junr Deputy Surveyor of the sd County", the land of Henry Reeves has been surveyed and processioned. Beginning at the lower side of Tigners Creek, the river bank, etc. Given in this 15th June 1716.

Robert Jones	Robt Elliott	Wm Smith
Salvator Muscoe	Jno Gaines	James Webb
Wm Covington Junr	Dan'll Brown	John Crow
Isaac Webb	Wm St John	John Wattkins

page 612. Inventory of Est. of Richd. Owen, decd, presented by Pr. Godfrey 10th July 1716. Total L 8: 15: 2 1/4

         Signed Jno Gaines
             Richd x Webb
             Fran: Moore
    Rec 17 July 1716.

page 613. Deed. 17 July 1716. Thos ffenwick, planter, of St. A. Par., sells to Thomas Short, for 2000 lb. tobo., 100 acres, adj. the line of Starke, of Pannell, of Blagborn, of Charles Brown.
Wit:
Tho Hipkins   Signed Thomas fenwick
John x hares
Elizabeth x haris
        Rec. 17 July 1716.

Note: Thus again it seems we must turn to the ladies - or at least to the petticoats. Thanks to Elizabeth we now know 'hares' means Harris.
                        B.F.

Ex 9

page 615. Appraisal of "som of Gibsons Estate for faruson" probably meaning for Ferguson. Total valuation 890 lb. tobo.
                                      Signed   Henry Shackelford
                                                        John Haile
                                                        Henry Boughn
                       Rec. 17 July 1716.

page 616. Inventory of Est. of Brigett Oneale, taken by Court order of 19 June 1716.
Includes:
To 1 old Sord and bolt 1 pale 2 pigings and one butter tob   00: 6: 6
Total valuation L 13: 16: 10
                                      Signed   Isaac Webb
                                                     James Webb
                                                     Dan'll Dobyns
                          Date of record not shown

page 617. At a Court 17 May 1719, Wm Young obtained an attachment agt. the est. of Henry Woodnot for L 9: 5: 0 Sterl. and 660 lb. tobo. Being returned was served on certain personal property listed, now in the hands of Henry Hudson. Capt. Isaac Webb, James Webb, Henry Adcocke and Wm Smith are appointed by the Court to appraise the goods and deliver enough to Young to pay the debt.
    The same regarding an attachment obtained by John Evans for 550 lb. tobo.

page 619. "I Jonathan ffisher doth make over to Benja ffisher x x all my wright Title or Claime and interest to and for the mill Benj'a ffisher and I did Build x x 28 of November 1715"
Wit:
Wm Cooper   Signed   Jonathan ffisher
Wm x Scott
                     Rec. 17 July 1716.

page 619. Bond. 17 July 1716. L 60. Sterl. Arthur Donelly as guardian of John Oneale and Katherine Oneale, orphans.
Wit: Signed   Arthur Donnolly
Ralph Gough   William Chase
                                                    Thomas Moore
                     Rec. 17 July 1716.

Ex 9.

page 620. "A true and perfect Inventory of the remaining part of the Estate of John Waggoner which being before forgott"
6 items, not appraised, presented by Rachel Waggener.
                        Rec. 17 July 1716.

page 621. Deed. 16 July 1716. John Moseley, planter, of St. A. Par., sells John Coffee and Edward Coffee, planters, of same Par., for 8000 lb. tobo., 200 acres commonly called Moseleys Quarters, in St. A. Par., on E. side of a branch of Occupation, a small branch of Gilsons, adj. land belonging to Mr Matrum Wright and land formerly belonging to Tho. Button.
Wit: Signed   John Moseley
Salvator Muscoe
John x Staton
Peter x Holland   Rec. 18 July 1716.

page 626. Bond. 18 July 1716. L 100. Sterl. James Webb and Ann his wife as guardians of Sarah, Jane and Peter Michell, orphans.
                                 Signed   James x Webb
                                                Richard Bush
                                                Wm Smith
                        Rec. 18 July 1716.

page 626. Bond. 18 July 1716. L 20. Sterl. Wm Berry as admr of Est. of Thomas Hathaway decd, who died without a will.
Wit:
Robert Jones   Signed   William Berry
                                                  Jno Ellitts
                                                  Rich'd x Long
                        Rec. 18 July 1716.

page 627. Power of Atty. Mary Tarent to Mr. Thomas Henman to relinq. dower rights in land sold James Rennolds Junr by her husband.
Wit:
G. Braxton (George Braxton)   Signed   Mary Tarent
J Walker   (James Walker)

page 628. Power of Atty. as above for land sold Wm. Brooking.
page 629. Power of Atty. as above for land sold Thomas Hipkins.

                        Rec. 18 July 1716.

Ex 9

page 629. "May the 19th 1716 Essex County Ss A Just and true envon'ry of the Estate of William Butler being ateached by William Dannill
To one old bed and bolster   00: 00: 00
And one old rug and blanket   01: 10: 00
         ffedricke (F) Coghill
         Wm Pickett
         Rich'd Booker "

"May 19 1716
Ess County Ss. A Just and true enverteary of the Estate of William Butler being ateached by Jorge Mitchell
To one old Druged Cote and Corse britches   00: 17: 00
To one gound and Pottecote   00: 10: 00
To one pare of bodeges and Stumeger   00: 7: 00
To Seven yds of broun linen and   00: 04: 00
To one rugg and blankett   00: 3: 06
To one old pare of Shooes   00: 00: 8
To a parsell of olde Lumber
         ffedricke (F) Coghill
         Wm Pickett
         Richd Booker   "

page 650. Bond. 19 July 1716. L 50. Aug't Smith as admr. of Est. of Place Powell, decd., he dying without a will.
Wit:
Salvator Muscoe   Signed Aug't Smith
            Robert Jones
      Rec. 19 July 1716.

page 631. Inventory of Est. of Thomas Pettross, Decd., taken by Court order dated 19 June 1716.
Includes:
To 1 small Tabell and six Rush bottom Chares   1: 2: 0
To old case of Pistolls and a Small Sword   0: 12: 0
To his wareing apparrell   3: 0: 0
Total valuation L 22: 00: 00
        Signed John Hawkins
            Bucken'm Browne
            John Miller
      Rec. 17 July 1716.

Ex 9.

page 632.
"Saunders   Essex County SS. In obedience to the within order wee
   ag   the Subscribers being first sworn have appraised a
  Evans   pair of brass Dividers to the value of Six pence Given
est of appm'r   under our hands this 16th day of July 1716
                                          A Somervell
                                          Henry Byrom
                                          Cha: Gresham   "

page 632. Bond. 15 July 1709. Thomas Harding of Accomack Co., promises
to pay to Buckingham Brown L 34. on demand.
Wit:
Robert Jones   Signed   Thomas Harding
John x ffellows
                        Rec. 17 July 1716

page 633. Will of William Scott. Dated 26 Nov. 1715. Prob. 21 Aug. 1716
To wife Margret his plantation during life. To son William at her death
To son William 200 acres more "at the end of the Land (next the white
oak swamp) x x which was given me by my brother James Scott".
"I give (if the Child which my wife now goes with be a boy)" balance or
    land being 300 acres. If a girl "then I give unto my three Daught-
    ers one hundred acres of Land a peice".
Personal Est. to be div. betw. wife and children.
Exors: wife Margret, James Scott and John Vawter.
Wit:
Paul Micou   Signed   William Scott
Thomas Meades
Jno x Cannaday   Rec. 21 Aug. 1716.

page 634. Bond. 21 Aug. 1716. L 200. Sterl. Margaret Scott as Extrx.
of Est. of Wm. Scott, decd.
Wit: Signed   Margaret x Scott
Ralph Gough   Tho Meades
                                          Jno Vawter
                        Rec. 21 Aug. 1716.

page 635. Bond. 21 Aug. 1716. L 100. Sterl. Anne Sutton admrx of Est.
of John Sutton, decd., who died without a will.
                                Signed   Anne x Sutton
                                          Thomas x Hilliard
                                          Richd x Long
                        Rec. 21 Aug. 1716.

Ex 9

page 636. Bond. 21 Aug. 1716. L 50. Sterl. Robert Harrison as guardian for George Green, an orphan.
Wit:
Ralph Gough

Signed Robert Harison
        Thomas x Griffin
        John Millatt

Rec. 21 Aug. 1716.

page 636. Deed. 21 Aug. 1716. Thomas Short of St. A. Par., sells Thomas Slaughter, planter, of Essex Co., for 1300 lb. tobo., 50 acres, adj. land of Benja Martin, the line crossing Crooked Swamp twice and adj. the land of Gouldman.
Wit:
Tho Hipkins
Saml Stallord
John Martin

Signed Thomas Shortt

Rec. 21 Aug. 1716.

page 639. Deed. 21 Aug. 1716. Thomas Short, planter, of St. A. Par., sells Elias Blackburn, planter, of same Par., for 1300 lb. tobo., 50 acres adj. the lands of Bentley and of Mr Xepher Blackburn.
Wit:
Sam'll Stallord
Tho Hipkins
John x Martin

Signed Thomas Shortt

Rec. 21 Aug. 1716.

page 641. Lease and Release. Both dated 4th Jan. 1715/16. John Bush of Essex Co., sells John Tood (Todd) of Stafford Co., for 200 acres in Stafford Co., 150 acres in Essex Co. This 150 acres being part of a Grand patent of John Prosser on puemansone Swamp and adj. the line of Mr ffrancis Tolipers (Taliaferro), etc.
Wit:
John x Jonnes
ffrancis x Maigkall

Signed Jno Bush
        Margrett x Bush

Margaret Bush, wife to John Bush, relinq. dower rights.

Rec. 21 Aug. 1716.

page 645. Inventory of Est of Thos Hathaway, taken by order of Court dated 18 July 1716.
Includes:

To a Gun 2 Swords a Spitt and 2 old Saddles att	1: 13: 6
To a Compass box a p'r of Spectacles a Looking Glass and a parcell of Ginger	-: 3: 6
To a old bible two books and a parcel of Thred	-: 6: -

Total valuation L 21: 13: 4

       Signed Saml Stallord
           Richd Goode
           Richd x Edwards

Rec. 21 Aug. 1716.

page 646. 1716 . The Estate of Thos Landrum decd Dr. to Wm Berry admr.

To pd Capt John Hawkins per Judg't	634	
To pd Richd Edwards	520	
To pd Silvester Patty	950	
To pd Jno Morgan for nursing his Child	1000	
To pd Robt Parker per Sherifs and Secys) fees and County Levys)	316	
To bill given Mr Herman per 150 cwt Tobo		1: 10: 0
To pd Thomas Taylor	150	
To attorneys fee abt the sd Estate	200	
To my Trouble ab't the adm'con of the sd Estate	300	
	3960	44: 2: 0
per Cred't		14: 1: 6
By the Inventory		
per Tobo rec'd of Rich'd Goode jr	690	
of Thos Hathaway	530	
of Edwd Hunter	104	
Two barrills and half Indian Corn		1: 05: 0
	1324	15: 6: 6
		30: 4: 0

      Signed William Berry

Rec. 21 Aug. 1716.

Ex 9

page 646. Bond. 18 Sept. 1716. L 30. Sterl. Robt Parker as guardian of Eliz'a Boulware an orphan.
Wit:
Ralph Gough
        Signed   Robt Parker
                        Nath'll ffogg
                        Joseph x Leeman
        Rec. 18 Sept 1716.

page 647. Inventory of Est. of Brigits Oneal decd., Court Order dated 18 July 1716. Taken 10 Aug. 1716. Total val. L 19. 0. 0
        Signed   Isaac Webb
                      James Webb
                      Dan'll Dobyns
        Rec. 18 Sept 1716.

page 647. Bond. 18 Sept 1716. L 50. Sterl. John Picket admr. est. of Jeffry Dyer, decd., who died without a will.
Wit:
Richd Covington
Ralph Gough
        Signed   Jno Pickett
                      James Edmondson
        Rec. 18th day of 7ber 1716 (Sept)

page 649. Power of Atty. 18 Sept. 1716. Susanna Wise of King & Queen Co., to Mr Orlando Jones of King William Co., to ack. in Essex Co. right of dower to 120 acres in Essex Co., lying at Piscataway Creek to Richd Price of K & Q Co. This land formerly sold by her husband Richd. Wise to sd Price, by Lease and Release, 6 - 7 April 1711.
Wit:
Edward Price
Theophilus Harford
Charles Phillips
        Signed   Susanna Wise
        Rec. 18 Sept 1716.

page 649. Deed. 15 Sept 1716. John Hodgson of St. A. Par., Essex Co., sells Thomas Ayres of ST. A. Par., for 3500 lb. tobc., 62 acres, part of land where sd Hodgson now lives. Adj. long bridge swamp, land of Wm Price, according to Hodgson's deed from Valentine Allen, etc.
Wit:
Wm Tiller
John Rouse
Samuell Bizwell
        Signed   John x Hodgson
        Rec. 18 Sept. 1716.

page 652. Inventory of Est. of William Scott, decd. By Court order dated 21 Aug. 1716.
Includes:

To his waring Cloaths and four gunns at	6:	7:	-
To two horses a pair of pistols houlsters Swourd and belt	5:	15:	-
To a parcell of Coopers tools and a pair of small stilards	1:	1:	6
To a parcell of Shoemakers tools and Lasts	-:	9:	-
To a serv't boy named John Cannadey	7:	-:	-
To a servant boy named James Cannadey	12:	-:	-
To Cash	1:	12:	7

Total valuation L 115. 16. 6

          Signed   Richard Booker
                         Richd Ship
                         John Miller
                         Thomas x Ayres
Rec. 18 Sept. 1716.

page 653. Power of Atty. William West, carpenter, in Essex Co., to "my wife Eliz'a West" to transact all business "untill I return home again having now sum verry urgent occations to goe from home and god willing shall return as oppertunity shall permit". Dated 4 Jan'ry 1715/16.
Wit:
Barna' x Ward (Bernard Ward)   Signed   William West
John x Ward
                    Rec. 18 Sept. 1716.

page 654. Bond. 18 Sept. 1716. 10000 lb. tobo. Richd. Taylor to keep an ordinary at his dwelling house.
Wit: Signed   Rich'd x Taylor
James Edmondson   Jos Baker
Ralph Gough
                    Rec. 18 Sept. 1716.

page 655. Bond. 18 Sept. 1716. L 40. Sterl. Ledia Beckham as Extrx of Est. of Simon Beckham decd.
Wit: Signed   Ledia x Beckham
Ralph Gough   Wm Winston
                                       Jno Bates
                  Rec. 18 Sept. 1716.

page 656. Inventory of the Est. of Benja. ffisher, decd. Court order dated 19 June 1716. Presented by Mrs Eliz'a ffisher Widdo and Extrx on 3 July 1716.
Includes:

1 laced hatt and band	-: 8:	-
1 Kaine	-: 5:	-
1 old Sword and 5 sickles 6/6	6:	6
1/3 of a gun	-: 10:	-
Pales and Piggins	8:	6

Total valuation approx; L. 120.

                          Signed   Wm Covington
                                        Thomas Bryan
                                        Fran: Moore
                 Rec. 18 Sept 1716.

page 658. Inventory of Est. of ffrancis Gibson, decd. Court order dated 18 July 1716. Presented by Samuel Henshaw admr. 18 Aug. 1716.
Includes:
To 1 ould Sourd 1 ould rasor and 2 ould knives   -: 3: -
Total val. L 2: 5: 6

                          Signed   John Boughan
                                      Thomas Ramsey
                                      John Andrews
                 Rec. 18 Sept. 1716.

page 659. Inventory of Est. of Isac Mercer, decd. Court order 20 Mar. 1715/16. Presented by Mr. William Winston, admr. Totals L 12: 7: 0
                          Signed   Thomas Munday
   Wm Winston   John Graves
                                        John Strang
                 Rec. 19 Sept 1716.

page 660. Inventory of Est. of John Gibson. Taken 18 Aug. 1716. Items listed indicate that he was a dress maker. Total val. 1318 lb. tobo.

                          Signed   Nath'll ffogg
                                        Tho Winslow
                                        Charles x Grisam

Ex 9.

page 660. Lease and Release. 18 - 19 September 1716. Richard Covington of St. A. Par., sells Thomas Haywerton Junr., of Essex Co., 100 acres in St. A. Par. adj. land of Wm St John, land formerly sold by sd Covington to Mr. Thomas Meriwether, the land of Mrs Mary Billington, and the land of Thomas Haywarton.
Wit: Signed Rich Covington
Wm Covington Junr
James Edmondson

page 665. "The Virble will of Simon Beckham deceased I Give and bequeath unto my Loving wife Lidia Beckham all my Estate wholey and Soleley for her use and the bringing up of my Children he not desiering the other should have any part haveing their part already"
Witness James ffoster
Eliz'b x ffoster
Xpher x Man
No date of record shown.

page 666. Deed of Release. 20 Nov. 1716. Augustine Smith, Gent., of Essex Co., having on 8 May 1712 mortgaged the plantation he lived on in St. A. Par., with other property, to Robert Beverley, for and to the use of Messrs Micajah Perry and Richard Perry of London, merchants, for L 550. 1. 02 with interest at 6 per cent, to be paid in five years, and having no prospect of paying, releases all equity in the property.
Wit:
T. Waring Signed Aug't Smith
Tho Herman
Ralph Gough Rec. 20 Nov. 1716.

page 667. Deed. 14 Nov. 1716. Edward and Richard Booker of St. A. Par., sell James Coghill and Tho Dickeson of same Par., for 1000 lb. tobo., 100 acres in St. A. Par., adj the land of Edwd. Booker, the land of ffedrick Cogghill, etc.
Wit: Signed Edw'd Booker
John Lowry Rich'd Booker
Samuel Bartlet
Rec. 20 Nov. 1716.

Ex 9

page 669. Will of Edward Coffey "being in bedd of Sickness".
Dated 14 Feb. 1715/16. Prob. 20 Nov. 1716.
To two sons John Cofey and Edward Cofey all land to be div. equally, at
    16 years if their mother is dead, otherwise at 18 years.
To daughter Marther Cofey a cow at 16 or her mother's death.
To son John a cow.
To wife Ann Cofey balance of personal property. At her death to be div.
    equally betw. "my six children John Cofey Edward Cofey Marther
    Cofey Ann Cofey Austes Cofey Elizabeth Cofey". The name Austes
    may be Anstes.

Wit: Signed   Edward x Coffey
Sam'll Edmondson
Themety Seleven   Rec. 20 Nov. 1716.

Bond. 20 Nov. 1716. L 100. Sterl. Ann Cofey as extrx of est. of Edward
Coffey decd.
Wit: Signed   Anne x Coffee
Robert Jones   Thomas x Graves
                                        John x Hart
                      Rec. 20 Nov. 1716.

page 670. Bond. 20 Nov. 1716. L 200. William Winston as admr of Est.
of Rich'd Brutnall deceased, who died without a will.
Wit:
Robt Jones   Signed   Wm Winston
Ralph Gough   Richd Covington
                                        Ephraim Paget
                    Rec 20 Nov. 1716.

page 672. Bond. 20 Nov. 1716. L 100. Sterl. Eliz'a Rhoden admrx of
Est. of Homer Rhoden decd., who died without a will.
Wit:
Samll Edmondson   Signed   Elizabeth x Rhoden
Ralph Gough   Rich'd x Cooper
                                        John Dickenson
                    Rec. 20 Nov. 1716.

page 673. Inventory of the Est. of Jeffery Dyer, Decd. Court order dated
18 Sept. 1716. Taken 17 Nov. 1716. Total val. L 9: 16: 6
                                  Signed   James Boughan
                                              John Harper
                                              Thomas Rallton
                    Rec. 20 Nov. 1716.

page 674. Lease and Release. 18 - 19 Nov. 1716. Sam'll Short, planter, of St. Marys Par., Essex Co., sells Caleb Lindsey, planter, of same Par and Co., 310 acres, being part of a patent formerly granted Enock Douchtey for 4763 acres. This 310 acres adj. land of Joseph Callay and land of ffrancis Browning.

Wit: Signed   Samuel Short
Jasper Coston
Jno Evans
Tho Ripley   Rec. 20 Nov. 1716

page 679. Bond. 21 Nov. 1716. L 2000. John Roy, Gent., as agent for a Storehouse on Rappahannock River. The name of this storehouse looks as though it were Nants or Harts. I ought to know what the record says it was, but I don't, and that's that.

Wit: Signed   Jno Roy
Wil Robinson   Richd Covington
Salvator Muscoe   Jno Lomax
Tho Henman
                           Rec. 21 Nov. 1716.

page 680. Will of Francis Gouldman of St. A. Par., Essex Co.
Dated 9 Jan. 1715/16. Prob. 21 Nov. 1716.

To kinsman Francis Gouldman 1200 a. purchased of Augt. Smith, Boughan and others, on branches of Occupation Creek and Mattapony. If he d.s.p. to kinsman Thomas Gouldman. If he d.s.p. to kinswoman Eliz. Waring wife to Thomas Waring.

To kinsman Thomas Gouldman all land on Hoskinses Creek in Essex County "whereon my Water mill now stands". If he d.s.p. to Francis G. If he d.s.p. to Eliz: Waring.

To kinswoman Elizabeth Waring 1100 a. "lying and being in Com'on" betw the heirs of Fran. Meriwether late decd., and himself, situated in King and Queen Co., on branches of Mattapony. She d.s.p. to kinsman Francis G. He d.s.p. to kinsman Thomas G.

To kinsman Thomas Gouldman 600 a. on Hoskinses Swamp on S. side in Essex Co., 200 a thereof given "me by my father", 200 a. purchased of Francis Awberry and 200 a. escheated from Katherine Long. He d.s.p to Francis G. He d.s.p to Elizabeth Waring.

To kinsman Francis Gouldman "all that my Tract of Land whereon I now dwell which was purchased of Arrabella Bird Daughter and Heir of Henry White". If he d.s.p. to Thomas G. If he d.s.p. to Elizabeth Waring.

If kinsman Thomas Gouldman when he attain the age of 21 would rather have dwelling plantation than the mill he to have his choice. Francis Gouldman to take the other.

Wife to have dwelling plantation during life. Also personal property.

(continued)

Ex 9.

Will of Francis Gouldman (continued)

That half of a water mill owned with Paul Micou be sold "by out Cry at Richmond Court", proceeds to be added to personal estate.
To kinsmen Francis and Thos. Gouldman certain stock in common until Francis be 21.
That L 13. Sterl. due from Capt. Pickarin and L 8. upwards due from Jno. Billups be added to personal estate. Also tobo. and money due from Robt. Elliot, Col. Richd. Covington, Thos Winslow and Jno. Billups.
That "all my own debts and the Debts due from my late Brother Edward Gouldmans Estate being the Childrens part or proportion be forthwith paid x x "
That "Thomas Waring aforesd take into his Custody my Desk with all my papers so soon as I shall depart this Life".
That "my negro Jack a Carpenter be free from Slavery".
To Thos. Waring certain money and tobo. That he settle a/cs of late brother's est. with William Winston.
That Thomas Waring manage certain property for Francis and Thos. Gouldman until they are 21. "and if it so happen that the sd Thomas Waring shall dye before my sd two kinsmen attaine the age aforesd that then my Sister Martha Winston shall take care of their Estates"
Refers to Francis and Thomas Gouldman as the orphans of his late brother.
To Thos. Henman "my silver hilted Sword and Belt"
Exors: wife Mary Gouldman and Mr Thomas Waring.
Wit:
Arth: Bowers   Signed   ffrancis Gouldman
Paschal Greenhill
Ro Brooke Jr
William Moss
Tho Henman

page 684. "Be it remembered that on the 7 day of July 1716 I ffrancis Gouldman do give unto Thomas Waring all the apple Treess growing in my Nurserie to be taken up when he shall think fit Except two hundred to my wife "
Wit:
Wm Winston   Signed   ffrancis Gouldman
Ro Brooke junr

Codicil proved 21 Nov. 1716.

Bond. 21 Nov. 1716. L 1000. Sterling. Mary Gouldman and Thomas Waring as Extrx. and Exor. of will of ffrancis Gouldman, deceased.
Wit:
Ralph Gough   Signed   Mary x Gouldman
                                                      Th. Wareing
                                                      John Bagge
                                                     Richd Covington

                            Rec. 21 Nov. 1716.

Ex 9.

page 685. Will of Thomas Edwards of St Anns Par., Essex Co.
Dated 26th Oct. 1716. Prob. 21 Nov. 1716.
To wife Katherin Edwards all personal estate. Real Est. to be sold, debt
    pd. and bal to wife. At her death to be div. equally betw. "my
    beloved Sister Mary, Thomas the son of my uncle Joseph Lewis,
    Thomas the son of my uncle James Thomas and Thomas the Son of
    Barbary Scandered my Coz"
Exors: wife Katherin Edwards and "the abovesd James Thomas"
Wit:
Owen Jones   Signed   Tho Edwards
Ro: Brooke
Ann Scandereds (Scandrett)

Bond. 21 Nov. 1716. L 300. Sterl. Catherine Edwards as Extrx. of will
of Thomas Edwards.
Wit: Signed   Kathene Edwards
Ralph Gough   John Bagge
                                            Salvator Muscoe
                           Rec. 21 Nov. 1716.

page 687. Bond. 21 Nov. 1716. 10000 lb. tobo. Robert Elliot to keep
an ordinary at his house in St. A. Par.
Wit:
Ralph Gough   Signed   Robt Elliott
                                            Richd Covington
                                            Robt Parker
                                            Jno Pickett
                           Rec. 21 Nov. 1716.

page 688. Bond. 22 Nov. 1716. L 20. Sterl. "x x in Essex County Court
in an action of Ejectm't brought by x x Thomas Pettet plt agt Godfrey
Stanton deft, upon a plea of the deft was dism't and the plt x x had
an appeal granted to the Eight day of the next Gen'll Court x x".
Wit:
Ralph Gough   Signed   Tho Petit
                                            R Beverley
                           Rec date omitted.

page 689. Inventory of Est. of Edward Cofey decd. Dec. 4th 1716. Total
valuation L 45: 10: 9
                           Signed
James Edmondson   Ann x Cofey
Will Taylor
Nich: ffaulconer
                           Rec. 18th Dec. 1716.

Ex 9

page 690. Inventory of Est. of Homer Rodin, decd. Court order dated 20 Nov. 1716.
Includes:
To a passell of Smiths Tools att   5: 0: 0
To 1 old Bible and Little Book   : 5: -
To 1 fire lock gun att   10: -
Total valuation L 23: 4: 7

                     Signed   Henry Purkins
                                  Benja Edmondson
                                  John Crow
                                  Wm Covington junr
               Rec 18 Dec. 1716

page 691. Deed. 7 January 1716/17. John Salmon of St. A. Par., Essex Co., son and heir of John Salmon late of the same Par. and Co. decd., sells to Charles ffarrell of same Par. and Co., planter, for 5 bbl. Indian corn and 1000 lb. tobo., 427 1/2 acres in St. A. Par. Adjs the lands of Col. Catlett, Richd Goode, the tract of 520 acres granted Wm. Moseley 1st Nov. 1656, the land of Robert and Thomas Mosse, etc., which sd tract of 427 1/2 acres was granted to John Salmon father to the said John Salmon party to these parts, Place Powell and William Powell by patent dated 2 May 1705. Salmon the father being the survivor of the sd patentees.
Wit: Signed   John x Salmon
Ja Alderson
Ann Alderson   Rec. 15 January 1716/17

page 694. Possession given and ack. 8 January 1716/17
                             before   Daniel x Tucker
                                        Henry Wood
                                        Ja Alderson

Power of Atty. 9th Jan. 1716/17. Sarah Salmon, wife of John Salmon, to Mr. Robt Jones to relinq dower rights.
Wit:
Daniel x Tucker   Signed   Sarah x Salmon
Henry Wood
                    Rec. 15 January 1716/17

page 695. Lease and Release. 20 - 21 August 1716. Edward Waller of the Par. of Stratton Major, King and Queen Co., sells Wm Upshaw of So. Farn. Par., Essex Co., 200 acres, "being part of 400 acres that belonged to Charles Waller w'ch he formerly purchased of the above named William Upshaw it being part of a pattent that did belong to Harry Beverley Scituate lying and being in the County of Essex on the North side of

(continued)

Ex 9

Lease and Release. Waller to Upshaw (continued)

Hoskinses Swamp", and adj. land "of one Thrachley", etc.
Wit:
Charles Waller   Signed   Edward Waller
Henry Shackelford
                Rec. 18 January 1716/17.

page 699. Power of Atty. 27th Dec. 1716. Christain Waller, wife of Edw. Waller of King and Queen Co., to Mr. Thos. Hemman to relinq. dower rights in 200 a. sold Wm Upshaw.
Wit: Signed   Christian x Waller
Charles Waller
Sarah Roane   Rec. 15 January 1716/17

page 699. Lease and Release. 8 - 9 October 1716. Samuel Prosser of Essex County sells Joseph Trowhare of same Co., for L 3. current money, 14 acres 126 perches of land. Adjs lower most corner of land heretofore purchased by Trowhere from Prosser. Also adjs lands of Robt. Kay junr, Mr. Richd. Buckner, etc.
Wit: Signed   Sam'll Prosser
Richard Buckner
Thomas x Hilliard
John x Powell   Rec. 15 Jan. 1716/17

page 704. December the 15th 1716. Inventory of the Est. of Jno. Sutton, dec'd. Total valuation approx: L 30.
                             Signed   Andrew Harrison
                                             Gabrill Long
                                             Will x Smith
                     Rec. 15 January 1716/17.

page 705. "Paid per me Ann Sutton of the debts of John Sutton after his decease
To Mr Booth   0900
To Peter Byram   01: 4: 6
To Coll Taylor   01: 8: 6
To Mr Turner   1: 0: 0
To Michael Ginnin   3: 9
To Mr Richard Buckner   1: 7: 3
To Sam'll Hawes 4 buckskins   1: 5: 0

                                  (continued)

Ex 9

Settlement of the Estate of John Sutton (continued)

To Mr John Taliaferro	0:	7:	0
To Elizabeth Tappine	1:	0:	0
To Nathaniell ffogg	0:	2:	6
To Mr Nicholas Wares	1:	0:	0

page 705. Deed. 11 Jan. 1716/17. Edward Skrimser of St. A. Par., planter, sells to James Gouge (Guggey) of same Par., planter, for 1300 lb. tobo., 50 acres, being part of land where Skrimser now has his dwelling house and orchard, and adj. lands of Wm Clapam and John Morgan.
Wit:
Sam'll Bizwell   Signed   Edward x Skrimser
Rob: Payne
ffrederick x Cogghill   Rec. 15 January 1716/17.

page 708. Division of Land. 2 January 1713/14. "x x we the subscribers being chosen and elected by an instrument in wrighting from under the hands and seals of Benja'n Watkins and John Watkins bearing date the fifth day of October 1713
     acordingly we did on the 30th day of December last devide the land that was left them by thare decea'd ffather Thomas Watkins as followeth (vizt) x x ". This land adj. land of abovesd Benja Watkins, William Coles, Samll Coates and Capt Wm Covington.
                               Signed   Wm Covington
                                         Nath'll Sanders

"We the subscribers do hereby agree to stand by the above award in the dividing of the above piece of Land In wittness our hands this 15 day of Jan'ry 1716 ". (1716/17)
Wit: Signed   Benj Watkins
Wm Covington Jun'r   John Watkins
James x Newell
                   Rec. 15 January 1716/17

page 709. Lease and Release. 14 - 15 Janry 1716/17. Benja Watkins of the County of New Kent and parish of Blissland sells to James Newbell and George Newbell of Co. of Essex and Par. of So. Farn., for L 65. Sterl., 200 acres in So. Farn. Par., and on the So. side of one of the branches of the Dragon Swamp. Adj. land of aforesd Benja. Watkins, the land of Wm Coles, Saml Conts and Capt Wm. Covington.
Wit:
James Turner   Signed   Benj Watkins
Wm Covington Junr
              Rec. 15 Jany 1716/17.

Ex 9.

page 715. Bond. 15 January 1716/17. 200.000 lb. Tobo. That Thomas Catlett, sheriff, shall make due payment of all notes delivered to him for paying Levys, Dues and fees, put in his hands to collect, etc. Justices names included in this bond are Joseph Smith, William Young, Reuben Welch and Tho Waring, Gents.

           Signed Thomas Catlett
                Jno Lomax
                Wm Daingerfield
       Rec. 15 Jan 1716/17

page 716. Will of James Webb of South Farnham Par., Essex Co. Dated 30 Nov. 1716. Probated 15 January 1716/17.
To wife Sarah, 3 slaves during life, at her death to surviving children
To son John "the plantation whereon I now live and all the Land belonging to me that lies on the lower side of the main road". He failing in heirs to son James.
To son John "my horse called fire w'th my saddle Holsters Sword and pistolls". Also 3 slaves.
To son James remaining part of lands lying above the road. He failing in heirs to son John. Also 3 slaves and an iron gray horse.
To daughter Catherine 3 slaves.
To daughter Mercy 3 slaves.
Refers to son James as being under 18 yrs. Refers to "my four Children"
Balance of Est. to be div. betw. wife and the 4 children, no division to be made until son John be 18 yrs. old.
Exors: "my beloved brother Isaac Webb" with sons John and James Webb. Brother Isaac Webb to do what is necessary toward education of children
Wit:
Giles Webb   Signed James Webb
Jno x Callicot
Pr. Godfrey

15 January 1716/17 will proved by Isaac Webb, "the other Exors being infants".
            Test Tho Henman C. Cur
"Examined with the original
    by W Beverley Cl Cur"

page 719. Bond. 15 January 1716/17. L 500. Sterling. Isaac Webb as Ex of will of James Webb deceased.
Wit: Signed Isaac Webb
Ralph Gough   Will Young
         Rec. 15 January 1716/17.

Ex 9

page 720. Inventory of the Estate of Thomas Edmondson, deceased. Taken by Court Order dated 20 Dec. 1715.
Includes:

To 1 fire lock gun at	1:	5:	-
To 1 do at	1:	0:	0
To 1 do at	-	15:	-
To 1 Cheafing dish at	-	3:	-
To 2 Spring locks and 1 padlock Do	-	3:	-
To 2 perewiggs and hatt	2:	-:	-
To 3 pair of french falls	-:	12:	-
To 4 felt hatts at	-:	12:	-
to 1600 Duble Tons at		13:	6
To 2000 single Tons at		10:	6
To 5000 4 penny nails		12:	6
To 22300 8 penny nails at	4:	9:	0
To 1 pare of mony Scales	-:	6:	0
To 4 papers of Ink powder	-:	2:	6
To 1 box and wafers	-:	2:	-
To 4 Doz'a of mottle buttons	-:	1:	-
To 3 Ivory Combs at	-:	3:	-
To 1 Suit of black Cloths	2:	-:	-
To 1 Coate and pr briches at	1:	5:	-
To 80 books	8:	-:	-
To 7 bibles	1:	-:	-
To 1 Silver headed Cane	-:	10:	-
To 1 Great riding Coat	1:	5:	-
To 6 leather Chairs and 3 Rushey Chairs	1:	2:	6
To 1 bell mettle skillet	-:	3:	-
To Sterling money	3:	2:	-
To 1 rideing Cloak	-:	12:	-

Total valuation of this long inventory approx: L 375.

Also:
By Tobo pd out of the Estate
To Natl Sanders	230
To Robert Elliot	-
Carey Coston	54
To Bryan Edmondson	220
1715 Lent to Bryan Edmondson	106

Signed   Wm Covington
Rich'd Tiler
Benja ffisher

Recorded 16 Janry 1716/17

Ex 9

page 729. Inventory of the Estate of Collo ffrancis Gouldman, deceased. Taken on 2 January 1716/17 by order of Court dated Dec. 18th 1716.

Includes:
Twenty and Seven Leather Chairs	6:	15:	-
40000 Nailes two old Chests	10:	-	-
Seven old chairs	-:	14:	-
one fowling peice	1:	-	-
one Tankard two Salts Do one Cup of silver	9:	-	-
Eight Diaper and 12 Course old knapkins	1:	-	-
Three Table Cloths one Diaper old	1:	-	-
a parcell of books	4:	10:	-
one doz mixt forks and Eight knives	-	7:	-
One Silver Case w'th a Cut Seal	-	5:	-
two lignum vite punch bowls	-	15:	-
one Earthen Do	-	2:	6

Belonging to the Home House
----
10 drinking Glasses one silver hilted Sword and belt one pr of Leather Baggs three Cyder Casks 4 small books 1 file 1 pr small stilliards and three stears
Two suits of wareing apparell and some shurts and other wearing Cloaths
And at the several plantations about 100 Barels of Corn

Total valuation of this exceedingly long inventory L 857: 11: 3

       Signed Salvator Muscoe
             Ja Alderson
             Edwm Moseley

page 733
Addl Inventory. Signed Mary Gouldman and Th Waring.

"At a Court cont'd and held for Essex County on Wednesday the 16th day of January 1716 (1716/17)
The Inventory within mentioned being returned is recorded
            Test
             Tho Henman
               Cl Cur"

FINIS

Ex 9   98

Essex County, Virginia.
Deeds and Wills   -   No. 15
1716 - 1718.

Due to my having out certain detail from the abstracts of entries in Number 14, all of which may be obtained easily by reference to the original in the Archives Division of the Virginia State Library, Richmond, Virginia, I have been able to include a few of the first items in No. 15. These follow.   Beverley Fleet.

No. 15. page 1. Lease and Release. 18 - 19 March 1716/17. Casper Coston, smith, and Mary his wife, of St. A. Par., Essex Co., sells to Robt. Farish of St. Steph: Par. King and Queen Co., 250 acres "being the reversion of a patton of 1000 acres of land formerly granted to Richard Jones and George Turner bearing date the eight day of ffebr 1672". This land being in Essex and K. & Q. Counties, upon the heads of the Dragon, Ashnamanseot and Piscatua branches. (if one could only see these serene, bland and beautifully blue waters so cursed with these awe inspiring names). Adjs a marsh at the head of one of the Dragon branches, by Maj'r Ajlots (ie. Ailet, Aylett, thereof the Hon. Patrick Henry Aylett and the still more inspired Cousin Emily Aylett) Quarter, formerly known by the name of Goodrichs land, the land of Sheffells old field, Alexander Youngers house and the head of a branch of ffishers mill. Also Capt Brereton's land. "the above patton descending to me the sd Mary Coston as being heir at Law to my only sister Sarah Shipley late deceased which was left by will of George Boyce to my sd sister Sarah Shipley"

Wit: Signed   Casper Coston
Jno Bates   Mary x Coston
John Boughan
Tho: x St John   Rec. 19 March 1716/17

Note: And it seems that I must further complicate this entry by remarking that the pronunciation hereabouts of the charming old English name of Sheffield is "Shuffles".   B.F.

No. 15. page 4. Lease and Release. 18 - 19 Feb. 1716/17. Danl. Smith of Essex Co., sells Geo. Robinson of same Co., for 3000 lb tobo, part of a tract formerly belonging to Thos. Meadows. Adj. land of Geo Loyd, Stony Hill, etc.
Wit: Signed   Daniell Smith
John Hill   Isabell x Smith
Thomas x Griffin
Robt Elliott

Isabell, the wife of sd Dan'll Smith, relinq. dower rights.
Recorded 19 March 1716/17
Test Will: Beverley Cl Cur

No. 15 page 6. Lease and Release. 7 - 8 Feb. 1716/17. Thos. Freshwater of Farn. Par. Richmond Co., Gent., sells Danl. Hornby, of same Par., Gent., for 20000 lb. tobo., 600 acres in St. Marys Par. Essex Co. being part of a pat. dated 1 Aug. 1665, granted Thos. Chattwood of 2000 acres. Adjs Moon Creek, etc.
Wit: Signed   Thomas x ffreshwater
James Juge
T Mountjoy
Martin Kemp   Rec. 19 March 1716/17

No. 15. page 7. Lease and Release. 15 - 16 March 1716/17. Richd. Price of Essex Co., sells Robt. Graves of same Co., for L 60. Sterl., 120 a. in So. F. Par., on S. side Piscattaway Creek, one acre excepted to be laid off square and commonly known as Storepoint Landing. Which tract was pur. from Richd. Wise by sd Price, and by sd Wise purchased of Daniel Austin and Susanna his wife. And all that Island of land and marsh lying in Piscataway Creek aforesd next above the ferry containing by patent 80 acres, "called and known by the name of Rogues Island", which sd Price likewise pur. of Richd. Wise, and by sd Wise pur. of Jno Picket.
Wit: Signed   Richard Price
Saml Clayton
Alexander Graves
Paul x Gibins   Rec. 19 March 1716/17

No. 15 page 9. Deed. 4 Jan. 1716/17. Wm Tharpe, planter, of St. A. Par. Essex Co., sells Cornelius Reynolds, planter, of same Par. and Co., for 3000 lb. tobo., 50 acres, adj. Cattail run, Cockelshell branch, the lan of George Andrews and Thos Tharpe, the corner of Tharps land which he formerly bought of Robert Paine, etc.
Wit: Signed   William Tharp
Samuel Bizwell
Thomas x Ayres
Henry Long   Rec. 19 March 1716/17

No. 15. page 10. Lease and Release. 18 - 19 Feb. 1716/17. Thos. Griffin of Essex Co., sells Geo. Robinson of same Co., 100 acres, part of a tract formerly belonging to Thos. Meadows.
Wit:
John Sanders   Signed   Thomas x Griffin
William Bramlitt   Ann   x Griffin

                               Rec. 19 March 1716/17

Ex 9

No. 15. page 12. Deed. 14 Feb 1717 (1716/17). Thomas Ayres, planter, of St. A. Par., Essex Co., sells Henry Long junr, planter, of same Par., for 2500 lb. tobo., 50 acres, wch sd Ayres bought of Geo. Andrews and lies in sd Par. Adj sd Andrews, line of Thos. Tharp, line of Jno Hackley, line of Geo. Proctor, etc.
Wit: Signed   Thomas x Ayres
Samuel Bizwell
Corneles Reynolds (sic)
William Tharp   Rec. 19 March 1716.

No. 15. page 13. Lease and Release. 18 - 19 Feb 1716/17. Wm Richardson, planter, of So. Farn. Par., sells John Smith Junr, planter, of same Par. for 4600 lb. tobo., 152 acres in sd Par. 102 acres of same being granted by Escheat Patent to Robt Richardson, deceased, father of sd William. The other 50 acres being pur. from Patrick Doring by sd Robt Richardson. The patent dated 10 June 1714 and the deed dated - --. The 152 acres adj lands of Henry Shackelford, John Cill and Daniel Brown.
Wit:
James Rennolds   Signed   William Richardson
James Boughan jr
Jos Baker

Dorothy the wife of Wm Richardson relinq dower rights.

Rec. 19 March 1716/17

No. 15. page 15. Deed. 9 Feb. 1716/17. Richard Bush of So. Farn. Par., sells Mary Merriwether of same Par., for L 100., 150 acres "including the plantation where the sd Richard Bush formerly dwelt and likewise the planta'con the sd Bush purchased of John Waters where the sd Bush now dwells", lying in sd Par., being part of 550 acres included in a patent of 700 acres granted to John Beby the 4th October 1653, and renewed 13 Feb 166- (1662 or 1664). Land adj. a gut issuing out of Piscataway Creek, the line of Richard Cauthorn near his house, a branch issueing out of Beaver Dam Swamp, the bounds of land the sd Bush sold to Francis Meriwether the 11th Dec 1708, etc.
Wit:
James x Webb   Signed   Richard Bush
Richard x Cauthorn
Benja Morris

Elizabeth, wife of Richd Bush, relinq dower rights.

Rec. 19 March 1716/17

Ex 9

No. 15. page 19. Will of Thomas Frank of So. Farn. Par. Dated 10 Oct. 1715. Prob. 15th Jan. 1715/16. Further proved 19 March 1716/17.
Land and plantation "I now live on to my son Thomas ffrank", he failing
    in heirs "to my three daughters to wit Catherine Anne and Mary
    ffrank"
Personal property to wife Martha Frank, son and three daus. If wife
    marry again then son Thos. to be of age at 18.
Exors wife and son Thos.
Wit: Signed   Thomas x ffrank
Nathan'll Sanders
Henry Purkins junr

No. 15. page 18. "An acc'ot of the estate of Alce Shipley come to my hands sence the Inventory returned
to empty Tobacco hogshed
                                John Shipley

At a Court held for Essex County on the 19th day of March 1716 (1716/17
    John Shipley Exor of the last will and testament of Alice Shipley
dec'd this day presented this additional Inventory of the sd dec'od
Alice's estate which was by the Court ordered to be recorded
                              Test
                                  Will: Beverley Cl Cur "

No. 15. page 18. Bond. 19 March 1716/17. L 500. Sterl. ffrances Critten den as Admrx of Henry Crittenden decd.
Wit: Signed   ffrances x Crittenden
Salvator Muscoe   Wm Upshaw
                                    Nath'l ffogg
                Rec. 19 March 1716/17.

No. 15. page 18. Bond. 20 March 1716/17. L 1000. Sterl. Jno Taliaferro as admr. of est. of Elizabeth Taliaferro deceased
Wit:
Jno Griffin   Signed   Jno Taliaferro
                                    Thomas Cattlett

                Rec. 20 March 1716/17

Ex 9   102

No. 15. page 19. Bond. 20 March 1716/17. L 500. Sterl. James Booth as guardian of William Booth an orphan.

Wit: Signed   James Booth
Thomas Edwards   Richd Covington
John Boughan   Ro Brooke junr

No. 15. page 20. Bond in duplicate of above excepting James Booth as guardian of Margaret Booth an orphan.

No. 15. page 20.   Williamsons estate Inv'ry

I Richard Brush the first subscriber being ordered by the Court the 18th of X ber 1716 to take care and charge of the estate of James Williamson deseasd therefore I have taken these two subscribes to see a right And true Inventory of the same estate as followeth Vizt

To 2 old pewter dishes and 3 plates one frying pan and a small Iron pott a siftin tray and a small wooden bowle
To one old fother bed and boulster two old pillows and cases two new Cotton blankets one rug and bedsted a straw matt and some cord one Cattale bed and boulster one old blankit and an old rugg
To one old sadle and sadlecloth one small pewter Tankerd one bason Do one saltseller and two scimers 16 old pewter spoons and one brass Candlestick
To one old cutting knife
To one pair brass scales 7 glass bottles one peck of salt and about 8 pd of Beef one box Iron and heiters one pr flesh forks a small pr potthooks one feyl one spere
To 2 old hoes a piggin 5 wooden bowles one rowling scrafe 2 old sifters one old hatt 2 old looking glasses one small picter one small faune skin one gimblet about 3 hundred single tenns a small hamer about 3 pd of woole one pr of Deer skins one little trunk wth papers one linen Do one half flick Do one swanskin petticoth one black gowne and pettecoth one scikerd aparen 5 do of pipes one large mugg and one small one do one small pr sisors one mans inkcloth one square pt bottle with some powder in it 5 yards of kirsy 2 doz Coth buttons (sic) 2 hanks of mohair and 2 skans of threed on hone and rasor one Eyfry comne about 8 pd of tallo one knife about 4 hundred sharp pointed nails one smale trunk with some heed linen one old trowell one old adse
To one Chost 2 old boxes 2 old chirshe and a little barskit one old sworde 4 books one beefs hyde

                                        Us
                                        Richard Bush
                                        Godfrey Pile
                                             his
                                        Georg R Roberts
                                             mark

I the subscriber have received an Inv'ry of Richard Bush drawed as within mentioned of James Williamsons deceassed estate which perticulers I

(continued)

Ex 9

The Estate of James Williamson (continued)

know to belonge to the said Williams (sic) estate since there hath appeared divers other goods w'ch in obedience to an order of Court dated January - 1716/17 and do return the within mentioned perticulers Vizt

To one old gun 8 head of cattle 5 head of hoggs 2 hoggs vallewed at by George Robberts and Richard Webb to be worth 80 pounds of tobacco per hogg and three hoggs that I killed weighed 223 pounds and 184 pounds of ground leaves unstemmed a parcell of Indian corn and an old axe 2 old hoes and a grubbing hoe and 2 small earthen potts

               Wm Smith

At a Court held for Essex County on the 20th day of March 1716 (1716/17)
This Inventory of the estate of James Williamson decd was this day returned by William Smith who made oath thereto and by the Court ordered to be recorded

            Test
              Will: Beverley   Cl Cur.

No. 15. page 21. Bond. 21 March 1716/17. L 20. Sterl. Peter Byrom as admr. of Est. of Jacob Sherwood decd., "during the minority of Jacob Sherwood son of the sd deced".
Wit: Signed Peter Byrom
Ro Brooke jr   Wm Winston
Thomas Edwards   Rec. 21 March 1716/17

No. 15. page 22. "In obedience to an order of Court dated the 17th of January Anno Domini 1716 we the subscribers whose names are underwritten being first sworn did meet on the land of William Hudson with Mr Robert Brooks (sic) surveyor on the 4th day of this instant and did then procession and lay of the land of William Hudson in manner and form following Beginning at a marked Red oak on the North side of Coxes Creek and thence runing North East by North seventy four pole to a marked red oak saplin and from thence South East by East one hundred eighty four poles to the Creek In witness whereof wee have hereunto set our hands this 4th day of ffebruary 1716" (1716/17)

Jos: Baker	Wm Moss	Tho x Burnet
Nath'll ffogg	James Booth	Cha: Grishun
Ephriam Paget	Wm Allen	Jno: Ball
Jn'o Bates	Richard Jones	Wm Dunn

At a Court held for Essex County on the 21st day of March 1716
This report being returned was by the Court ordered to be recorded
            Test
              Will: Beverley   Cl Cur

Ex 9

No. 15. page 21. Bond. 20 March 1716/17. L 20. Sterl. John Hawkins appeals to the Genl. Court from judgt. to deft. in case "John Hawkins plt agt Mr Matthew Page deft".
Wit: Signed   John Hawkins
Thomas Edwards   John Boughan
                       Rec. 20 March 1716/17

Note: The columns in the list to follow are headed in the original; "What the Books Contain", "When Begun", "When Ended", "In What Condition", "Alphabetted or Not", all abbreviated here in an attempt not to crowd the page.   B.F.

Book 15. page 22.   "List of Essex Court Records"

A List of Essex County Court Records taken the 11th day of March 1716.

In Bound Bookes

Contents	Begun	Ended	Condition	Index
Conveyances Bonds Lr atto &c	1663	1665	Cover worn off	some of the Alphabet torn
Ord'rs	May 3d 1665	Novembr 5th 1679	Cover much worn	not alphabetted
Conveyances &c	1666	1676	Cover worn	Alphabetted
Conveyances	1677	1683	Good	Not Alphabetted
Inv'rys and Wills	1682	1686/7	Good	Alphabetted
Wills & Inv'rys	1672	1683	Loose in the binding	Alphabetted
Ordrs	April 7 1679	Jan'ry 8th 1683	Loose in the binding	Not Alphabetted
Conveyances	1682	1692	Good	Alphabetted
Wills & Invrys	1672	1683	Loose in the binding	Alphabetted
Ord'rs	April 7th 1679	Janry 8th 1683	Loose in the binding	Not Alphabetted

Ex 9.

List of Essex County Records 1717 (continued)

Contents	Begun	Ended	Condition	Index
Conveyances	1682	1692	Good	Alphabetted
Ordrs	ffebry 6th 1683/4	Septembr 1st 1686	Good	Not Alphabetted
Ordrs	Octobr 6th 1686	April 6 1692	Good	Not Alphabetted
Wills & Invrys	March 1686/7	April 1692	Good	Alphabetted
Ordrs Deeds Bonds Wills Invrys &c	May 10th 1692	Decembr 10th 1695	Good	Alphabetted
Ordrs	ffebry 10th 1695	June 21st 1699	Good	Not Alphabetted
Deeds Bonds Wills Invrys &c	ffebry 10th 1695	June 21 1699	Good	Alphabetted
Ordrs Deeds Bonds Wills &c	August 10th 1699	March 11th 1702	Good	Alphabetted
Ordr's	June 10th 1703	March 11th 1707/8	Good	Not Alphabetted
Conveyances &c	1704	1707	Good	Alphabetted
Conveyances &c	July 1707	October 1711	Good	Alphabetted
Conveyances &c	November 1711	Janry 1714	Good	Not Apbt.

In Unbound Bookes

Conveyances Wills Invrys &c	1656	1659	Good	Alphabetted
Ordrs	ffebry 4th 1656	ffebry 2nd 1659	Indifferent	Not Apbt'd
Ordrs	May 2d 1660	September 8th 1664	Torn at both ends	Not Apbt'd
Conveyances &c	1660	1663	Torn at both ends	Alphabet torn

(continued)

Ex 9   106

List of Essex County Records 1717 (continued)
Unbound Books.

Contents	Begun	Ended	Condition	Index
Depositions	1660	1671	Good	Alphabetted
Ordrs	Septembr 8th 1664	March 3rd 1664 (1664/5)	Good	Not Alphabetted
L'rs Atto Dep's) Protests &c)	1672	1675	Good	Alphabetted
Lrs Atto Protests &c	1675	1681	Good	Alphabetted
Bonds Lrs Atto) Protests &c)	1680	1681	Torn at the Beginning	Not Alphabetted
Bonds Lrs Atto &c	1681	1683	Good	Alphabetted
Depo: Bonds Procla) &c)	1683	1684	Torn at the latter end	Not Alphabetted
Bonds &c	1684	1685	Indifferent	Not Alphabetted
Depo: Bonds &c	1685	1687	Torn at the beginning	Not Alphabetted
Depo: Bonds &c	1687	1689	Good	Not Alphabetted
Bonds Lrs atto &c	1689	1690	Good	Not Alphabetted
Conveyances &c	June 1703	June 1704	Good	Alphabetted

At Essex March 19th then the above list examined in the office

      Joseph Smith
      Reub'n Welch

At a Court held for Essex County on the 21st day of March 1716
This list being examined was by the Court ordered to be recorded

      Test
      Will: Beverley Cl Cur

Ex 9.

No. 15 page 23. "Jurys report on processioning the bounds of Craswells land". By order of Essex Court dated 19 July 1716 the subscribers surveyed and processioned the land of James Craswell in So. F. Par. granted by pat. 18 Apl. 1670 to Amy Johnson. The land adjs a little branch of Yorker swamp. Another part of Craswell's land adj line of a pat. granted to John Sharp. Dated 15 Aug. 1716.

Ja Edmondson	James Boughan jr	Henry Alcocke
James Webb	Dan'll Browne	Edward Smart
Wm St John	Henry Perkins	John Adcocke
Thos Bryan	John Dyke	Richd x Dobbins

Ro Brooke junr D S E C
(Deputy Surveyor Essex Co.)

Rec. 22 March 1716/17

No. 15. page 24. Appeal Bond. 22 March 1716/17. L 50. Current money of Virginia. Judgt. being given in Essex Co. Court in dif. betw. William Johnson and William Hudson, and Johnson ord'd to pay costs: and Johnson appealing to the Genl. Court, etc.

Wit: Signed   Wm Johnson
R Beverley   John Boughan
Wm St John   Rec. 22 March 1716/17

No. 15. page 24. Power of Atty. 25 June 1716. Saml Randall Jr of the City of Cork, merchant, and Mary Randall als Pope, his wife, to "our well beloved friend Thomas Wills of Bristoll mercht", to collect money in Virginia. Also to sell "the plantation and lands lying and being at or near Popes Creek in Westmorl'd County in Potomac River in Virginia"

Wit:
Jonathan rennells   Signed   Saml Randall Junr
William x Brewer   Mary Randall
William Maybery Jr
Essex Bosher

Proved in Westmorland Co., 27 March 1717 by oath of Wm Maybery
            Test
                Thos Sorrell   Cler Com
"Recordat Decimo sexto die April 1717"

Prov. Essex Co., by oath of Essex Bosher 21st May 1717.

No. 15. page 25. Lease and Release. 20 - 21 May 1717. William Smith and Anne his wife of So. Farn. Par., Essex Co., sell Mr Lewis Latane of sd Par. and Co., Gent., for 4000 lb. tobo., 200 acres adj main swamp of

(continued)

Ex 9.

Piscattaway Creek, "being part of a devident of land belonging to Mr James ffullerton decd and by the sd James ffullertons last will and testament bearing date the 21st day of March 1677/8 was given and bequeathed unto his daughter Hannah ffullerton mother to the aforemen'coned Anne Smith".
Wit: Signed Wm Smith
Jos Baker Anne x Smith
Wm Dobyns
David x Lewis   Rec. 21 May 1717.

No. 15, page 27. Lease and Release. 20 - 21 May 1717. John Sanders of St. Marys Par. Essex Co., planter, sells Laurence Taliaferro of same Par., for L 25. Sterl., 100 acres in St. M. Par., part of a pat. granted sd Jno. Sanders 23 Mar. 1715/16. Adj. land formerly granted to Warwick Camock, the land of Meader and Pertous (or Pertons).
Wit:
Jno Taliaferro Junr   Signed John Sanders
Jno Taliaferro
Jno Boughan   Rec. 21 May 1717.

No. 15, page 29. Sanders bond to Taliaferro.

No. 15. Deed. 12 Feb. 1716/17. Wm Stokes of St. A. Par., Essex County, planter, sells Salvator Muscoe of Sd. Par., planter, for 1200 lb. tobo., 150 acres in same Par., adj. Moseleys Swamp, the main road below Stokes dwelling, Arthur McDaniels plantation, William Jones bridge in Moseleys Swamp, corner tree to Aaron Perry, etc.
Wit: Signed William x Stokes
John Smith
Thomas Jones
William x Stokes
John Hunter
Jno. Simcock   Rec. 21 May 1717.

No. 15, page 31. Memo. that full and peaceable possession, etc. Dated 13 Feb. 1716/17. Witnessed by:
Andrew x Pritchet
Arthur x McDaniel
Elizabeth x McDaniel

Rec. 21 May 1717.

No. 15, page 31. Lease and Release. 17 - 18 May 1717. Wm Smith of "Abbington" parish, Gloucester Co., gent., sells Richd. Johnson of St. Marys Par. Essex Co., for L 50. Sterling, 200 acres in St Marys Par.,

Ex 9.

on S. side Rappahannock River, adj. land of John Gresham, Giles run, etc.
Wit: Signed Wm Smith
Law: Taliaferro
Jno Taliaferro Junr
Robt Taliaferro Recorded 21 May 1717.

No. 15. page 33. Lease and Release. 20 - 21 May 1717. Augustine Smith of Essex Co., sells Robert Taliaferro of same Co., 200 acres in Essex, on S. side of Rappa., being lower part of 600 acres granted to Charles Grimes.
Wit: Signed Aug't Smith
Jno: Taliaferro junr
Richard Johnson
Richard x Long Recorded 21 May 1717.

No. 15. page 35. Lease and Release. 1 - 2 January 1716/17. John Todd of Stafford Co., sells John Cattlet Jr., of Essex Co., 15o acres formerly purchased by John Bush of William Pannell, Thomas Pannell and James Phillips, adj. lands of Coll Jno. Catlet and land of Henry Brice.
Wit:
Wm Harrison Signed John x Todd
Andr: Harrison
Wm Dixon Recorded 21 May 1717.

INDEX

Adams, Jam 58
Adcocke, Henry 68. 78
          John 107
Alcocke, Henry 107
Alderson, Ann 92
          James 4. 5. 6. 9
                15. 18. 40. 57.
                74. 75. 92. 97.
Allen, Dinah 65.
       Erasmus 11. 35. 64. 65.
                69. 72.
       John 11.
       Margaret 65.
Allin, Ross 36.
       Valentine 21. 84.
       Wm. 33. 65. 103
Amax, Wm. 3
Andrecos, Jno. 67
Andrews, Geo. 99. 100.
         Jno. 75. 86.
Attwood, Wm. 58
Austin, Danl 99
        Susanna 99
Axam, Wm 3. 5.
Awberry, Francis 89
         Henry 50
Aylett, Major Wm. 15. 18. 98
Ayres, John 71
       Thos. 10. 42. 46. 53.
             65. 66. 77. 84.
             85. 99. 100.

Bagge, Rev. John, 3. 5. 23. 35.
              38. 48. 49. 90. 91
       Mary 3.
       William 49
Baker, Jos. 22. 38. 48. 51. 85.
            100. 103. 108.
Ball, John 103
Barbee, John 3.
Bartlett, Patience 71
          Saml. 87
          Tho. 37. 71
Bates, John, 54. 57. 85. 98. 103.
Baxter, Chas. 62

Beby, Jno. 100
Beckham, Ledia 85. 87
         Simon 39. 85. 87
Beesly, Wm. 43
Beeswell - see Biswell, Bizwell
Bell, Jno. 66
Bene, Thos. 39
Bentlet - 82
Berkeley, Sir Wm. 66
Berry, - 55
       Henry, 1
       Margaret 21
       Wm. 21. 24. 34. 79. 83
Beverley, Mr. 60
          Christopher 36. 47.
          Harry 92
          Robert, 2. 3. 35. 38.
                 39. 87. 91. 107.
          William 11. 22. 95.
                  98. 101. 103. 106
Biesle (prob. Bizwell)
       Henry 73. 74.
       Wm. 73
Billington, Mrs Mary 87
Billups, Dorothy 50
         John 50. 61. 72. 90.
Bird, Arrabella 89
Bizwell - Beeswell, Bizwell and
          prob. Biesle.
       Ann 69
       Danl 69
       Erasmus 69
       Jeremiah 13. 66. 67. 69.
                71.
       John 69
       Robt. 69. 71
       Sarah 69. 71
       Saml. 21. 44. 55. 66. 71
              84. 94. 99. 100.
Blackburn, Elias 82
           Christopher 82
Blagborn - 77
Booker, Edmund 46. 64.
        Edw. 87
        Richd. 44. 45. 51. 65. 66
               67. 80. 85. 87.

Booten, Joshua 4
Booth, Mr. 93
    Humphrey 9
    James 23. 54. 102. 103.
    John 9.
    Margaret, 23. 54. 102.
    Phebe 23. 54.
    Wm. 23. 54. 102.
Borne, Hester 64
    Wm. 64
Bosher, Essex 107
Boughan - 89
    Major 59
    Henry 24. 78
    James, 7. 11. 15. 18.
        22. 38. 48. 70.
        73. 75. 88.
    James Jr. 75. 100. 107
    John 1. 5. 19. 23. 34.
        46. 47. 52. 53. 54.
        65. 67. 69. 70. 71.
        72. 73. 75. 86. 98.
        102. 104. 107.
    Mary 19
    Sarah 43. 75.
Boulter, Jno. 12
    Margarett 12
    Wm. of Eggbury 12
Boulware, Eliz. 84
    James, Jr. 46
    Jno. 1
    Mark 46
Boulwares Storehouse 6.
Bowers, Mr. 35. 37.
    Arthur, 16. 68. 90.
    Charles 55.
Boyce, Geo. 98
Brame, Richins 63.
Bramlit, Wm. 58. 99
Braxton, Geo. 79
Brewer, Wm. 107.
Brereton, Capt. 98
Brice, Henry 14. 76. 109
Bristow, Jno. 63
    Nicholas 63
Broch, Geo. 2
Broock, Wm. 4
Brooke, Mr. 4
    Hum. 16. 18.

Brooke, Robert Jr. 5. 7. 9. 10. 12.
    18. 38. 40. 57. 59. 77.
    90. 91. 102. 103. 107.
Brooking, Susanna, 75
    Wm. 75. 79
Brooks, Mary 7.
Brown, Buchingham (?) 3
    Buckingham 80. 81
    Buckner 2. 3.
(Can it possibly be that the origin
of the Virginia name 'Buckner' is
'Buckingham' ?)
(2nd note: We all remember those Va.
tournaments, when the knights of
this and that rode to the rings. I
amongst them. Now it comes to me
that the greatest gentleman of all
all Europe, who kept the nude portrait of Anne of Austria, behind a
curtain, over the alter in his
chapel, and who rode so well to
the rings, was known to his in-
timates as 'Buckner'.   B.F.
Brown, Charles 21. 37. 77.
    Charles, Jr., 77
    Danl. 70. 77. 100. 107.
    Danl. Sr., 11
    Eliz. 69
    Francis, Sr., 15
    Henry 15.
    Margaret 46
    William 46
Browning, Anne 19
    Francis 19. 21. 89
Brush (Bush) Richd. 102
Brutnall, Richd. 88
Bryan, Thos. 73. 86. 107.
Bryant, Thos. 51
Buckner, Eliz. 22. 100
    Richd. 1. 6. 22. 36. 39.
    60. 93.
Bull, Jacob. 24
Burnett, Thos. 11. 62. 103.
Bush, Jno. 82. 109.
    Margaret 82
    Richd. 51. 53. 79. 100.
Butler, Jno. 69
    William 80
Button, Tho. 79

Ex. 9.

Button's Range 7
Byrom, Henry 81
       Peter 7. 38. 65. 93. 103

Callicot, Jno. 95
Calloway, Jos. 19
Cammock, Warwick 108
Cane, Richd. 39.
Cannaday, Jas. 85
       John 81. 85
Camebridg, Edmund 56
Cappell, Geo. 15. 16. 17
Cardin, Jno. 55
Carter, Richd. 63
       Saml. 55
Caston see Coston, Cosston,
       Costone, etc.
Catlett - 70
       Col. 92
       John 109
       Tho. 63. 72. 95. 101.
       Wm. 70
Cauthorn, Richd. 100
Chace, Wm. 74. 78
Chamberlain, Jno. 23. 62. 70.
Chance, Wm. 63
Chattwood, Tho. 99
Cheeke see Chick
Cheeke, Sinor 11
Chew, Larkin 33
Chick, Jno. 11. 22. 48.
Chiswell, Cha. 33
Churchill, Mrs. 35.
Cills, Jno. 100
Clapham, Wm. 94
Clarke, Jno. 20.
       Wm. 50
Clayton, Saml. 57. 75. 99.
Clowder, Jeremiah 35
Coates, Saml. 59. 94
Coatleland, Jas. 63
Cocke, Wm. 9. 10
Coffey, Ann 3. 88. 91
       Austis 88
       Edw. 3. 79. 88. 91
       Elizabeth 88
       Jno. 79. 88
       Martha 88

Coghill, Fredk. 44. 45. 46. 64. 66.
       80. 87. 94.
      James, 55. 66. 77. 87
      Mary, 44
      Sarah, 66
      Susanna, 45. 66
      Thos. 44
Colegate, Richd. 24
Coleman, Capt. 60
      Mrs. Ann 15. 18
      Edw. 70
      Robt. 15. 70
      Spilsbe 68
      Thos 15. 75
Coles, William 94
Collier, Jno. 16
Collins, Matthew, 46. 58. 77
Connelly, Anne 22
Cooke, Jno. 35. 52. 53
      Susanna 52
Cooper, Richd. 88
      Wm 78
Copeland, Nicho. 47
Corbin, Col. Gawin 42
Cornew, Jane 3
Costono, Carey 96
      Casper 64. 98
      Mary, 52. 98
Coutance, Jno. 3
Courtney, Patrick 36
Covington, Richd. 6. 14. 18. 23. 39.
         46. 63. 68. 69. 84
         87. 88. 89. 90. 91.
         102.
      William 68. 86. 94. 96.
      Capt. Wm. 94
      William, Jr., 10. 17. 24.
         48. 68. 69. 75. 77.
         87. 94.
Cox, Ann 57
      Lem. 16
      Thos. 57
Crittendon, Francis 101
         Henry 101
Crosswell, Jas 56
Crow, Jno. 70. 77. 92.
      Thos. 63.
Crutcher, Hugh 45

Dangerfield, Wm. 2. 31. 52. 56
    63. 65. 68. 73. 95
Daniell, Wm. 21. 24. 77. 80.
Davis, Matthew 39
    Thos. 10. 36.
    Wm. 37
Deverell, Benj. 16. 39. 40
Dickinson, Jno. 88
    Thos 55. 87
Dier see Dyer
Dike, Jno. 51
    Judith 51
Diskin, Danl. 14. 17. 35
Dixon, Wm. 109
Dobbins, Danl. 63. 78. 84. 107
    108.
Donelly, Arthur 78
Doores, Charles 66
    Charles Jr. 66
    James 66
Doring, Patrick 100
Doubly, Jno. 40
Doughty, Enock, 19. 21. 89.
Dowers, Chas 75
    Sarah 75
Downing, Geo. 16
Driscoll, Kath. 63
    Timothy 12. 63. 76
Duckbary, Geo. 44. 51. 66
    Mary 44. 45. 51
Duden, Thos. 64
Dunbar, Jno. 55
Dunn, Wm. 103
Dyer, Andrew 11
    Jeffrey 84. 88
    Mary 62
Dyke, Jno. 107

Earle, John 28
Edmondson, Benj. 92
    Bryan 7. 42. 43. 96
    James 7. 42. 43. 84.
        85. 87. 91. 107
    John 42. 43.
    Joseph 42. 43
    Judith 7
    Mary 42. 43
    Saml 7. 43. 88
    Thos. 42. 43. 96
    Wm. 7. 42. 43

Edwards, Kath. 91
    Mary 91
    Richd 21. 34. 83
    Thos. 91. 102. 103. 104.
Elliott see Ellitt and variations.
    Johanna 37
    Robt. 7. 16. 17. 23. 37. 39
        77. 90. 91. 96. 98.
Elliot's Ordinary 72
Ellitts, Jno. 14. 19. 58. 76. 79.
    Robt. 16
Elton, Isaac 31. 32.
Emerson, Tho. 62
Evans - 81
    John, 40. 50. 62. 68. 78. 89
Evans Mill 68
Evered, Wm 68

Farish, Robt. 98
Farmer, Margaret 42
    Thos. 42. 53
Falconer, Nicholas 38. 91
Farguson see Ferguson
Farrell, Charles 56. 92
Fellows, John 81
Fenwick, Thos. 3. 77
Ferguson, Jno. 49
    Joshua, 70
Ferry bond 5
Fisher, Benj. 5. 24. 36. 50. 73. 78
    86. 96.
    Mrs. Eliz. 73. 86
    Francis 12
    James 73
    John 73
    Jonathan 39. 73. 78
Fitzhugh, Henry 32
    John 32
Fleming, Alex 8
Flowers, Martha 52
    Sarah 52
Fogg, Nath'l. 5. 35. 39. 56. 60. 84
    86. 94. 101. 103.
Forbush, Mary 38
Foster, Anthony 54
    Eliz 54. 87
    Geo. 54
    Jas. 54. 87
    Jno. 54
    Margaret 54

Ex 9.

Foster, Richd. 54
    Robt. 54. 87
    Thos. 54
    Wm. 54
Frank, Anne 101
    Catherine 101
    Martha 101
    Mary 101
    Thos. 101
    Thos. Jr. 101
Freshwater, Thos. 19
Fullerton, Hannah 108
    Jas. 9. 18. 31. 108
    Thos. 99

Gaines, Bernard 36. 37
    John 62. 77
Garnett, James 37
    Thos 54
Gatewood, Jno. 18. 72
    Richd. 2. 4. 11. 23. 37
Gefferys, Wm. 63
George of Brunswick and Lunen-
    burg (George I) 6
Gibins, Paul 99
Gibson - 78
    Francis 52. 86
    John 86
Gillson, Mr. 19
    Andrew 48
Ginkins see Jenkins
Ginnin (?) Michael 93
Goare, Jno. 12
Godfrey, Eliz. 57
    Peter 9. 57. 73. 77. 95.
Golding, Cassandra 8
    John 8. 18
Goode, Richd. 42. 83. 92
    Richd. Jr. 21. 83
Goodrich, Coll. 98
Gordon, Geo. 3
Gouge, James 94
Gougey, Eliz. 58
    Richd. 58
Gougey see Guggey
Gough, Ralph 51. 52. 53. 56. 63. 64. 65. 66. 67. 69. 70. 72. 74. 81. 82. 84. 85. 87. 88. 90/ 91. 95.

Gouldman, Edw. 7. 59. 90
    Col. Francis 3. 4. 6. 7. 35. 39. 52. 54. 56. 57. 63. 89. 90. 97.
    Martha 39
    Mary 90. 97
    Thos. 56. 89. 90
Gouldman's land 82
Gray, Abner 66
Graves, Alex 63. 99.
    Jas. 40.
    Jane 22
    John 35. 86
    Mrs. Mary 63
    Robt. 99
    Thos. 88
Gray, Abner 66
    Wm. 66
Green, Geo. 82
Greenhill, Paschal 55. 62. 90
Gregsby, Jno. 32
Gregory, Cath. 22
Gregson, Thos. 4
Gresham, Chas. 81. 86. 103
    John 109
Griffin, Ann 8. 99
    James. 9. 18
    Jno. 101
    Kath. 34 A
    Thos. 8. 14. 51. 69. 76. 82. 98. 99.
Griggs, Jno. 11. 61.
Grymes, Charles 109
Gugge, Richd. 66
Guggey, Eliz. 55. 56
    Richd. 55. 56. 66.

Hackley, Jno. 100
Haile, Jno. 57. 73. 78.
Hakes, Wm. 39.
Hall, Martin 62
    Tho. 58
Halloway, Jno. 3
Hamer, Wm. 39
Handerkin, Kath. 11
    Thos. 11
Handerkin see Henderkin
Hardee, Andrew 59. 61. 62.
    Joseph 61
    Robt. 40. 59
Harding, Thos. 81
Hardwicke, George 12

Hardwicke, James 12
Harford, Theophilus 84
Haris, Eliz. 77
Hares, Jno. 77 (Harris)
Harper, Jno. 75. 88
    William 1
Harrison, Andrew 66. 67. 93. 109
    Andrew Jr. 76
    John 21
    Robt. 82
    William 76. 109
Hart, Francis 20
    John 88
Hartnell, Saml 58
Harwar, Sarah 63
Hathaway, Thos. 79. 83
Hawes, Saml. 93
Hawkins, Capt. 35
    John 1. 5. 16. 70. 80. 83. 104.
Hayes, Danl. 22. 57. 74
Hayman, Ann 43
Haymon, Jno. 2
Haywerton, Thos. Jr. 87
Henderkin, Jno. 11
Henman, Thomas, 6. 11. 14. 17. 20. 22. 31. 32. 34. 37. 39. 61. 71. 72. 79. 83. 84. 87. 89. 90. 93. 95. 97.
Henman, Tho. App. Clerk E. Co 9. 10
Henshaw, Keziah 52
    Saml. 52. 53. 86
Hickman, R. 51. 53. 57.
Hide, Jonathan 24. 25
Hill, Henry 76
    John 35. 98
    Leonard 15. 16. 17. 23. 59. 68. 69.
Hilliard, Thos. 81. 93.
Hipkins, Cordela 74
    Thos. 74. 77. 79. 82
Hodgson, Eliz 21
    Jno. 21. 84
Holland, Peter 79
Holloway see Halloway
Hornby see Onbee
    Danl. 99
How, Alex. 61

Howerton, Thos 68
Howlet, Wm. 7
Hubbard, Jno. 12
Hucklecot, Tho. 11
Hudson, Edw. 55. 62
    Henry 78
    John 3. 21. 73. 74. 76
    Rebecca 2. 55. 62.
    Wm. 32. 50. 55. 62. 74. 103. 107
Hunter, Edwd. 83
    John 15. 36. 71. 108

Ingram, Thos. 39
Ireland, Richd 55. 62

Jackson, Thos. 55
Jeffries see Gefferys
James, Jno. 14
Jameson, Jas. 33. 55
Jenkins, David 13
Johnson, Constance 48
    Richd 76. 108. 109
    Saml. 46. 53
    Wm. 22. 38. 48. 107
    Wm. Jr. 48
Jones, Eliz 55
    Geo. 19
    Orlando 35. 59. 84
    Owen 91
    Richd. 15. 16. 17. 73. 98. 103.
Jones, Robert, as a witness, 2. 7. 8. 17. 18. 23. 24. 52. 54. 55. 59. 79. 81. 88
Jones, Robert, other entries, 6. 10. 16. 23. 40. 56. 73. 77. 80. 92.
Jones, Thos. 108
    Wm. 10. 34. 55. 108.
Jonnes, Jno. 82
Juge, Jas. 99
Junys, Jere 58
Jewell, Frances, 49
    Thomas 19. 35. 48.

Kay, Robt. 76
    Robt. Jr. 76. 93
Kelly, Wm. 1
Kemp, Ann 23
    Eleanor 70
    Martin 99
    Richd. 2. 23. 70
Kendall, Jno. 45
Kephill, Geo. 15
Key, Robt. 14
Kilpatrick, Saml. 39
King, Armstrong, 48
    Eliz 5. 9.
    Geo. 3
    John 58.
    Richd. 48
    Walter 16. 58
Kirby, Henry 37
Kirk's land 37
Kirk - 71

Landrum, Jas 46
    Saml. 46
    Thos. 24. 34. 83
Latane, Lewis 68. 107
Lea, Henry 45
Leach, David 36
Lee, Richd 42
Leeman see Lemon, Leamon, etc.
Leftwich, Thos. 23. 47
Lemon, Jos. 1. 5. 9. 51. 64. 84
Lewis, David 108.
    Jno. 59
    Joseph 91
    Thos. 91
    Zachary 15. 69
Ley, Augt 67. 69. 71
    Thos. 5. 16. 23. 47
Lilliard, Thos. 35. 36. 37.
Lindsey, Caleb 89
Lomax, Jne. 6. 13. 20. 89. 95.
London, Jne. 38. 48
Long, Gabriel 22. 93
    Henry 99
    Henry, Jr 100
    John 76
    Kath. 89
    Richd 24. 79. 81. 109
Loveing, Barbary 54
    Richd. 54

Lowry, Jno. 87
Loyde see Lyde.
Loyde, Mrs Elizabeth 30. 33
    George 20. 35. 37. 39
    James 30. 31. 32. 33. 34
    Johanna 37
    John 22. 35.
    Lyonel 31. 34
    Stephen, 25...34. 34A. 60.
Lucas' Creek 43. 76
Lyde, David 34A
    Mrs. Elizabeth 34A.
    Stephen 34A.

McDaniel, Arthur 108
    Eliz 108
Macker, Mary 8
Mackew see Micou (all of which goes
    to show that they did not
    know how to spell in Eng-
    land any better than we
    did here in Virginia. BF.
    See next item. What do you
    think of that ?
Maigkall, Francis 82
Man, Christopher 39. 87
Marriott, Jno. 56 (Merrit)
Marsh, James 63
Martaine, Jno. 65
Martin, Benj. 82
    Eliz. 43. 44. 49. 51.
    Geo. 12
    John 43. 51. 82.
    Mary 43. 44
    Richd 12
    Thos. 12
Massey, John 50
    John, Jr. 50
Masters, Jas. 46
Maybery, Wm. Jr. 107
Mayfield, Abraham, 22
    Isaac 22
    Jacob 22
    John 22
    Robt. 22. 34
    Sarah 22
Meader see Meador, Meadows, etc.
Meader - 108
Meador, Addra 64
    Ann 64

Ex 9.   117

Meador, Richd. 64. 72
Meadows, Thos. 46. 59. 98. 99
        Susanna 59
        Wm. 64
Meades, Thos. 45. 53. 64. 81.
Mekenny, Jno. 69
Mercer, Isaac, 36. 56. 86
Merchant, Lewis 20
Meriwether, Eliz. 50
        Francis, 89. 100
        Mrs. Mary 57. 62.
            100.
        Thomas 87
Merritt, Jno. 34
        Thos. 37
Merritt see Marriott.
Micou, Paul 4. 18. 20. 34.
        81. 90.
Miller, Jno. 53. 65. 66. 71.
        77. 80. 85.
Millett, Jno. 71. 82
Mills, Jno. 12. 48
        Robt. 48
Mitchell, Jane 79
        John 53
        Jorge 80
        Peter 79
        Sarah 53. 79
Monglothly, Timothy 46
Montague, Wm. Senr. 50
Moore, Fran: 76. 77. 86
        Geo. 57
        Thos. 78
Morgan, Jno. 19. 58. 77. 94
Morris, Benj. 3. 12. 73. 100
Moseley, Benj. 1. 38.
        Edw. 38. 53. 54. 97
        Edwn. 75
        Jno. 79
        Robt. 1. 38.
        Wm. 92
Moseley's Quarters 79
Moss, Jno. 103
        Martha, 1. 36. 38
        Richd. 71
        Robt. 10. 12. 92
        Thos. 92
        William 6. 90. 103
Mountjoy, T 99
Munday, Jno. 40.

Munday, Mary 45
        Thos. 5. 16. 17. 86
Muscoe, Mary 10
Muscoe, Salvator, 9. 10. 12. 17.
        23. 35. 36. 38. 54. 57.
        63. 70. 77. 79. 80. 89.
        91. 97. 101. 108.

Naylor, Jno. 33
Neale, Garet 4
        Jane 4
Newell, Geo. 94
        James 94
Newton, Nicholas 15
Nicholson, Antho 20
        Jacob 20

O'eson, Thos. 77
Offley, Mr. 60
        Loury 24
Olive, Jane 69
Onbee, Arthur 52
Oneale, Brigett 78. 84
        John 78
        Kath 78
Owens, Richd 2. 73. 77

Page, Mathew 104
        Thos. 46
Paget, - , 39. 60
        Ephriam 74. 75. 88. 103.
        Francis 35. 37.
Paine (Payne) Jno. 16
        Robt. 52. 53. 70. 94. 99
Palmer, Martin 35
Pannell - 77
        Thos. 109
        Wm. 5. 109
Parker, Jeremiah 35
        John 19. 33. 36. 38.
        Margaret 3
        Martha 35
        Robert. 3. 4. 21. 36. 37.
            39. 43. 71. 83. 84.
            91.
        Thomas Senr. 57
Patty, Silvester 43. 44. 83

Peacock, Jane 69
Peatross, Ann 73. 74
    Eliz 73. 74
    John 73. 74
    Matthew 73. 74
    Thos. 21. 73. 74. 80
Pellow, Jasper 44. 45
    Jno. 45
Perry, Aaron 10. 108.
    Micajah 42. 87
    Richd. 60. 87
    Saml. 42
Pertous - 108
Peters, Henry 58
Pettet, Thos 91. 2.
Pow, Capt. 39
Phillips, Charles 84
    Jas. 8. 24. 109
Phillpots, Paul 24
Pickarin, Capt. 90
Picket, Jno. 6. 33. 48. 59. 61
    62. 64. 73. 84. 91
    99.
    William 8. 45. 51. 64.
    80.
Pile, Godfrey, 37. 51. 102.
    Jasper (?) 44
Pillow see Pellow
Pitts, Eliz 44
    Jno. 43. 46.
    Wm. 21
Place, Francis 8
Pley, Elizabeth 19
    Robt. 3
Pope, Mary 20. 107.
    Thos. of Cork 20
Powell, Jno. 93
    Place, 8. 18. 80. 92
    Wm. 92
Price, Edw. 84
    Henry 14
    Richd 84. 99
    William 36. 67. 77
Pritchet, Andrew 108
Prockters, Geo. 8
    Wm. 8
Proctor, Geo. 100
Proclamation at Death of Queen
    Anne 6
Prosser, Saml. 21. 22. 76. 82.
    93.

Purkins, Henry 63. 92. 107
    Henry, Jr. 101
    Tabitha 63
Pursell, Eliz. 72

Rallton, Thos. 88
Ramsey, Tho. 3. 4. 5. 65. 67. 75. 86
Randall, Mary 20. 107
    Saml. Jr. 20. 107
Ransone, Frances 50
    Robt. 50
Rappahannock (ship) 58
Rebey, Margaret 12
    Thos. 12
Reeves, Henry 7. 38. 77
    Joseph 39
Reson, Thos. 48
Rennolds, Cornelius 99. 100
    James, 100
    James, Jr. 36. 47. 68. 75.
    79
    James, Senr. 36
Rennells, Jonathan 107
Rhoden, Eliz 88
    Homer 88
Richardson, Dorothy 100
    Jane 11
    Peter 50
    Robt. 11. 100
    Stephen 20
    William 11. 100
Ridgdaile, Jno. 66
Ripley, Thos. 89
Roane, Sarah 93
Roberts, Geo. 102. 103
Robinson, Geo. 45. 46. 51. 58. 76. 98
    99.
    Henry 63
    William 89
Rodes, Jno. 62
Rodin, Homer 92
Rogues Island 99
Rodyford, Jno. 59
Rotterford - 71
Rouse, Jno. 84
Rousey, Capt. 36
Rowzee, Edw. 1. 9. 57.
    Jno. 57
    Ludowick 57
    Ralph 1. 9. 47. 71.

Roy, Jno. 89

Sale, Cornelius 7. 22. 34 36 53.
Salmon, Jno. Jr. 92
    Jno. Sr. 92
    Sarah 92
Samuel, Antho. Jr. 49. 54
Sanders, Jno. 19. 76. 99. 108
    Nath'l. 94. 96. 101
Sanderson, Richd 20
Saunders - 81
Savage, Jno. 51
Scandered, Barbary 91
    Thomas 91
Scandrett, Ann 91
Scott, James 18. 81
    Margaret 81
    William 78. 81. 85
Schrimshaw, Edw. 77
Seleven, Themety 88
Shackelford, Henry 11. 78. 93. 100.
Sheffield, - 98
Sherwood, Jacob 103
    Jacob Jr. 103
Ship, Eliz 21
    Josias 21. 37. 59. 74
    Richd 21. 53. 85
Shipley, Alice 52. 67. 101
    John 52. 67. 101
    Sarah 98
Short, Cath 15
    Mary 44. 51
    Miles 15
    Saml 89
    Thos 45. 49. 77. 82
    Thos. Jr. 21. 43. 44. 51. 65
    Thos. Sr. 51
Sills see Cills
    John 11
Simcock, Jno. 108
Skrimser, Edw. 94
Skey, Jno. 74
Sky, Eliz. 59
    John 59. 65
Slaughter, Tho. 82
Smart, Edw. 107

Smith, Ann 38. 107. 108
    Augt. 3. 7. 8. 63. 80. 87. 89. 109
    Daniel 52. 53. 98
    Eliz 59
    Francis 19. 52. 53. 70. 71 77.
    Henry 53. 64
    Isabell 98
    John 18. 58. 59. 60. 70. 108
    John Jr. 100
    Joseph 6. 23. 31. 33. 35. 39. 52. 56. 63. 68. 73. 95. 106.
    Mary 44. 45
    Nicholas 8. 16. 58. 70. 76.
    Nicholas Jr. 9. 23. 59. 68
    Thos. 44. 50.
    William 50. 55. 62. 77. 78. 79. 93. 103. 107. 108. 109
Smithee, Gabrill 55
    William 54
Somervell, A 9. 22. 40. 57. 81
    Martha 40
Sorrell, Tho. 107
Southings ferry 67
Spearman, Job 49. 51. 65. 74.
Spicer, Jno. Jr. 7. 70
Spotswood, Lt. Gov. Alex 42
St Aicson, James (?) 62
St. John, William 68. 75. 77. 87. 98. 107.
Stallord, Saml 1. 2. 3. 5. 6. 9. 34. 47. 65. 74. 82. 83.
Stanton, Dorothy 1. 2.
    Godfrey 1. 2. 91
Stapleton, Geo. 63
Strang, John 86
Starke - 77
Staton, Jno. 79
Stokes, Wm. 10. 108
Storepoint Landing 99
Streshley - 93
Streshley see Threshley
    Thomas 62

Streshley, Thos. Jr. 3. 5. 16. 49.
Stubbleson, Ann 49
        Stubble 48. 49
Sullivan, Timothy 88
Sutton, Anne 81. 93
       John 81. 93
Swillivant, Danl. 75
Swinney, Morgin 63

Taliaferro, Eliz 101
       Charles 2. 59.
       Francis 82
       John 7. 8. 59. 72 94. 101.
       John, Jr. 109
       Lawrence, 59. 108. 109
       Robert 109
Tandy's Mill 4
Tarent, Leonard 4. 7. 17. 18. 19 35. 70. 71. 74. 75.
       Mary 19. 79
       Mary Brooks 7
Tayloe, Miss Estelle 34 A
       John 31. 32. 34. 34 A
Tatlor, Col. Jas. 11. 35. 93.
       Richd. 5. 24. 85
       Thos. 83
       Wm. 18. 37. 38. 91
Templeton, Jno. 58
Thacker, Mrs. 35
       Edwin 11
       Mary 3
       Saml 3. 7. 33
Tharpe, Thos. 99. 100
       Wm. 99. 100
Thomas, Edwd. 50
       Jas. 91
       John 8
       Robt. 8. 10. 13. 14
       Susanna 8
       Thomas 20. 91
Thompson, Wm. 1. 19. 52. 64
Thorp see Tharp
Thorp - 71
Thornton, Francis 7. 8. 10. 72
       J. 59
       Robt. 10
       Rowland 7. 8.
       William 58

Threshly, Thos. Jr 37
Throwhere see Trowhere
Tiler, Richd. 96
Tiller, Cath. 37
       Thos. 37
       William 46. 53. 84
       William, Jr. 37
Tinsley, Philip 55
       Sarah 55
       Thomas 55. 64
Todd, Christopher 24
       Eliz 24
       John 82. 109
       Martha 24
       Philip 24
       Robt. 24
       Thos. Jr. 24
       Thos. 3rd 24
       Thomas 24. 47
       William 24
Tomlin, Robt. 19
Toppine, Eliz 94
Touchberry, Jas. 39
Trowhere, Joseph 21. 36. 93
Tucker, Danl. 92
Turner, Mr. 93
       Geo. 98
       James 94

Upshaw, Mr 36
       William 92. 101.

Vass, John 4
Vawter, John 2. 36. 46. 81
Velden, Abr'm 11
Virgett, Eliz 52
Virginia Coffee House, St. Michaels Alley, Cornehill, London. 17

Waggoner, Waggner, etc.
       Benj. 65
       Herbert 11. 65
       John 65. 76. 79
       Rachel 65. 76. 79
       Saml. 65
       William 65
Walker, Capt. 35
       James 79
       John 3. 5. 18

Waller, Charles 92. 93
    Christian 93
    Edwd. 92. 93
Walls, James 38
Walter, Henry 58
Ward, Bernard 85
    John 85
Ware, Nicholas 76. 94
Waring, Eliz. 56. 57. 89
    Thomas 47. 50. 56. 57
        63. 73. 87. 89
        90. 95. 97.
Warren, Tho. 3. 52.
Warrener, Ralph 3. 5.
Waters, Eliz 38
    John 100
Watkins, Benj. 94
    Hohn 77. 94
    Thos. 94
Webb, Ann 79
    Catherine 95
    Giles 95
    Isaac 76. 77. 78. 84. 95
    James 9. 17. 53. 68. 76.
        77. 78. 79. 84. 95.
        100. 107.
    James. Will of 95
    John 95
    Mercy 95
    Richd 77. 103
    Sarah 9. 95
Welch, Reuben 2. 35. 36. 39.
    73. 95. 106.
West, Eliz 85
    Richd 4
    Wm. 85
Wheeler, Ann 61
    Tho. 48. 57. 61. 62
White, Henry 89
    Wm 46
Whitehorn, Ann 56
Whiteside, Francis 20
    William 20
Wiles, Thos of Bristol 20
Willard, Jno. 46. 51
    Martin 43
    Sarah 43
Williams, Hugh 68
    John 1. 4.
    William 7. 35. 43. 58.

Williamson, Eliz 57. 72
    James 36
    James' Est. 102-103
    John 72
    Joanna 72
    Thomas 57
Willis, Mary 44
    John 44. 45
Wills, Thos. 107
Willson, Wm 38
Wilson, Wm 38
Winslow, Thos. 3. 18. 35. 86. 90
Winston, Martha 90
    William 5. 16. 18. 39. 54.
        56. 62. 65. 68. 85.
        86. 88. 90. 103
Wise, Richd 84. 99
    Susanna 84
Wood, Jno. 8
    Henry 92
    Thomas 15
Woodnot, Henry 2. 3. 62. 78
Worden, Jno. 35. 39
Wright, Mottrom 7. 79
Wyatt, Cath. 2
    Fr: 50
    Richd 2
    Thos 1. 2

Young, Kath. 50
    William 4. 14. 35. 50. 63.
        78. 95
    William, Jr. 63
Young, Will a Scotch Indentured
    Servant. 47
Younger, Alex. 11. 15. 17. 98.

www.ingramcontent.com/pod-product-compliance
Lightning Source LLC
Chambersburg PA
CBHW031413290426
44110CB00011B/360